ADAMS

❧ BRITAIN'S OLDEST POTTING DYNASTY ❧

William Adams III (1772-1829)

ADAMS

❦ BRITAIN'S OLDEST POTTING DYNASTY ❦

Philip Nanney Williams

First published in Great Britain in 2022
A Llwyn Estates Publication, Llwyn, Manafon, Welshpool, Powys, SY21 8BJ
www.adams-history.com
ISBN 978-0-9955337-1-4

© Philip Nanney Williams, 2022
Unless otherwise stated, the photographs and graphics
are by the author.

Philip Nanney Williams asserts his moral right under
The Copyright, Design and Patents Act, 1988, to be
identified as author of this work.

All rights reserved. No part of this book may be reproduced,
stored in a retrieval system, or transmitted in any form or
by any means, electronic, electrostatic, magnetic tape, mechanical,
photocopying, recording or otherwise without permission
in writing from the above publishers.

Cover and internal design by jenksdesign@yahoo.co.uk

Printed and bound by 1010 Printing International Ltd. China

I come from the Five Towns of Stafford,
Where manners are exceedingly odd;
For while Wedgwoods speak only to Adams,
The Adams speak only to God.

An old rhyme often quoted in the Potteries in days gone by, a likely parody
of John Bossidy's poem , *On the Aristocracy of Harvard.*

FOREWORD

If there were a Debretts for the aristocracy of English craftsmen, the Adams family would occupy pride of place. Owning lands in Tunstall, North Staffordshire, as far back as 1299, members of the family were in 1448 known to be potters and documentary evidence proves that William Adams who lived in the reign of Elizabeth and James I., was a Master potter.

Review of *Ten Generations of a Potting Family* by Robert Nicholls in the Yorkshire Post 11th August 1931

This is a remarkable book, detailing as it does this notable family's history since the reign of Edward I and their unparalleled commercial activities that spanned an astonishing five hundred years.

Through research of considerable scholarship and depth, we witness each family member in Technicolor detail as they grew their business from generation to generation to become one of the largest commercial enterprises of the early nineteenth century, eventually producing ceramic ware in epic proportions.

We witness the Adams family history set in high relief against the backdrop of wider regional and national events, their changing fortunes chronicled as they unfold through turbulent times, successfully negotiating seismic and disruptive events such as the American War of Independence, the French Revolution, through to the comparatively quieter times of the later Victorian era, and then on to two World Wars, the Wall Street Crash and the brave new world of the 1950s.

But who really were these people? What were their indelible traits that emerge recorded over this five centuries of turbulence and opportunity? Certainly they were God fearing, diligently carrying out their duties as church wardens for countless generations; well-educated and cultivated with boundless entrepreneurial energy; successfully riding the ever-changing waves of the industrial revolution and indeed fulsomely contributing to it.

Overwhelmingly we observe family traits that reflect an indomitable spirit of enterprise and adventure, with an ingrained sense of decency, probity and moral scruples, limited in their endeavours only by the extent of their own talents and imagination.

Despite at times accruing considerable wealth, they never fell for any form of *folie de grandeur*. Whilst of course living well in delightful houses, 'the business' in the wider sense – serving the local community and recognising the need to do one's duty –seems to have been the mainstay of successive generations.

A family of such note deserves an enduring monument to their history and this fascinating book admirably serves that purpose, enabling the reader to follow the development of Staffordshire's potting industry through the prism of this unique family.

Profusely illustrated and well documented it is interesting, informative and entertaining in equal measure.

Michael Tree

Llanfair Waterdine
March 2022

To Pauline whose incredible support
and encouragement
made this book
possible

CONTENTS

Forward		i
Introduction and Acknowledgements		v
Chapter 1	Early Adams Ancestors (1299-1563)	1
Chapter 2	Hulton Abbey and the Dissolution (1223-1536)	15
Chapter 3	Butterpots, Tygs and Quagmires (17th & 18th Century)	27
Chapter 4	The Mysterious Dutchmen of Bradwell (1688-1700)	39
Chapter 5	Adams of Longcroft, Brick House & Cobridge Hall (1563-1869)	53
Chapter 6	Adams of Greengates (1746-1821)	107
Chapter 7	Adams of Bagnall & Fenton Hall (1660-1829)	131
Chapter 8	Adams of Greenfield – William Adams IV (1798-1865)	155
Chapter 9	Dawn of the Twentieth Century – William Adams V of Greenfield and Wolstanton (1833-1952)	207
Chapter 10	The Last of the Adams Master Potters (1909-1966)	287
Photographic Credits		300
Bibliography		302
Index		315

INTRODUCTION

The history of the Adams family of North Staffordshire is remarkable. Stretching back to the 13th century, generations of this distinguished line have practised the ancient art of pottery while clinging tenaciously to their ancestral lands.

The Adams clock tower in Tunstall Park records that a William Adams held lands in Tunstall in 1307, and two of his descendants, William and Richard Adams, enter the historic record in 1448 when they are fined for digging clay from a Burslem roadside.

Since 1617 twelve generations of the Adams family have proudly borne the title of *master potter*, allowing the family the legitimate claim of being

> *one of the longest instances of continuous family control to be met with in the annals of the British ceramic industry.*

'The Business World, Messrs. William Adams & Sons (Potters) Ltd.' Dod's Publications Ltd. London

The Adams' potting heritage was passed down to at least twelve elder sons who all bore the name of William. They were men of grit and talent who left their mark on the history of the Potteries, and none more so than their three most famous protégées, the three cousins: William Adams I, II and III, who flourished in the reign of George III.

William Adams I, the most gifted member, was a formidable rival of Josiah Wedgwood, Spode and Turner and other great potters of the late 18th century, all working at a time when it is said the Staffordshire Potteries reached the very apex of its reputation.

All three cousins achieved excellence; William I through his beautifully embellished jasper ware inspired by Grecian mythology; William II by being the first to attempt copperplate printing in Staffordshire–a secret he so carefully guarded that he forced his workers to work behind locked doors; and William III by building up one of the largest businesses in the country and being the first to introduce blue printed ware to the area–a process that enabled him to develop a huge trade with America.

Through these early Adams master potters and their descendants, the name of William Adams has been indelibly impressed on the history of potting. All have played their part in making Staffordshire pottery world famous.

Being directly descended from the senior Adams branch through my great grandmother, a daughter of William Adams IV, I grew up surrounded by Adams pottery and family heirlooms, some embossed with the Adams boar's head crest. Nothing, however, was more fascinating to me than Percy Walter Lewis Adams' magnificent tome, undoubtedly his magnum opus,

A History of the Adams Family of North Staffordshire.

Throughout my research I felt very much as if I was following in Percy's footsteps, building on his impeccable genealogical research, ever in awe of his determination to unearth long-lost family connections.

It is my sincere hope that this book will be a lasting tribute to a long and distinguished family who made such an impact on North Staffordshire, not only as potters but also as entrepreneurs and philanthropists.

ACKNOWLEDGEMENTS

It has been my ambition for many years to produce a definitive book on the Adams family of potters of Staffordshire. The research was begun in early 2018, and the book was completed during the stringent conditions of lockdown. I sincerely acknowledge a deep gratitude for the many individuals and institutions who assisted in the development of the book, in particular the Adams family members whose support and encouragement were invaluable. Foremost among them were Joanna Adams and Robert Adams, who were constantly bombarded with queries and cries for assistance. Their staunch support for the book was truly magnificent. Likewise, Virginia Adams, Christopher Adams and Letitia Adams also assisted greatly in the venture.

Others deserving of special thanks include:

Gemma Williams; Dr. Helen Pendry; Charles Evans Art; Bethan Rowlands Wiffen (Artist); Malcolm Jenkins (Graphic Designer), Robert Nanney Williams; Alan Ludovic Nanney Williams; David and Sherril Kelly; Michael Tree; Jeremy Rye (Wales Fine Art); Lucy Lead and the Staff of The V&A Wedgwood Collection, Barlaston; Staff of The Potteries Museum and Art Gallery, Hanley; Staff of the Staffordshire Record Office; Jonathan Gray (President of the English Ceramic Circle); The Victoria and Albert Museum; The British Museum; The Nelson-Atkins Museum of Art, Kansas City, Missouri, USA; Ali Burdon, St. Margaret's Church, Wolstanton; Staff of St. John's Church, Burslem; Dr. Shaun Evans (I.S.W.E., Bangor University); J. Richard and Judith Wagner; John H. Roth III; Claire de Lune; Theresa Lange; Claire Houston-Brown.

1. *Tunstall Manor Court Leet.*
Oil on Canvas. 27 x 35 inches
by John Copey

2. right: Cartouche from Christopher Saxton's Map of Staffordshire dated 1577

1

1299-1563
EARLY ADAMS ANCESTORS

The Adams family of North Staffordshire have a long and fascinating genealogy, tracing their ancestry back to the reign of Edward I.

Established within the Manor of Tunstall, successive generations have bought, sold and inherited lands, passing down their skills and expertise to descendants who have, since Elizabethan times, been designated Master Potters.

The earliest tentative family reference records a certain William Adams in 1299 as holding one bovate or oxgang (about 15 acres, the area four yoke of oxen could plough in a day) at a yearly rent of eleven pence, payable to Nicholas, lord of the manor of Tunstall. Self-government at a local level had existed in England since the 12th century and this manifested itself in the manorial court structure, which consisted of:

THE COURT LEET – Presided over by the Lord of the Manor or his steward. A jury tried minor breaches of the peace and public order committed within the jurisdiction. More serious cases were reserved for itinerant justices and after the 16th century the court's duties were increasingly transferred to the Justice of the Peace.

THE COURT BARON – Presided over by the Headborough or Reeve, who in turn was elected to office by the manor freeholders, with the brief of dealing with defaulters who failed to provide services or pay fines due the Lord of the Manor, and with other issues such as disputes between tenants and the succession of heirs.

Manorial lands were held as customary freehold or copyhold; the latter category meant that landholders could not be dispossessed provided they paid the dues to the Lord and performed the stipulated services. Records were entered on the Court Rolls and tenants were issued with copies of such titles, hence the origin of the term copyholders.

3. right: Man ploughing with oxen. Early 13th-century English manuscript (BL MS Royal 12F XIII f.37v)

*4. above: The Old Court Leet in Cross Street, Tunstall
Drawn by William Scarratt, 1906*

The earliest manorial court records were written on parchment, which were stitched together and formed into rolls. The Tunstall Court Rolls, written in Latin, shed much light on the early Adams family and are a rich source of information on a time before the appearance of parish records in the 16th century. Courts met locally, often in the manor house or an inn, but in Tunstall proceedings were conducted in a purpose-built building, the Tunstall Manor Leet, which miraculously survived until 1888, when it is thought to have been demolished.

In the 14th century most surnames were not fixed but based on descent or occupation, a William Adams being William son of Adam (patronymic). It is highly likely, due to the isolated and stable population, that many of the Adams individuals represented in the Tunstall Court Rolls are members of the same family; they are shown on the early Adams family tree in red, denoting that their membership of the family is speculative.

Tunstall Court records reveal that a certain William Adamesson was Reeve of Tunstall Manor in 1373, and his likely descendant, William de Adams, held the post of Headborough of Burslem in 1416, but no record of this era gives any indications of the family emerging as pottery workers, however primitive their pottery work was likely to have been. Likewise, the Tunstall Subsidy Rolls of taxpayers of 1327 and 1333 reveal no individual being designated as a potter. Later 14th-century Tunstall Court Rolls allude to certain individuals being involved in potting; a William the Pottere makes an appearance in the records in 1348 being given a licence to make 'earthen pots' for the grand sum of 6d.

A few other isolated records suggest individuals with leanings to pottery making but there is nothing significant until 1448, when, with total genealogical certainty, the brothers William and Richard Adams of Sneyd and Burslem 'burst' into the historic record by appearing in the Tunstall Court Records for, of all things, being fined for the misdemeanour of damaging a road!

The Little Court held at Tunstall on 9th October 1448 states that

> *Richard Adams & William his brother dug clay in the road there between Sneyd & Burslem and so damaged the said road.*

There can be little doubt that such offences clearly establish our enterprising brothers as being actively involved in pottery making, and, as such, most probably the earliest recorded potters in Staffordshire.

The Adams brothers were not alone in their wanton destruction of the Burslem highways. The keeper of the Ashmolean Museum, Dr Robert Plot, commented in the 1680s that

> *the greatest pottery they have in this county is carried on in Burslem, where for making their several sorts of pots they have as many different sorts of clay which they dig round about the town all within half mile distance.*

(The Natural History of Stafford-shire, Dr Robert Plot)

Itinerant labourers are known to have scoured the area, digging for the most accessible seams of clay, and selling each load for a few shillings. The roadside was naturally seen as the easiest place to dig as the ground had been broken and softened by waggons and packhorses. Interestingly, the term potholes is thought to have been coined as a result of the illicit practice the Staffordshire potters carried out in order to acquire the raw materials of their trade.

Such unlawful digging resulted in a landscape pockmarked by craters that filled with stagnant water and made roads dangerous and often impassable.

The condition of the roads figures often in the Tunstall Court Rolls, with many examples of fines issued to individuals who illegally dug the roadside. Such fines were, however, minimal and sometimes seen as almost an inducement, or a form of 'licence', to undertake this unlawful but cost-effective activity. Perhaps our pioneering brotherhood were not the shadowy criminals we first imagined?

In the 15th century the making of pottery was at a very primitive stage of development, overwhelmingly carried out by yeomen farmers and peasants whose output would have only supplied local demand. They produced basic utilitarian wares such as jugs and pitchers while higher classes of society still used pewter and wooden utensils.

North Staffordshire in the Middle Ages was a wild and isolated area with a sparse population, and in challenging times a sideline of earthenware production was a useful supplement to meagre incomes. There was the added bonus of a readily accessible supply of coal, a vital component to the potting process. Potting would also have been an attractive proposition for the younger family members who might have otherwise been forced to leave the family farm. Such are the likely scenarios that the early Adams family potters found themselves in at the close of the 15th century.

The more entrepreneurial members would expand fledgling potworks, taking on workmen and adding work sheds, thus beginning to differentiate the work. Originally the whole potting process would have been carried out by only one or two individuals but as work became more specialised the quality improved.

An illuminating description of an early Staffordshire moorland potworks is to be found in *The Life of Josiah Wedgwood* (E. Meteyard):

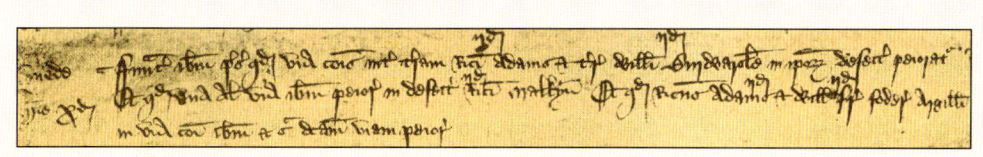

... and that Richard Adams & William his brother dug clay in the road there, and so damaged the road.

5. above: Tunstall Court Roll - Extract of the fine imposed on Richard and William Adams

6: The bleak Staffordshire Moorlands

7. above: An illustration of an early 17th-century pottery from Dr. Plot's Natural History of Staffordshire *(1686)*

the oven – only one – was eight feet high and six feet wide. It was surrounded by a wall of broken saggers to keep the heat in, and this wall, later on, became the hovel. It stood in a secluded spot, most often at the crossing of two roads, near a little stream of water. Round the oven clustered the open shed where the different operations necessary to complete each piece were performed, and the family dwelling, a small thatched cottage. The thrower worked in one place; the contrivance he used was of the simplest description, being rather a 'whirler' than a potter's wheel. The potter's wheel is kept in rotation, while the hand that fashions the clay into shape remains fixed ... Next to the thrower sat the handler, sticking on the handles and spouts; what tools he used were certainly very primitive, being nothing more than a pointed bit of iron and a flattened strip of wood. In another shed were the man who traced upon the best pieces fanciful scrolls and lines of slip, and he who through a course cloth dusted upon them the pulverised galena for glazing. Very often the same man performed all these different tasks. Close by, the diluted clay evaporated in the sun-pan, until it became thick enough to be conveniently worked, or else the moistened clay was thrown against a dry wall, from which, the water becoming evaporated, the lumps fell upon the ground, ready to be stored in a damp place for further use. Isolated from the rest of the world the potter worked there, attended by his sons and wife. Sometimes a labourer or two completed the staff, which never seems to have numbered more than eight people. When the stock was ready for sale, the wife took it to the nearest fair, leading, pipe in mouth, the double-panniered asses, and there either sold her goods to the crate-men, or exchanged them at the town shops for such articles as she wanted to take back home.

The potter in charge needed an overview of the whole process and high levels of the necessary manufacturing skills. In due course, this key person took on the persona of the widely admired and revered Master Potter.

Other valuable documents shine a light on early Adams' history; foremost among these are the Muster Rolls. Dating back to feudal times, the rolls exist in the form of inventories that the Lords of the Manors were obliged to keep, detailing all the able-bodied men between the ages of 16 and 60 who were eligible for military duty.

The Muster Roll of 1539 is of particular interest as John Adams (1461-1544) is specifically named; he is

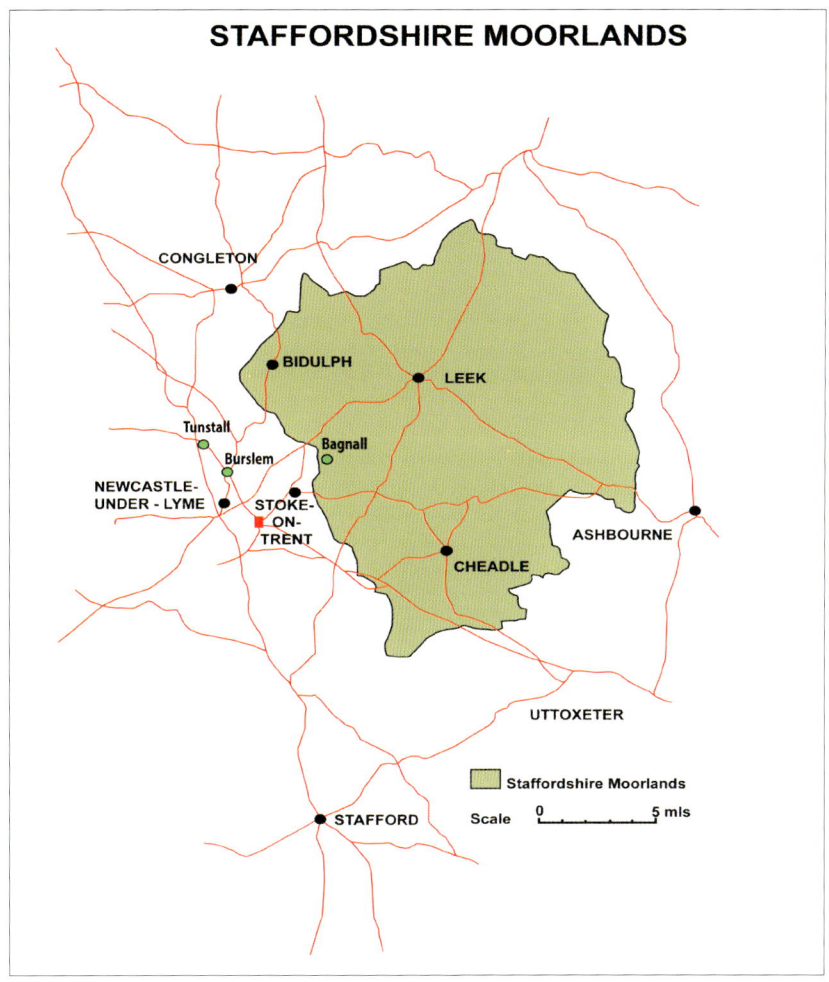

8. above: The extent of the Staffordshire Moorlands and their relation to Stoke-on-Trent

returned under Staffordshire, in the Hundred of Pirehill, as an

abull man with a bowe and a sheff of arwes, and willing also to supply artillaire to serve the King's Grace in his wars.

The 1539 Musters were taken against the backdrop of a threatened war with France. The contemporary Holinshed Chronicles of 1577 records that

the King being informed that the Pope by instigation of Cardinall Pole has moved and stirred divers great princes and potentats of Christendome to invade the realme of England, without all delaie rode himself towards the sea coasts, and sent diverse of his nobles and councellors to surveie all the ports and places of danger on the coast, where any meet and convenient landing place might be doubted, as well as borders of England, as also of Wales: in which dangerous places he caused bulworks and forts to be erected. And further, he caused the Lord Admerall, Eerle of Southampton, to prepare in readiness his navie of ships for defense of the coasts. Beside this, he sent forth commissions to have general musters, taken through the realme, to understand what number of able men he might make account of: and further to have the armor and weapons seene and viewed.

9: An oil painting of what is thought to be an early Adams Moorland Mill with potworks attached. (artist unknown)

10. below: Early Adams Family Tree – individuals highlighted in red are speculative

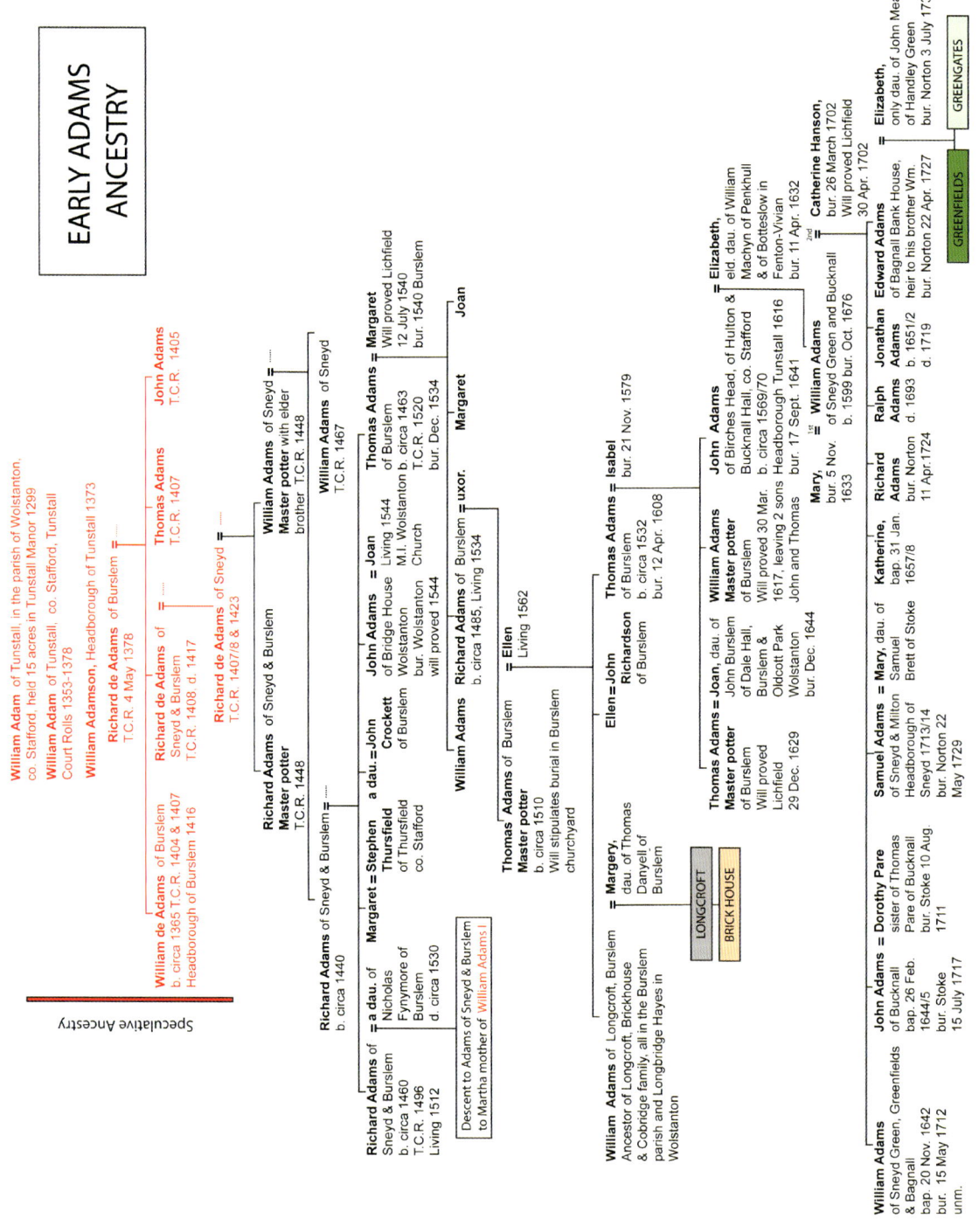

Henry VIII, concerned about the possible effectiveness of the local militia forces for home defence, appointed a Lieutenant in each county with specific responsibility for ensuring the defence of their territory. To ascertain the fighting capabilities, men from each township throughout the kingdom were required to muster for inspection, and on such occasions the equipment each individual possessed was recorded.

While listing the able bodied, the Rolls also record individuals who were excused for various reasons, with age or illness being the most likely scenarios. The majority possessed their own weapons, and the more affluent pieces of defensive armour or horses and harness.

Two main arms in use in the Tudor time were the bill (bylle) and the longbow. The former was a vicious weapon based on a spear with an axe blade on one side. The bill's origins hark back to the agricultural billhook, but in its weapon form it had a pronounced spear and often a hook on the reverse side to the blade. This weapon could be used to drag an unlucky horseman off his charger, to be finished off with bill or sword.

The English longbow, made of yew and up to 6 feet long, was a formidable weapon. A skilled archer could fire ten to twenty 3-foot arrows per minute, which en-masse could be devastating to the enemy. Since the 14th century, state ordinances had commanded Englishmen not to spend their free time on pointless games and hobbies, but on archery practice.

For our John Adams, the fact that he is mentioned as 'an abull (able-fit for military service) man with a bowe and sheff of arrows' almost certainly denotes that he was a well-practised archer; and the term 'willing to supply hernes' (defensive armour or harness) signifies that he was typically of the gentry class.

Defensive armour for archers could mean a jack–a protective sleeveless tunic of quilted leather or, later, plated with iron for additional protection; far lighter than armour, it was seen as effective protection in the cut and thrust of battle.

John Adams' nephew Nicholas is likewise named in the 1539 Muster Roll and mentioned as

an abull man with a bylle, a gesterne, and a pair of splentes.

While probably not as skilful as his uncle, he was well equipped with a bill, a dagger and armour (in the form of strips of metal splints attached longitudinally to a cloth or leather backing, commonly used as protection to the limbs).

As early as the 14th century, Adams family members had been actively involved in coal mining in the Burslem area. Successive lords of the Tunstall manor had leased out their Burslem mines and Richard Adams (1460-1530) seized on such an opportunity, leasing a title in the Great Row Mines near the monastery of Hulton in the year 1487.

John Adams' (1461-1544) will, dated 23rd April 1544, states that he wanted to be buried within the parish church of Wolstanton, a privilege reserved to higher status parishioners who inevitably endowed the church as a means of acquiring salvation for their souls. John's son Nicholas's will, dated 22nd November 1567, stated that he wanted

To be buried in the church of Burslem.
To Richard Adams my eldest son certain heirlooms …
To Richard and William Adams my sons my part of the lease … coal mine Small Row.
To Elizabeth my wife to have sufficient coal for her own fire at Sneyd.

… and various other legacies and, intriguingly, the following:

I give one plank of wood to the mending of the Fowle Ley Bridge at Dakyns and one other plank to mend the Bridge at the Fowle Ley going from Shelton to Penkhyll.

The Fowle brook rises in the north of Tunstall, joining the Trent at Stoke; in the 16th century the bridge in question carried the pack way from Tunstall to Burslem and is now represented by the present

11. above: A group of 15th-century re-enactors with Italian and English bill-hooks during a display at Cardiff Castle

Longbridge Hayes. No specific mention of any potting activity is made in Nicholas' will, but he is stated to be

seized of 40 and a half acres in Snead.

Thomas Adams (1510-1563) is a pivotal member of the family. From him descend all the historically important potters of this ancient dynasty, most notably the Adamses, successively of Greengates, Brick House and Greenfields, whose influence on the potteries has been so profound.

Thomas's will yields tentative proof of his involvement in potting as he leaves his

best iron chimney to his son William ... and to Ellen my daughter my other chimney.

A chimney was an important component of any potwork and indicated his likely occupation as that of master potter.

Thomas Adams, Master Potter of Burslem, was rated in the Tax Subsidy Roll of 1559 at 5s for his lands and 8s 3d for his goods. Sir William Sneyd, the principal landowner under the Tunstall Court, is assessed amongst the highest at £30 and taxed at £4. Noted gentry families such as the Burslems and Colcloughs were assessed at 20s, which places the enterprising Adams family clearly in the emerging gentry class at the close of the 16th century.

12. top opposite page: The chancel of St. Margaret's Church, Wolstanton with the 16th-century tomb of Sir William Sneyd and family of Bradwell– far left

13. above: Close-up of Sir William Sneyd's family tomb with recumbent effigies of Sir William and his wife

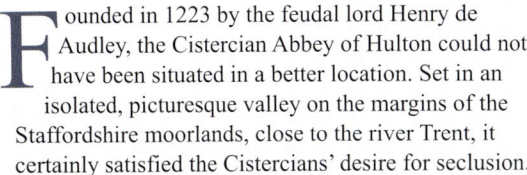

15. *right: Stained-glass representation of St. Bernard of Clairvaux from the Upper Rhine, circa 1450*

2

1223-1536
HULTON ABBEY AND THE DISSOLUTION

Founded in 1223 by the feudal lord Henry de Audley, the Cistercian Abbey of Hulton could not have been situated in a better location. Set in an isolated, picturesque valley on the margins of the Staffordshire moorlands, close to the river Trent, it certainly satisfied the Cistercians' desire for seclusion.

Henry de Audley's family was illustrious, descended through the female line from Richard de Toeni, who was the Standard Bearer of Normandy, a relative of William the Conqueror.

Henry, in line with other landed benefactors of the middle ages, donated a significant amount of land in the vicinity to the newly established Hulton Abbey and later provided a yearly grant of 10 marks, on the proviso that the brotherhood would celebrate mass for the souls of Henry, his predecessors and successors for

> *all the days of the world*

Although Henry and later family members continued as patrons of Hulton Abbey, it was never destined to become significant, remaining small and relatively poor in comparison with some of the great Cistercian abbeys of England.

The Adams family, living and eking out an existence within the sphere of influence of Hulton Abbey, could well have been associated with the monastery, particularly with regards to potting ventures. Long-held family traditions certainly allude to this, but nevertheless remain unsubstantiated.

Written records emanating from the Abbey are virtually non-existent; however, recent archaeological excavations have certainly been illuminating, especially regarding Hulton Abbey's potting activities.

Lack of documentary evidence is not the only missing aspect with regards to Hulton Abbey, in that

> *modern developments on the several sites of monastic activity since the mid-sixteenth century have conspired to wipe out virtually all visible traces of monastic activity from the landscape. No fine ruins survive above ground level to simulate and inspire the romantic imagination of later generations.*

(John L. Tomkinson, *A History of Hulton Abbey,* 1997)

14. left: Remains of Croxden Abbey, a 12th-century Cistercian foundation

■ Hulton Abbey - Site Location

16. above: The location of Hulton Abbey in relation to Burslem and Bagnall

It is somewhat troubling to note that part of the blame, for at least the eighteenth-century destruction of Hulton Abbey, lies squarely in the lap of a certain William Adams of Bucknall Hall.

Hulton Abbey was the smallest and last Cistercian abbey to be built in Staffordshire. The first, Croxden Abbey, founded in 1176, was followed by Dieulacres near Leek in 1214 and Hulton in 1223. Hulton Abbey was the daughter house of the Cistercian Combermere Abbey in Cheshire and was dedicated to the Virgin Mary.

The Cistercians, also known as the 'White Monks' because of the distinctive colour of their un-dyed habit, are a Catholic religious order of monks and nuns. They had branched off from the Benedictines in 1098, and traced their origins back to Citeaux Abbey in France. Under the direction of their highly influential Abbot Bernard of Citeaux, their monasteries rapidly spread throughout Europe during the Middle Ages. They followed the Rule of St. Benedict as their guiding principles, aptly encapsulated by the following:

Idleness is an enemy to the soul: and hence at certain seasons the brethren ought to occupy themselves in the labour of their hands, and at others in holy reading

Monastic communities often included many lay brethren (conversi) who acted as farm workers, shepherds, carpenters and, significantly, masons, whose contribution to Cistercian architecture was profound.

Hulton Abbey represents a fine example of a small Cistercian Abbey whose layout clearly conformed to the conventional Cistercian plan, having a cruciform church and a square tower.

The monastic buildings at Hulton were constructed from sandstone, most probably quarried from nearby Wetley Moor. Intriguingly, it is thought that the Cistercian abbeys of Dieulacres and Hulton were probably constructed by the same skilled workforce, as similar masons' marks have been identified at both sites. Regrettably, as is the case regarding Hulton Abbey, very little remains of the Abbey of Dieulacres today.

MONASTIC GRANGES

The outlying monastic landholdings, or granges, were worked by the conversi or by paid labour. Land in the immediate vicinity of the Abbey would have been utilised for food for the monastic community while the outlying granges would have farmed livestock or grain

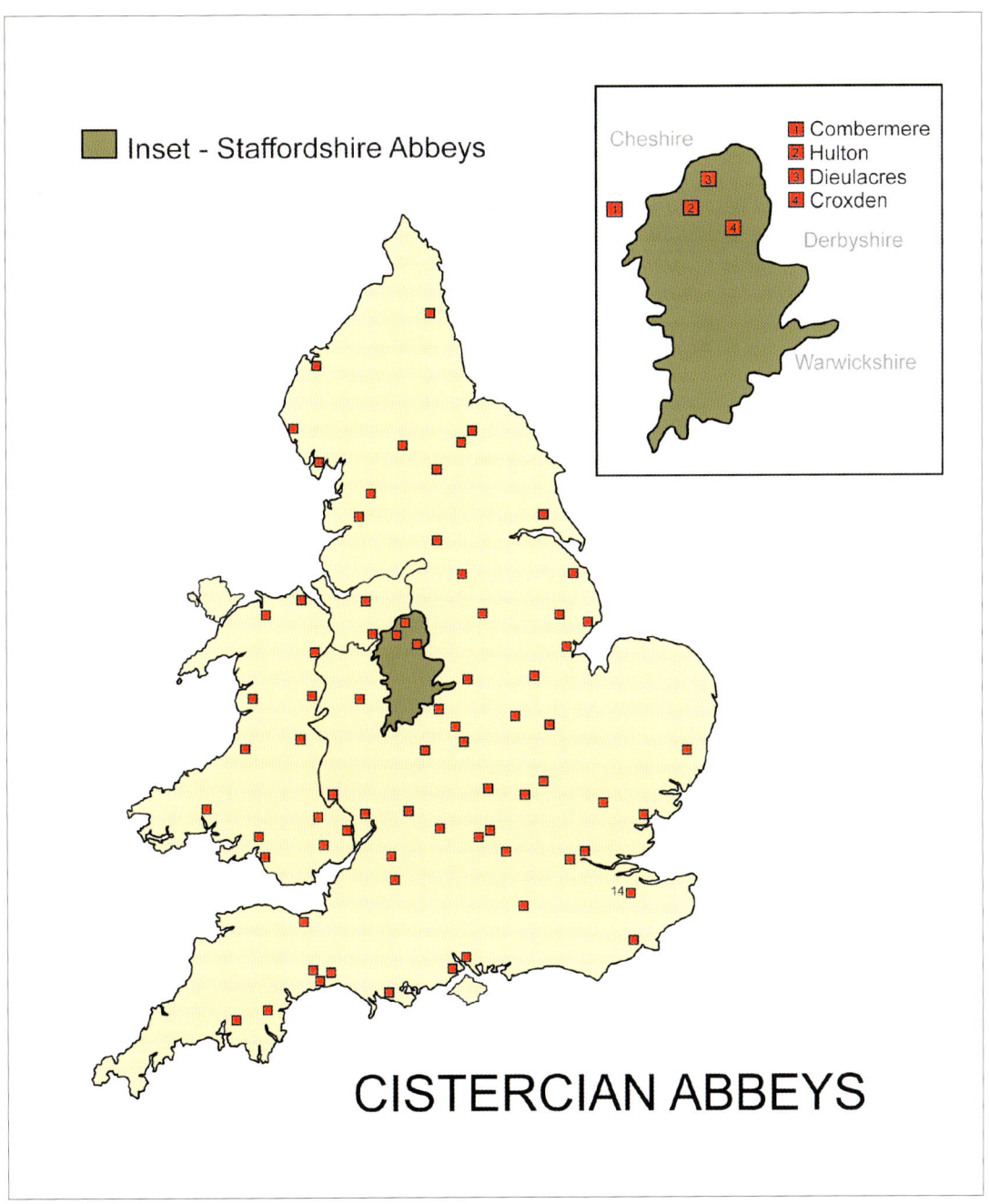

17. above: Cistercian Abbeys in England and Wales

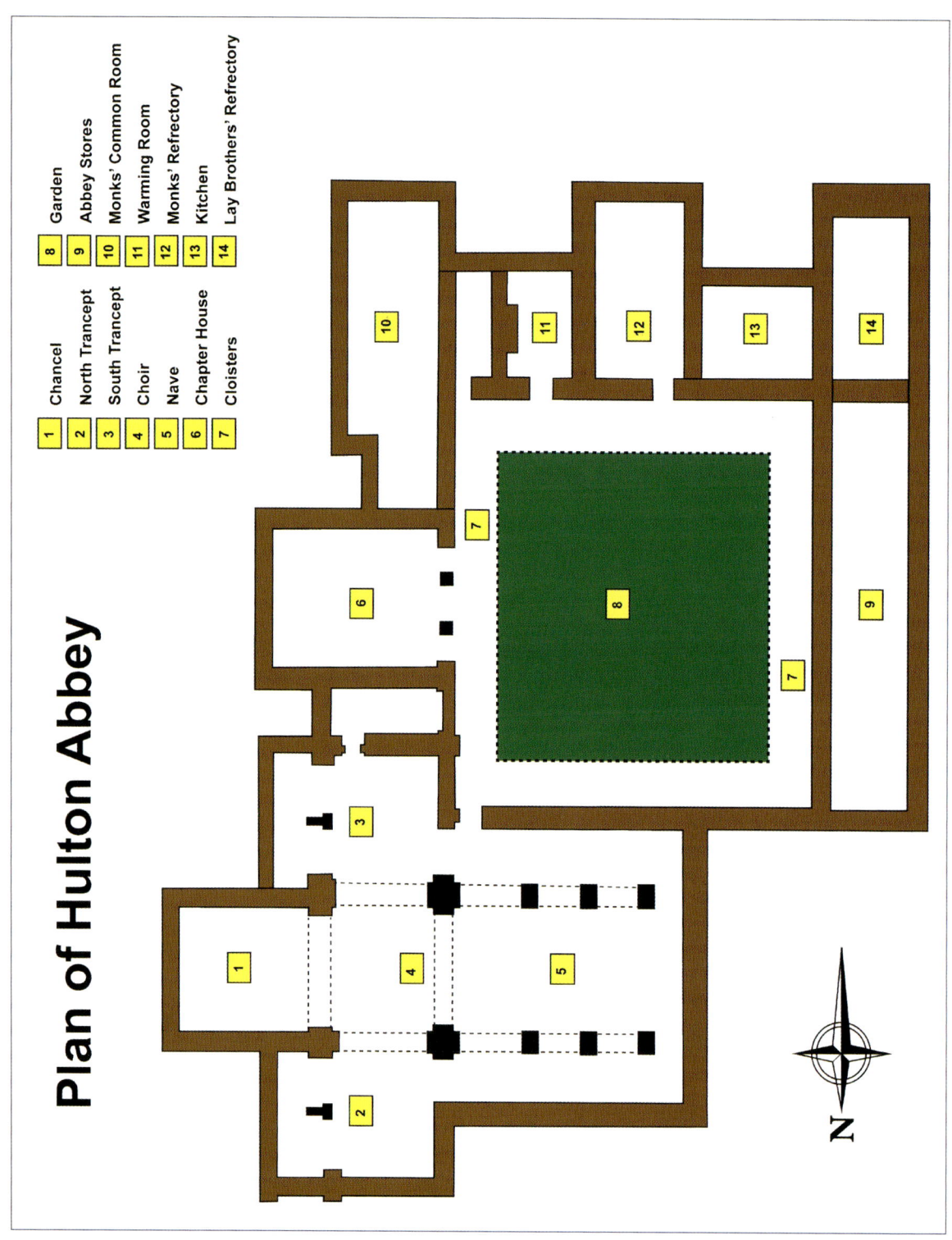

18. above: Plan of Hulton Abbey's buildings in the 13th century

crops, the latter being an important source of wealth for the monastery. In common with other abbeys, Hulton would undoubtedly have benefitted from the sale of wool, widely recognised as the Cistercians' most important source of wealth in the early years of the foundation.

According to the records of the *Taxatio Ecclesiastica* of Pope Nicholas IV, compiled in 1291-2, Hulton Abbey Granges consisted of:

Hulton Grange   - 2 carucates (approx. 240 acres)
Rushton Grange - 3 carucates (360acres)
Normacot Grange - 4 carucates (480 acres)
Bradnop Grange - 1 carucate (120 acres)

(Average size of Grange – approx. 300 acres)

Throughout the 13th century the monasteries enjoyed a degree of prosperity, with thriving numbers of monks and conversi swelling their ranks, until

ill fortune reached a grisly climax with the visitation of the plague known as the Black Death, which seemed to have reached the North-West Midlands early in 1349

(John L. Tomkinson, *A History of Hulton Abbey*, 1997)

By the time the pestilence had worked its gruesome way through the population, it was stated that

the monasteries of Dieulacres, Combermere and Vale Royal had insufficient income to support the small numbers of monks remaining in them after the plague had carried away their brothers.

(John L.Tomkinson, *A History of Hulton Abbey*, 1997)

Hulton's income certainly diminished as a result of the onset of the Black Death, falling from £26 in 1291 to just £14 in 1354; worse was yet to come as the deadly pestilence reappeared in 1361 and 1369.

The religious houses probably never fully recovered from such a devastating blow, but for smaller foundations such as Hulton it would have been bleak in the extreme. The once plentiful supply of conversi vanished in the wake of the Black Death, compelling already financially compromised abbeys such as Hulton to take on hired labour, moving to letting some of their landholdings as a source of desperately needed income.

OTHER COMMERCIAL ENTERPRISES

Although primarily engaged in agriculture, Hulton Abbey is known to have owned tanneries, fulling and grist-mills, coal mines and a pottery of some kind, all of which would have supplemented their diminishing revenues. Historically, branches of the Adams family have often been linked to Hulton Abbey's industrial heritage, particularly with regards to the abbey's potting and milling enterprise. 17th-century court records intriguingly reveal that in 1487/8 Richard Adams had a title in the Great Row Mines near the

19. above: Cistercian monks at work in the field from Scenes from the Life of Saint Bernard *by Jörg Breu the elder (1475-1537)*

20. Artists impression of Hulton Abbey as it might have appeared in the 13th century (pen and ink by Bethan Wiffen)

1223-1536 Hulton Abbey and the Dissolution

21. right : Bucknall Mill, near the Trent, worked by John Adams (1645-1717)

Monastery of Hulton–direct evidence of the family's long-standing connection to the Abbey.

Given the abundance of suitable raw materials for potting found in the vicinity, it is inconceivable that industrious Cistercians would not have established a pottery nearby, especially as

very near the abbey, the coal crops out, and both clay and coal were close to the spot, they, the monks, had very little obstacle to indulgence in branches of experimental investigation into methods of ceramic production.

(Simeon Shaw, *History of the Staffordshire Potteries*, 1829)

P.W.L. Adams, in his book *History of the Adams Family of North Staffordshire*, vigorously asserted that the Adams family took over the Hulton Abbey pottery on the dissolution of the Abbey in 1538. However, excavations on the Abbey site seem to contradict this claim: very little medieval pottery was excavated and nothing with regards to pottery waste, which would have been evidence of a flourishing pottery works.

It is interesting to note that the Abbey's excavated medieval fragments bear strong resemblance to pottery emanating from kilns found in Burslem and Sneyd Green. The inevitable conclusion must be that there was no pottery industry at Hulton Abbey. The fact that Burslem was such a thriving centre for potting even in the 13th century meant that the Abbey could easily obtain necessities locally. Given that the Adams family were actively producing utilitarian wares at this time, it is highly probable that Adams, among others, supplied the domestic needs of the Abbey.

22. above: Abbey Hulton Mill, a grist-mill worked by Hulton Abbey monks, and after the Dissolution by John Adams (1645-1717)

23. left: Red earthenware floor tile impressed with a design of a hare and foliage, circa 1332-1350 from Reading Abbey, Buckinghamshire

Other ceramic activities, however, were flourishing at Hulton Abbey, most notably the production of encaustic tiles. Strong excavation evidence points to a thriving tile production centre based at the Abbey as early as the 14th century.

Encaustic tiles were ceramic tiles in which the surface pattern was not a product of glazing but a result of utilising different colours of clay, meaning that the design remained as the tile wore down. The fact that we are still able to appreciate the medieval designs after centuries of monastic footfall is an enduring legacy to the skilful medieval monastic tile makers.

The Cistercians expended great care in the production of their beautiful ceramic tiles and lavishly installed them on floors within their magnificent monasteries.

A. Hayden, in *Chats on Old Earthenware,* 1909, pointed out that

designs found on medieval tiles consist of figures of animals, mythical and heraldic, of birds, of human heads and grotesques, as well as conventional, floral, and geometric patterns … they are highly artistic and of great technical excellence.

After three centuries of relatively peaceful contemplation, the occupation of Hulton Abbey came to an abysmal end with the dissolution of the Abbeys in 1536 and the seizure of Church properties by the State. Over a period of two years, eight hundred monasteries were dissolved and their buildings systematically demolished, with the exception of a small number that were converted to churches. Hulton Abbey's fate was determined early, along with smaller abbeys whose annual incomes were less than £200 each.

A third of all religious houses were closed by the 1536 Act of Suppression, and the Crown immediately took possession of all the precious metals, roofing lead and bells, which were summarily salvaged and sold. Farm stock was sold and Crown tenants sought for the vast acreages that had been seized. It has been stated that

the prime interest of the government in the Dissolution was, from start to finish, in the money that could be raised.

(G.W.O Woodward, *The Dissolution of the Monasteries,* 1985)

A second Suppression Act of 1539 led to the dissolution of the larger monasteries and religious houses. The monastic land was sold off, much of the proceeds funding the King's military campaigns.

The bells of Hulton became the property of a certain Stephen Bagot, possibly destined for the foundry in the Tower of London, to be recast into canons. The roofing lead, amounting to some 16 tons, was valued at £63 4s 7d.

Whether or not local pottery manufacturers such as Adams gave employment to the redundant monks or workmen of the Abbey on dissolution is a matter of conjecture, but perhaps it might have led to the family's assertion that they took over the Abbey pottery. As no mention is made of the existence of a pottery in the Abbey's final closing accounts in 1538, their assertion is highly unlikely.

Left roofless and ruined, the Abbey soon became a source of building material, a veritable quarry for the

24. above: **A drawing from the Adams family archives of old Bucknall Church in the late 18th century (much of the stone appropriated from the Hulton Abbey ruins)**

local population. Stone from the ruined abbey can still be seen in buildings in the vicinity of Abbey Hulton.

In 1718, causing yet further destruction to the ancient ruins, William Adams of Bucknall appropriated much of the remaining masonry to rebuild Bucknall church, of which he was churchwarden. A stone tablet exists in modern day Bucknall church commemorating this event:

> *This memorial stone, handing down to posterity the names of Rev. Samuel Lea and his warden William Adams, and the date when the church was rebuilt, was unfortunately lost when the church was again rebuilt in 1856, but a replica of the stone (red sand-stone), with a framework of brass, carefully executed by Messrs. Robert Bridgeman, of Lichfield, has recently been placed in the chancel of the church.*

(P.W.L. Adams, *The Adams Family of North Staffordshire*, 1914)

Today, virtually nothing survives of Hulton Abbey–no fine ruin to fire the imagination of bygone times–and all traces of monastic life have been wiped from the landscape that the monks so carefully nurtured for centuries.

POST-DISSOLUTION CONNECTIONS

The Adams family of Bucknall Hall and Bagnall are undoubtedly the branch of the family with the most connections to Hulton Abbey post Dissolution. William Adams of Milton, great grandson of William Adams of Sneyd and Bucknall Hall (1599-1677), was intriguingly described as master potter of Hulton Abbey in 1772. William's grandfather, Ralph, had worked the pottery at Holden some 50 years earlier with his brother Edward Adams. Edward's elder brother William (1642-1712), is further stated by Shaw as being *a manufacturer of salt glaze earthenware at Holden Lane (or Abbey) pottery in 1680.*

(Simeon Shaw, *History of the Staffordshire Potteries,* 1829)

The location of Holden, or more precisely Holden Farm, was thought to be on the ancient pathway from Hulton Abbey to their associated grange at Rushton, near Cobridge.

Given the proximity of Holden Farm to the Abbey, it is feasible that it might have been the original site of the Hulton Abbey's pottery, or that the family adopted the name some time after the Dissolution. It is well known that the Adams of Bucknall Hall, like their contemporary cousins, combined potting with the farming of their estates–in addition to working coalmines in the vicinity. So industrious was William Adams of Milton that he is even known to have learnt and practised the art of weaving.

In a photographic album circa 1900, taken by Cecily Adams (1866-1946), there exists a detailed photograph of Holden, the home of Edward Adams.

John Adams (1644-1717), brother of Edward Adams of Holden, owned and worked the mills at Bucknall and, it is thought, also the Abbey Mill at Hulton.

While it is clear that the Adams family's links to the ancient abbey were many and varied, it is impossible to say whether they gained any skills or secrets from the enterprising brethren within their immediate neighbourhood, although it is difficult to believe that they did not.

25. below: Holden near Hulton, possible site of Holden Lane, otherwise known as Abbey Pottery, worked by William Adams 1642-1712 (photograph by Cecily Adams circa 1900)

27. right: *Stoneware vessel made in Germany and extensively copied in England*

3

17th & 18th Century
BUTTERPOTS, TYGS & QUAGMIRES

The Staffordshire potteries don't rise to any significant prominence until the latter years of the 17th century, when Dr. Robert Plot published his *The Natural History of Staffordshire* in 1686.

Dr. Plot, keeper of the Ashmolean Museum at Oxford, provided a valuable account of the conditions of the emerging pottery industry as he progressed through the county. His book affords us the only first-hand account of the fledgling pottery business as it transitioned from its peasant-based origins.

Through Plot's perceptive observations we not only build up a comprehensive picture, of the potting processes and products; we also gain revealing glimpses of the furiously independent Staffordshire character, in some cases warts and all.

Plot visited the Potteries in about 1680 and commented that

the greatest pottery they have in this county is carried on at Burslem, near Newcastle-under-

26. left: *Three Shires Head - old packhorse bridge over the River Dane, Staffordshire Moorlands*

28. right: *Portrait of Dr. Robert Plot, an English naturalist, the first keeper of the Ashmolean Museum and author of* The Natural History of Staffordshire *published in 1686*

Lyme, where, for making their several sorts of pots, they have as many different sorts of clay, which they dig around about the town, all within half a mile distance: the best being found nearest the coal, and are distinguished by their colours and uses.

Foremost in terms of production at the time was the butterpot, a coarse, cylindrical vessel. The chief market for these pots was Uttoxeter, where they were filled with butter and sold to London dealers. Significant trade must have ensued, as Plot explained that dealers

27

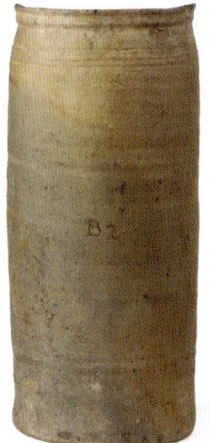

29. left: Butter pot – a tall cylindrical earthenware pot made to hold 14lbs of butter, destined for the Uttoxeter market

30. below: A tyg made by George Richardson of Wrotham in Kent dated 1651. Many such multi-handled pottery mugs were made in Staffordshire in the 16th and 17th centuries

frequently laid out £500 in these articles on a market-day.

The once plentiful butterpots are now a rare commodity. Made of coarse clay and about 14½ inches high, they have been compared to a chimney pot in appearance. They were designed to hold 14lbs of butter, but often the consumer was cheated out of the full amount through a variety of devious means, such as false packing and the producing of unduly thick pot bases. To prevent such abuses, an Act of Parliament was passed in 1661 that regulated the size and weight of the pots, and surveyors were employed to enforce the legislation. Armed with an iron instrument called a *butter boare*, the surveyors would have thrust it to the bottom of a pot to gauge the amount of butter, therein avoiding the necessity of weighing. Smaller butterpots were produced for sale locally, probably purchased by famers around the Burslem area.

Plot generally regarded the Staffordshire potter as a poor scheming knave, indeed referring to a certain Richard Cartwright of Burslem as a *poor butter pot maker*. This hardly rings true, as the Richard in question was a man of considerable property, who in his will devised £20 a year for ever to the poor of Burslem.

The output of the 17th-century Staffordshire potter was not confined to butterpots; the tyg or drinking-cup had been popular since before the reign of Elizabeth I. Tygs were manufactured with two or more handles; the idea was that different people used a separate handle and their lips touched different parts of the rim as they drank communally. Tygs are known to have had as many as ten handles, used no doubt in riotous, disorderly beer-drinking sessions.

Then there was the Bellarmine, an ale-mug that originated in Germany but was later copied in England. Its ugly expression is thought to be the origin of the word 'mug' as a representation of the human face. The ugly face on the neck also gave the bottle its name, as its gruesome design was meant to be a representation of Cardinal Bellarmine. The detested cardinal, one of the Catholic leaders of the Counter-Reformation, was perceived by many protestants in England and Germany as a villainous monster.

The curiously named posset pot was universally used on Christmas Eve to hold a beverage made up of a mixture of hot ale, milk, sugar, spices and diced bread or cake. A silver coin and a wedding ring were often dropped into the simmering posset and the assembled guests in turn partook of a spoonful of the

32. left: Salt-glaze pottery tombstones photographed at Wolstanton Church, circa 1900

33. below: Earliest known Adams ware–a slipware salt cradle, circa 1700, attributed to William Adams of Holden (H. 7.25 x W. 10.75 inches)

mixture as it was passed around. The guest who fished out the coin would, it was believed, have good luck in the coming year, and fishing out the wedding ring would foretell a happy marriage. Possets were a mainly British creation, universally used by the population; even Oliver Cromwell and Samuel Pepys were said to have partaken of the seasonal concoction. Used only once a year, the posset pot often became a prized possession and a family heirloom which perhaps explains their relative abundance today, compared with the utilitarian tygs or butterpots that have virtually disappeared.

Seeking to broaden the range of manufactured items, the potters were known to have produced tombstones and memorial tablets out of clay, although virtually none have survived to the present day, except for rare examples found in museums.

Perhaps the most emotive item created by skilled hands of the 17th-century Staffordshire potter took the form of an elaborately decorated miniature cradle. These classic earthenware cradles often bore a date and occasionally a name and, it is thought, were presented to parents on the occasion of the birth of the first child. The simplicity of their design, moulded in the plainest of fashions, takes us back to a distant time when peasant potters worked their humble magic among the pigs and fowls.

31. left: A German stoneware bottle called a Bartman (bearded man) known in England as a Bellarmine, circa 1660-1665

The earliest known Adams pottery item is a charming slipware salt-glazed cradle of circa 1690, attributed to William Adams of Holden (1642-1712), an early proponent of the salt-glazing process in Staffordshire. William's grandfather, confusingly also William Adams (1599-1677), possesses the accolade of being the earliest mentioned master potter in Staffordshire, appearing in a document of 1617.

By 1670 there appear to be many references to potters in Burslem, and in 1712 records show that there were forty-two master potters in residence in the area, although it was still a fledgling industry as

34. above: Extract of Speed's Map of Staffordshire dated 1610 showing the location of Burslem in relation to Uttoxeter

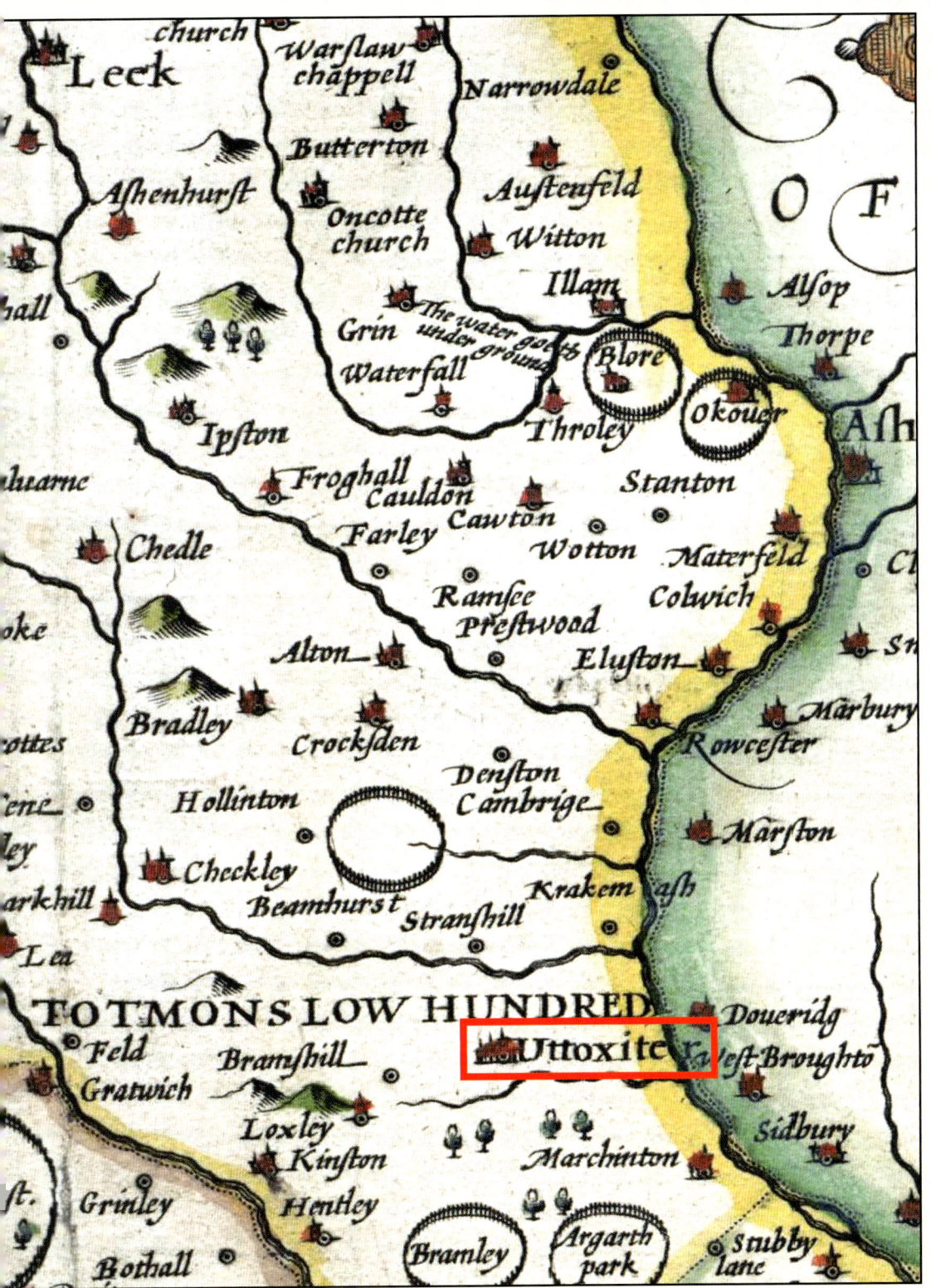

17TH & 18TH CENTURY Butterpots, Tygs & Quagmires

not one of the whole number, turned out more than £6 worth of goods a week.

(William Burton, *Josiah Wedgwood and his pottery*, 1922)

A fascinating account of the conditions in Burslem at the end of the 17th century is to be found in Eliza Meteyard's *The Life of Josiah Wedgwood*:

Burslem was at this period a mere village of thatched cottages somewhat crowded together on the top of a low-lying hill; the old church and Dale Hall resting in the hollows beneath it ... comparatively crowded as the houses were together, most of them had a patch of garden ground; and occasionally both croft and garden; wide strips and angular patches of the original waste intersected the lane-like streets, and on these, in many places, were piled vast amounts of sherds and ashes; whilst around were the hollows from which the potters dug their clay, as at an earlier day they had their coal. In some places the waste had a wider extent, and yet free from the potters 'shard rucks' was intersected by pleasant pathways and little streams; and occasionally where the springs were not gathered into pools, but stagnated near the spot where they rose ... the houses stood singly or in groups; and behind most of them were to be seen thatched working sheds and potters' hovels. The alehouses were very numerous; and their signs creaking in the wind, answered to such names as the 'Turk's Head', the 'Jolly Potters', the 'Court House' the 'Bear', the 'Talbot', the 'Red Lion', the 'George and Dragon' or the 'Packhorse'. A farmyard, a barn, a smithy, a croft, or a wheelwright's shop, broke the line or group of pot-works and tenements; and here and there in the more public portion of the village the butcher had his open shop-baulk, the barber displayed his pole, the cobbler his shoes ... the lanes, for highways they could be scarcely called, which led into the village from the surrounding neighbourhood, were of the worst possible description; that leading through Tunstall to Lawton being literally a 'hollow-way' and in winter-time all but impassable, even to pack-horses.

The 17th-century pottery works did not possess the familiar bottle-shaped pot oven we identify with the potteries today, but had ovens that were only about 8 feet high and 6 feet round with a domed roof. Subsequent developments led to the encasing of the oven with bricks to conserve heat and resulted in the classic bottle chimney that dominated the potteries landscape for centuries.

35. below: Old packhorse route between Burslem and Tunstall drawn by William Scarratt in 1906 from personal memory and the recollections of others

36. right: A man selling pots and pans by Paul Sandby. Grey and brown wash with graphite and black chalk on textured laid paper (H. 7.5 x W. 5.8 inches)

Raw materials for potting were available in abundance. L.N. Solon states:

Clays and coal could be had, by merely scratching the soil. The tilewright, a name given to the worker in clay whether he made tiles, butter-pots, or crocks was at no loss for his materials.

(Solon. L.N., The Art of the Old English Potter, 1906)

Despite its isolated location and poor communications, the Staffordshire industry expanded, the readily available natural resources more than adequately compensating for any geographic disadvantage.

Plot's reflection on the condition of the roads in the Potteries is short and explicit, describing them as *'impossible to get into and almost impossible to get out of.'* To describe them as abominable would be an understatement. Being no better than a series of drovers' tracks, primitive in origin, they became quagmires in winter and heavily rutted in the summer.

For the fledging 17th-century Staffordshire potter, getting his products out to distant markets was challenging in the extreme, what with impassable roads and the nearest navigable river some 30 miles away. The use of packhorses to get their pottery to distant markets was the only solution; wheeled vehicles would have floundered in the miry, pot holed lanes. Endless streams of heavily laden horses, muzzled to prevent their biting the hedgerows, would have plied the countryside, and even they would have had to seek higher ground when low-lying tracks became too treacherous.

The canny potter would also employ the services of chapmen or pedlars. This hardy band of fellows carried the finished pottery on their backs through neighbouring villages, wandering from farm to farm in search of trade, occasionally taking in more populous events such as fairs and markets.

By employing such simple distribution methods, the fame of the Staffordshire potter gradually spread

37. above: Pack Horse Lane, Burslem–the old road between Burslem and Newcastle-under-Lyme, which once ran down the side of Enoch Wood's pottery works

17TH & 18TH CENTURY Butterpots, Tygs & Quagmires

39. below: The original bust of John Wesley, modelled by Enoch Wood, when Wesley sat for his likeness to be taken in 1781

40. inset: Detail below

throughout the countryside, and their products were extended to increasingly important markets. The use of superior glazes, more elaborate decoration and other innovations facilitated marked improvements in pottery making, this fuelling the ever-increasing demand by the close of the 17th century.

Isolated in their moorland towns and villages, the Staffordshire potters inevitably developed a strong independent attitude, seeming rude and outspoken to the outsider. John Wesley, first visiting the Potteries in 1760, was highly critical of the habits and manners of the area, influenced no doubt by the reception he was given. His diary entry vividly explained that one clearly disgruntled observer even aimed a clod of earth at the distinguished preacher, hitting him squarely on the head. It is gratifying to learn that the outlook was somewhat more favourable when he returned in March 1781, his diary recounting,

> *I returned to Burslem. How the whole face of the country changes in about twenty years! Since which, inhabitants have continually flowed in from every side. Hence the wilderness is literally become a fruitful field. Houses, villages, towns, have sprung up: and the country is not more improved than the people.*

The popular amusements of the day were hardly less conducive to civilised behaviour, counting bull and bear baiting, and cock and dog fighting among their most popular attractions at fairs and festivals, with drunkenness and rowdy behaviour being a key feature of these events.

It seems it would have been futile to look to the master potter of old as an example to follow, as according to Tellwright they were

38. left: St. John's Church, Burslem, where items from the Wood family vault are carefully preserved

THE REVEREND JOHN WESLEY, M.A.
FELLOW OF LINCOLN COLLEGE, OXFORD,
AND FOUNDER OF METHODISM,
HE SAT FOR THIS BUST
TO
MR. ENOCH WOOD, SCULPTOR,
BURSLEM,
1781,
AND DIED IN
1791
AGED
88
YEARS.

IS NOT THIS A BRAND PLUCKED
OUT OF *THE FIRE*

17TH & 18TH CENTURY Butterpots, Tygs & Quagmires

41. above: The Old King and Queen at Sneyd Green with the bull-baiting ring clearly visible in the foreground

very much one of the boys and part of the crew men who liked a good time ... just as soon as they had placed the ware in the ovens off they'd go and make straight for ye alehouse on Swan Bank and there they'd drink 'till the ware would be ready to be taken out or so they thought relying on guesswork and the state of intoxication they found themselves in. The master potters always took their labourers with them to go to the alehouse and when they were all half drunk many a row or fight would break out each man taking his turn in the arena arguing over whose turn it was to pay.

It was into this rough and somewhat primitive society that two aristocratic Dutchmen chose to settle in 1690, taking up residence at Bradwell near Burslem, a rather secluded spot, where they established a clandestine factory. As aliens in a foreign land, among a populous that were distrustful of strangers, let alone foreigners, they rapidly became the source of much rumour and speculation.

42. below: Bull-baiting in the 19th century – oil painting by Samuel Henry Alken (1810-1894)

44. right: Tea canister, porcelain with underglaze blue; Chinese, 1790-1810

4

1688-1700
THE MYSTERIOUS DUTCHMEN OF BRADWELL

The uneducated butter-pot makers and tilewrights were just beginning to feel the first stirrings of an ambition to improve their coarse productions, when Elers came among them, their taste for beauty and refinement; such a feeling, hitherto unknown in the district, was in itself sufficient to give an impetus to the latent desire for perfection.

(L.M. Solon, *The Art of the Old English Potter*, 1906)

The first appearance of the Elers in Staffordshire is somewhat uncertain and, in common with their general subversive practices, clouded in mystery, but it is likely that they settled in the area around 1690, establishing a potting factory at Bradwell Hall, a very secluded spot near Burslem. The unique pottery they produced was stored at their residence at Dimsdale Hall, an Elizabethan manor house, some one mile distant from their works. The house was unsurprisingly encircled by dense clumps of ancient woodland, seemingly far enough away from the prying eyes of the local population.

Of Dutch extraction, brothers John and David Elers came over to Britain, as did so many of their countrymen, in the train of William of Orange in 1688. Their father, Martin Elers, had been an ambassador to several European courts and was undoubtedly of noble birth. That John Philip Elers is noted as a godson of the Elector of Mentz, and that his godmother was the Queen of Sweden, confirms their elevated status.

On their arrival in Britain the brothers would have witnessed the new court craze for tea drinking, which had swept the whole country, and they were no doubt familiar with the 'China drink' as it had taken Holland by storm some years earlier. Tea was imported by the East India Company and was a very valuable commodity, at times selling for up to twice its weight in silver. A London merchant, Thomas Galway, extolled the benefits of the oriental beverage in a circular, stating,

The drink is declared to be most wholesome, preserving in perfect health until extreme old age.

Samuel Pepys also noted, when arriving home one day:

found my wife drinking of tee, a drink which Mr Pelling, the Potticary tells her is good for her cold and defluxions.

43. left: The Old Pottery Kiln, Bradwell Wood (artist unknown)

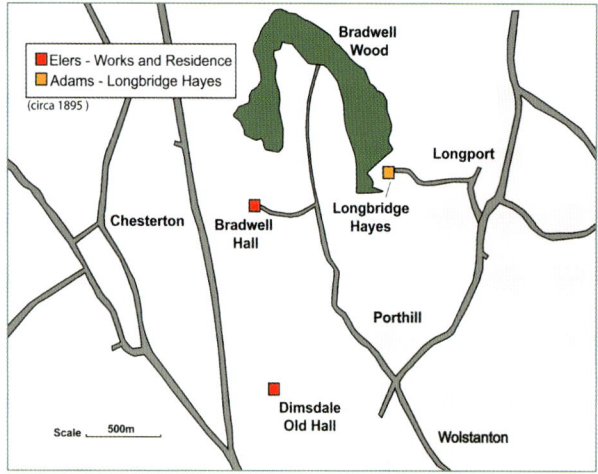

45. left: Location of Dimsdale Old Hall and Bradwell in relation to Wolstanton

Polite society demanded that its unique beverage be served from elegant Chinese pots, which became increasingly available from Dutch manufactories. Indeed, the Elers brothers' uncle was involved in importing such commodities to serve the expanding British appetite for Chinese tea ware.

The entrepreneurial brothers, trained as silversmiths, initially set up a business practising their trade, but by 1690 are known to have switched their attention to pottery and are found to be operating a potwork in Fulham. They were associated with the famous Fulham potter John Dwight, himself of Dutch extraction, who was actively involved in producing patented copies of red clay Chinese teapots. The scene was set: the Elers brothers were poised to capitalise on the lucrative market for copies of the red Chinese Yi-xing ware imported by the East India Company, but to action the plan a ready supply of red clay was necessary.

How Elers became aware of the excellent supply of red clay to be found in the Burslem area is a matter of conjecture; possibly it was through Dwight himself, who had surveyed the area for clay deposits while based at Chester; or conceivably it was through contact with the Sneyd family, landed proprietors of Bradwell and large swathes of North Staffordshire. They wasted no time in relocating to the area, with John Philip Elers taking command of the production side in Bradwell and brother David establishing a shop in London in the Poultry. There he marketed their dainty imitation teapots and cups at somewhat exorbitant prices, a teapot fetching between 12 and 20 shillings each (approximately equivalent to £70-£120 in today's value).

Although not an experienced potter, J.P. Elers is known to have produced some exquisite pieces, prompting one Chinese senator to comment that the clays formulated by Elers were even finer than ones used in Yi-xing. It is evident that the talented Dutchman's output achieved such a high level of sophistication that in some respects they were superior to the items they were copying.

Given that they were trained silversmiths, it is easy to understand how they achieved high levels of mastery regarding the applied decorations. Such ornamentation often took the form of plum trees, produced by pressing clay into copper moulds. These were then pressed onto the teapot surface and finished off by hand tooling, a technique later used to great effect by Wedgwood in his jasper productions.

No doubt J.P. Elers' skill as a chemist greatly assisted him in the preparation of the clay and the mixing processes. However, one is left with the opinion that he must have, to a great extent, chosen Bradwell not only for the ready access to the raw materials in the form of a plentiful supply of red clay and coal, but also because of the vast pool of pottery expertise that

46. above: A coffee-pot in the style of Elers brothers, Staffordshire, 1750-75

47. above: Two teapots – left by the Elers; right Chinese Yixing ware of 1627

was to be found in the vicinity of Burslem, the mother town of the potteries.

Very few authenticated Elers wares are in existence today and–being devoid of makers' names–with the exception of pseudo-oriental seal markings–it is difficult to establish a genuine Elers example. The situation is made more complex as the term 'Elers ware' is often applied in the generic sense when describing items with similar characteristics.

Dimsdale Old Hall, seat of the Brett family in the 17th century, was situated about a mile from Wolstanton and just over two miles from Burslem. In Elers' time, it would have been a high-status building and an appropriate residence for our aristocratic potters. Dimsdale's front elevation of Jacobean style, was cased in brick by the Bretts in the early 17th century, while the back retained its early English half-timbered appearance.

A description of the old hall, as it stood in the late 19th century, gives a sad and faded reflection of its long-lost glory:

We had a cursory sight of the principal rooms in the old Hall, which was occupied by a farmer, who stored his potatoes in the reception-room. There was a danger of these vegetables rotting the finely carved wainscot which covered the walls; we took the liberty of suggesting that the carved portion of the wainscot was of some value, and some time after, perhaps eighteen months we heard of a portion of these carvings being offered for sale in the form of old chests, by a dealer in antique furniture ... [and some years later, inspecting the hall found] ... *the walls stripped of panelling, which lies in heaps about the bedrooms, leaving the walls bare ... one wing had been taken down, and the northern side of the house is open 'to all the winds that blow'.*

A later description of the decorative panelling gives an evocative impression of the once-imposing mansion:

The panels ... are in squares, twelve or fourteen inches across, and five or six inches apart, with a fluted frieze at the top, beautifully cut. In each

48: *Rear of Dimsdale Old Hall.*
Photographed by Cecily Adams, 1898

49. above: **Dimsdale Old Hall Staircase, June 1901, pencil sketch**

panel is a circular smear, which it appears was formerly a painted landscape in the manner of Claude, together with representations of birds and animals. The panels, landscapes, etc., were thickly encrusted with dirt, through the rooms being used for live-stock, and when they were scraped the paintings were practically destroyed. The mansion, we believe, is soon to be demolished; but its generally forlorn condition – the bags of turnips in the corners of the rooms, the empty sacks stuffed in the broken windows, the lively clucking of poultry, and the egotistical grunting of a litter of young pigs – cannot rob the place of a certain mournful dignity.

(G.W. & F.A. Rhead, *Staffordshire Pots and Potteries*, 1907)

In 1908, Percy W.L. Adams speculates that there were signs that a moat once protected the ancient hall, further evidence of the site's antiquity. Likewise, he postulates that the stone building to the rear of the old mansion could conceivably have been a chapel belonging to the house, possibly erected in Saxon times by the earliest occupant, the Wolstans, from which the name Wolstanton was derived.

Cecily Adams's emotive photograph, taken in August of 1898, mournfully captures the grim circumstances to which the historic mansion had sunk, having been gutted by fire in 1895. Little was standing when the estate and house were sold around 1925, when it apparently received a reprieve and was restored, only to be sadly demolished in 1947. The site is presently part of Wolstanton Golf Club. It is interesting to note that the golf club have preserved part of the ancient building, visible only in their restaurant, for posterity, explaining on their website that

we have preserved part of the oak-framed wall with wattle and daub rendering, which we have encased in glass. It's a reminder of our very ancient past.

50 right: Dimsdale Hall Barn dating from around the early 17th century, photographed in 1957

Bradwell Hall, in common with Dimsdale, was built on ancient foundations and encased with bricks in the late 16th or early 17th century. In 1670 Dr. Plot specifically mentions Bradwell, together with other local seats, which

> *doe shew a great deal of present or past magnificence ... the mansion [Bradwell] has been practically pulled down, and the extensive deer park, which Robert Parker was the quondam keeper disparked.*

Evidently, by the time of the arrival of the Elers brothers Bradwell appears to have been greatly reduced in size and status, a common fate for seats that had been relegated in importance, due in this instance to the Sneyd family relocating to Keele Hall at the end of the 16th century.

It is thought that the Elers potworks lay on the southern edge of Bradwell Wood, just above Longbridge Hayes, in view of the population of Burslem who, no doubt catching glimpses of the strangers' furious activities, understandably wondered what was going on. Locals attempting to gain closer inspection of the clandestine operation were seemingly encouraged to leave; this in itself would have contributed to the intrigue and general wild speculation and no doubt spawned the plethora of myths and legends concerning the foreigners' covert activities.

It is interesting to note that John Adams (1652-1717) inherited a number of potteries from his father, most particularly one at the family homestead of Longbridge Hayes only a hundred yards or so away from Elers' potworks at Bradwell on the old packhorse way from Newcastle to Burslem. John Adams would have been well placed to witness Elers' day-to-day activities but disappointingly no mention is made in the family archive of the two brothers except a tantalising link to later Dutchmen. The Warburton, Daniels and Adams potting families (all interrelated by marriage) are known to have carried out a considerable trade with Holland and are on record as having brought over Dutchmen to Bagnall to assist with their attempts at enamelling salt-glaze ware. The arrival of these Dutchmen happened when Richard Adams (1739-1811) was a 'young lad', which tentatively dates the visit to the later 1740s, four decades after the departure of the Elers brothers from Staffordshire. Whether or not these Dutchmen were in any way connected to Elers can only be a matter of conjecture, but it is intriguing nevertheless.

Tales of the paranoid levels of secrecy employed by the Elers in protecting their manufacturing processes seem to have emanated from the pen of Simeon Shaw, as elucidated in his *The History of the Staffordshire Potteries*, 1829. Relying on local oral traditions, Shaw

51. above: Front elevation of Dimsdale Old Hall with brick pedimental gables and large lateral chimney stacks

*52. below: **Rear elevation of Bradwell Hall.** Photographed by Cecily Adams, circa 1900*

53. below: Drawing of Bradwell Wood by William Scarratt, 1906 (the location of Elers' pottery is thought to have been on the summit of the wood, top left)

outlined that, in order to protect their trade secrets, the Elers resorted to employing the stupidest workmen they could find, safe in the knowledge that they would not be able to articulate the innovative processes to competitors, thus mitigating any chance of industrial espionage. John Astbury is named as one perpetrator who feigned idiocy in order to gain access to the works, but this is hardly feasible as Astbury would have been a mere child when Elers established the pottery at Bradwell.

Further adding to the intrigue, in 1900 workmen unearthed a number of interconnected earthenware pipes while excavating the cellars at Bradwell; the house by then had become a tavern. It has been suggested that these pipes formed an early form of speaking tube connecting Bradwell to Dimsdale, possibly used to alert the works to approaching intruders. Specimens of the actual pipes were loaned to the Hanley Museum by Mr Rhead of Newcastle.

Ultimately, the Elers must have been successful in safeguarding their trade secrets, as history has shown that their most innovative processes did not become common practice until some forty years after their departure from Staffordshire.

One is left to consider what were the possible processes or techniques that the Elers took such pains to protect? The answer is to be found indirectly, in a letter written by Josiah Wedgwood to his business partner in January 1777, in response to a request received from J.P. Elers' son Paul. The content of Paul's letter had infuriated Josiah who had been

55. right: **Josiah Wedgwood by George Stubbs,** 1780 – enamel on a Wedgwood ceramic tablet

directed to inscribe a jasper medallion in honour of J.P. Elers with the words:

'Johannes Philipus Elers, Plastices Britannica Inventor.'

(John Philip Elers, Inventor of the Art of Pottery in Britain)

Josiah's reactions were understandably uncompromising:

This inscription, if I understand it, conveys a falsehood, and can therefore do no honour to the memory of his father, who was not the inventor of the art of Pottery in Britain, if there be any difference between inventing and improving the art.

54. above: **Medallion of John Philip Elers, England (Staffordshire),** 1775. Jasper ware, 4 $1/8$ x 3 $1/4$ in. The Nelson-Atkins Museum of Art, Kansas City, Missouri

Josiah goes on to detail the improvements in potting that he considered were as a direct result of Elers, these being:

Glazing our common clays with salt.
Refining our common red clay by sifting and making it into tea and coffee wares in imitation of the Chinese manner of ornamenting.
Casting of ware in a plaster mould and turning it on the outside upon lathes.

He further goes on to explain:

For these improvements, and very great ones they were for the time, we are indebted to the very ingenious Messrs. Elers, and I shall gladly contribute all my power to honour their memories, and transmit to posterity the knowledge of the obligations we owe them, but the sum total certainly does not amount to inventing the Art of Pottery in Britain.

Excavations and further research cast doubt on the idea that the Elers practiced salt glazing, with current thinking being that salt glazing was introduced to Staffordshire some ten years before the arrival of the Elers.

1688-1700 The Mysterious Dutchmen of Bradwell

56. below: **Stoneware bust of John Dwight, Master potter of Fulham, circa 1673-1675**

Potter of Fulham, who sought to hinder the defendants from making imitations of his red-coloured porcelain and undercutting him on price. Included in the injunction was the allegation that they had enticed an employee of Dwight to work for them, thus stealing patented secrets.

It seems that Dwight managed to reach an agreement with Elers, allowing them to licence his patents until 1698 when the licence duly ran out, coincidentally the very year in which John Philip Elers quit his lease at Bradwell and returned to London in an allegedly financially distressed circumstance.

The entry in *The London Gazette* of 12th December 1700 comes as no surprise, in that it mentions

a Commission of Bankruptcy being awarded against David Elers and John Philip Elers, late of Foxhall in Surrey, Potmakers.

J.P. Elers is thought to have been involved in a glass works in Chelsea and subsequently became established as a highly successful glass and china merchant in Dublin, while his brother David remained in London.

While their Staffordshire ventures had ended in failure, their legacy was perpetuated, subsequently inspiring generations of potters to strive for perfection, and undoubtedly bridging

the great chasm between the grand, massive, quaint yet clumsy course and cumbersome tygs and posset-pots of the latter half of the 17th century and the dainty light, and sharp turned tea sets and fine red stoneware that not even Wedgwood afterwards could rival with all the appliances of a century later.

(A.H. Church, *English Earthenware*, 1884)

Undoubtedly, the refining of clay and turning and finishing techniques were the two greatest assets left behind by Elers, techniques which have been developed and enhanced through the early 18th century by such influential potters as Thomas Astbury, Ralph Wood and Thomas Whieldon (the latter two once pupils of Astbury).

In 1693 the Elers brothers had, along with a number of other Staffordshire potters, become embroiled in a court action instigated by John Dwight, the Master

57. above: *Miss Bennett at Dimsdale, circa* 1890

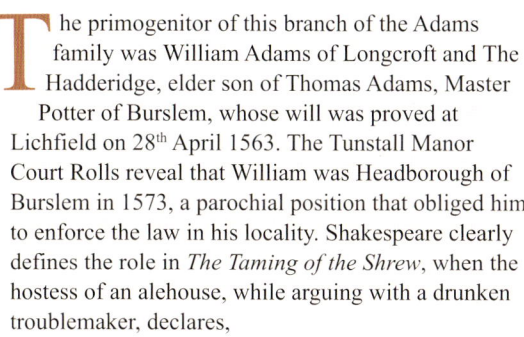

59. right: An early example of Wedgwood's Queen's Ware made in Josiah's Brick House works, circa 1765

5

1563-1869
ADAMS OF LONGCROFT, BRICK HOUSE & COBRIDGE HALL

The primogenitor of this branch of the Adams family was William Adams of Longcroft and The Hadderidge, elder son of Thomas Adams, Master Potter of Burslem, whose will was proved at Lichfield on 28th April 1563. The Tunstall Manor Court Rolls reveal that William was Headborough of Burslem in 1573, a parochial position that obliged him to enforce the law in his locality. Shakespeare clearly defines the role in *The Taming of the Shrew*, when the hostess of an alehouse, while arguing with a drunken troublemaker, declares,

I know my remedie, I must go fetch the Headborough.

William, in common with many of his family members, looked to a local potting family to find a wife, marrying Marjery Danyell, a member of one of the oldest potting families in the area, a union which no doubt added to William's status within the Burslem community.

As the elder son, William would have inherited the majority of the family wealth that at this time included the Longcroft estate, Velvet Croft, Wilberstones and The Hadderidge, property that mostly centred in and around the town of Burslem.

By the time William's son John (1570-1640) came into his inheritance, he would have been a well-established man of property and, following his father as Headborough of Burslem in 1606, a pillar of the community. John is known to have purchased more property, adding to the family's expanding estate.

John's first wife Elizabeth died in October 1610, having produced two sons and four daughters. Seemingly in no rush to remarry, he waited until 1619, when he took Margery Bagnall as his second wife, who was of collateral descent from the distinguished Staffordshire Bagnalls.

Sir Ralph Bagnall of Dieulacres Abbey had been Member of Parliament for the county of Staffordshire in 1555-9 and Newcastle in 1563-7. When Dieulacres Abbey fell in 1538 it was initially granted to Edward, Earl of Derby. Having been stripped of anything salvageable, the site, together with 12,000 acres, was given to Sir Ralph Bagnall, who was noted as being a committed Protestant. Ralph's younger brother, Sir Nicholas Bagnall MP also rose to high office as Marshall of Ireland 1547-53.

Further proof of the family's ascent in status is evident in the marriage of John and Margery's eldest daughter

58. left: Wedgwood Institute, Queen Street, Burslem, which stands on the site of the Adams' Brick House works

60. below: *Family tree of Adams of Longcroft, Brick House and Cobridge Hall*

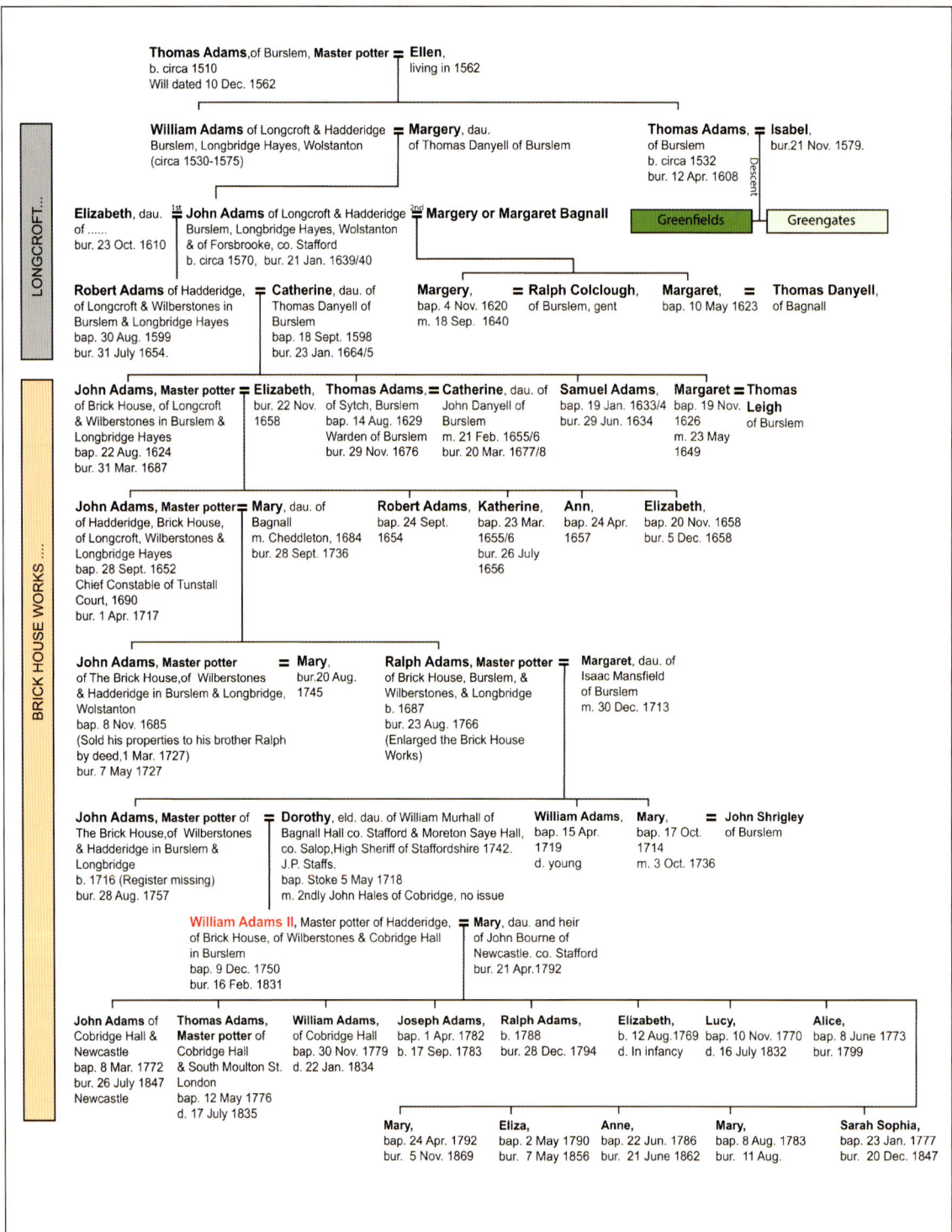

61. right: Memorial tablet to the early Adams family in St. John's Church Burslem. Inset – Adams' coat of arms quartered with Heath and Breeze

to Ralph Colclough gent, whose family had long served as MPs for Newcastle and were originally lords of the manor of Hanley and Baronets of Tintern, County Wexford.

John Adams' will, proved in Lichfield 1639, reveals through its myriads of legacies that he was a prosperous individual who provided well for his family, leaving elder son Robert well equipped to expand their potting ventures. That he left his son Robert all his ploughs and harrows reveals that farming was still an important activity for the family as they made the tentative transition from agriculture to the burgeoning potting industry.

Robert, emulating his entrepreneurial father, continued to acquire property centred around the Burslem, Tunstall area, and, with an eye to the future, seemingly paid off mortgages taken out by previous generations. It comes as no surprise to find that in the early 1640s he embarked on building a new family home in Burslem, constructed not of the traditional reddish-grey stone and wood, but unconventionally, of brick. Its standing out from the local houses no doubt spawned the name the 'Brick House'. When Robert's eldest son John (1624-1687) added a small pottery adjoining the family residence and christened it the 'Brick House Works', little did he know that his humble manufactory would become one of the most historically important potworks in Burslem, indeed in the potteries as a whole.

Specimens of the black and mottled ware produced by John Adams at the Brick House Works were discovered in excavations made on the site and preserved as museum exhibits. These items give us a unique insight into early Adams wares before markings were employed.

Life in the 1640s was challenging in the extreme; the country was beginning to recover from the effects of the first English Civil War and harvests in that period were nothing short of disastrous, culminating in the catastrophic harvest of 1647, during which time the yield was reduced by more than fifty percent. The price of grain rose sharply, doubling in the five years to 1647. The poorer families were hit the hardest, malnourished and more susceptible to disease.

It was against this bleak and troubling time that the parish of Burslem was further devastated by an outbreak of plague. The pestilence is said to have come from Italy, being brought in some clothing belonging to a governess who was employed to educate the Biddulph family of Rushton Grange. Victims of the plague were not buried in Burslem churchyard, for fear the wider population of the town would catch the disease, but were interred in a hollow at the back of Rushton Grange, henceforth called *Singing Kate's Hole* after the poor Italian governess who locals thought brought the deadly plague into their midst.

Burslem parish registers are somewhat silent on the subject of the plague, due in part to the ban on churchyard burials, but also as a direct result of parish

1563-1869 Adams of Longcroft, Brick House & Cobridge Hall

records being lost in the fire of 1717. The fire necessitated the rebuilding of St. John's church, with the exception of the 12th-century tower, which had miraculously survived.

Almost three centuries after the Black Death of 1348, the country had witnessed another plague of epic proportions. An estimated 205 of the population of the parish of Burslem had been struck down with the dreaded infection, but fortunately it seems to have been contained to outlying areas and the town itself was miraculously reprieved.

Both Robert Adams and his son John would have lived through the challenging times of the plague but it is highly probable that Robert, as churchwarden of St. John's church, Burslem, was intimately connected with assisting with the relief for the afflicted population. An entry in the churchwardens' accounts for Stoke-on-Trent noted:

A whole lune made by the present churchwardens and overseers of the poor, for the relief of the poor that were visited with the plague at Burslem.

Leek's experience of the plague as represented in the parish records, reveal that the vicar and some of the churchwardens perished in the heroic attempts to halt the progress of the deadly outbreak.

Less than a decade after the grim events of 1648, John Adams (1624-1687) embarked on a major rebuild of his Brick House Works in 1657, an event commemorated by the Adams family of potters in the 20th-century pottery mark they employed, namely, *Established 1657.*

Under his father's will, the eldest son, John Adams (b.1652), inherited a significant portfolio of property and an impressive collection of potteries, among which were Adams' oldest pottery, The Hadderidge, and the famed Brick House Works, which was their principal enterprise.

Centred in Burslem, John would have witnessed the rapidly developing potting industry which was transforming the town: by 1700, thirty five potworks had sprung up in the vicinity with twenty two salt-glaze ovens regularly firing up on a Thursday night until Saturday. Accounts graphically describe the occasions during the firing process when

the salt was cast upon the ware and the dense white cloud arising from the 'firing up' so completely enveloped the town as to cause persons to run against each other in the streets.

(William Chaffers, *Marks and Monograms on European and Oriental Pottery and Porcelain*, 1891)

The furious pace of development must have gripped the locality, as by 1750 it is further stated that there

62. left: Etching of the west elevation of St. John's Church, Burslem

63. below: **Bust of Ralph Adams** (1687-1766) *of the Brick House, Burslem*

were no fewer than sixty-five factories in the Potteries making salt-glaze ware and it is said that

the whole country was black with the smoke of burning salt – so black, it is said, that people groped their way through the streets of Burslem.

(Josiah C. Wedgwood, *Staffordshire Pottery and its History*, 1913)

Given the family's entrepreneurial flair, it is somewhat surprising to find his son, yet another John (b.1685), somewhat financially embarrassed, owing considerable sums of money locally. Two years after the death of his father in 1717, he is noted to have made a deed of gift of all his goods, personal estate, leases etc. to his wife, perhaps motivated by a desire to protect his assets from creditors. By 1727 his possible reckless spending came to a head. Fortunately for John, his younger brother Ralph came to the rescue, paying off his debts but with the proviso that the family conveyed to Ralph Adams:

The Brick House estate including the Brick House which Mary Adams Senior doth inhabit also the Wilberstones and Lower Wilberstones and Velvet Croft and also that other house in Burslem, which John Adams doth inhabit. Mary Adams Senior, John Adams & Mary his wife to have the smaller house at Brick House for their lives or the life of the survivor of them, & John Adams to have the yearly sum of £9 10s & Mary Adams the sum of £5.

(Extracts of the 1727 Conveyance)

Whether or not John was a spendthrift is difficult to ascertain; that he was left in reduced circumstances is undeniable. Adding to the grief and anguish, we find he died soon after the conveyance dated 7th May 1727, leaving his brother Ralph in sole charge of the family enterprise.

RALPH ADAMS, MASTER POTTER OF THE BRICK HOUSE

Under Ralph's tenure, the family's potting ventures flourished and this necessitated the enlargement of the Brick House Works in 1727 to cope with the

64. below: **Site of historic potteries in Burslem**

expansion of the range of wares produced. Greatly improving his wares naturally led to increased trade and ultimately profitability.

Ralph's son John was only eleven when his father took over the family potting business, but it appears that John was apprenticed in 1723/4, at the age of 8, to the well-known master potter John Simpson of Handley Green. It was common for potting families to apprentice their sons to other potteries and, in signing the legally binding indenture of apprenticeship, Ralph would have committed his son to a term of seven years with the expectation that his son would learn the craft of potting and eventually become a master potter in his own right. As part of the agreement, £5 was paid to the master, a fee that ensured that the child would be trained and given appropriate food, clothing and lodging for the duration of the apprenticeship. In order for the Indenture to become legally binding, the signature of a Justice of Peace was required and two copies were usually made, one for the parent and the other for the master.

Ralph would indeed be amply rewarded, as John flourished in his chosen trade, eventually becoming a celebrated manufacturer of salt-glaze ware. William Turner (*William Adams: An Old English Potter*, 1923) noted that

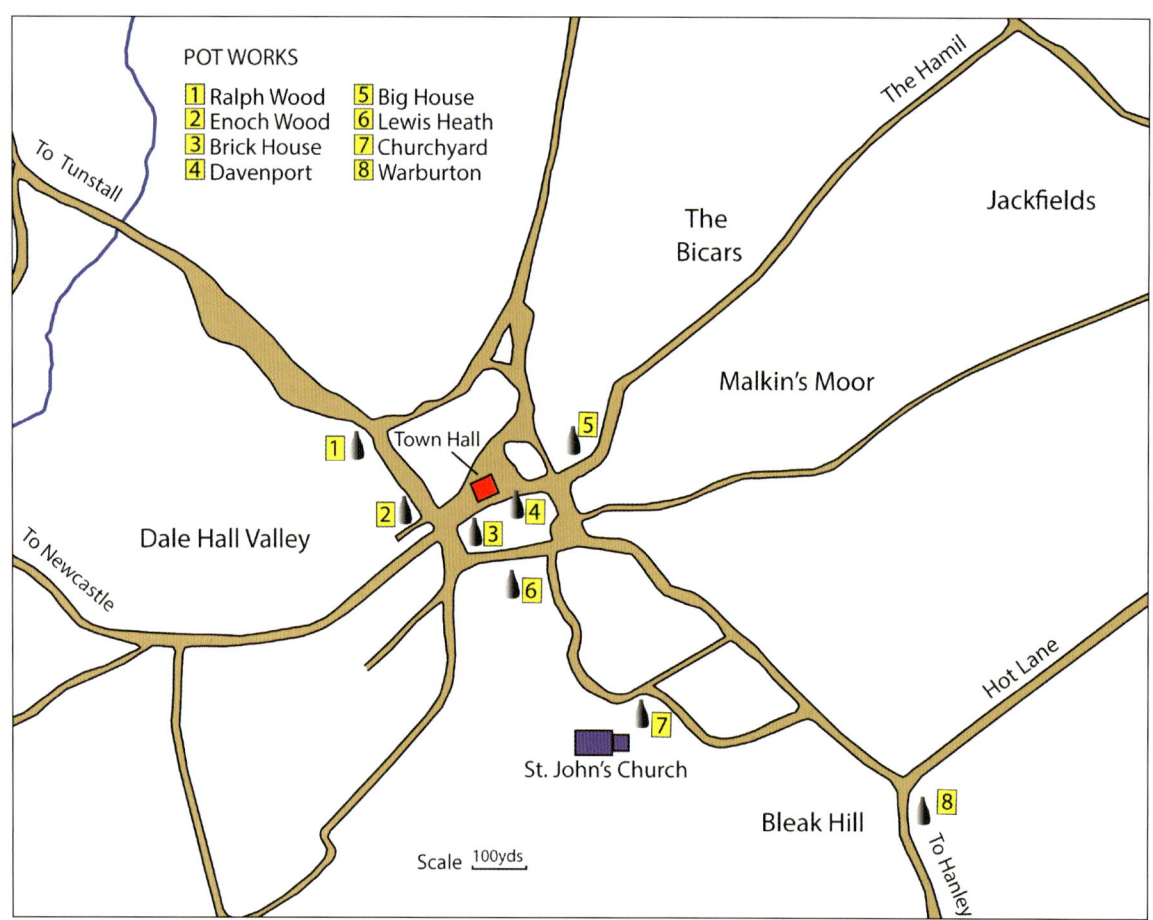

58   **ADAMS** Britain's Oldest Potting Dynasty

65. below: The Leopard Inn, Burslem – a late 18th century inn once owned by the Brick House Adams

John was a clever potter ... and his works were extensive for the period in which he lived.

Evidently not overlooking his civic duties, Ralph's name regularly occurs as a juror in the Tunstall Manor Court Rolls from 1709, and his role as churchwarden is immortalised by having his name incised on one of the church bells at St. John's, Burslem, in 1720. The role of churchwarden was significantly different to today; their brief in the 18th century involved:

1. Looking after the church.
2. Attending to the welfare of the parish.
3. Maintaining order and when required punishing wrongdoers by putting them in the stocks etc.

Two years before Ralph's appointment, St. John's, Burslem, had caught fire and was partially destroyed. With a thatched roof and much of the structure being of timber and plaster, the blaze would have spread rapidly. It is thought that many early records were destroyed in the fire, and some of the surviving registers have scorched edgings–a grim testament to the devastation that occurred.

It is interesting to note that every generation of the Adams family, in all their varying branches, have diligently occupied the role of churchwarden from the earliest of times, as did so many of Staffordshire's great potting families.

Around 1736, Ralph Adams is known to have 'lent' his son-in-law, John Shrigley, the Adams family's oldest property, The Hadderidge estate, which included a pottery works. The Hadderidge had been in the family since at least the 14th century and it is likely it formed part of a marriage settlement signed and dated 22nd September 1736 between Ralph Adams and John Shrigley.

John Shrigley, who was probably the son of Edward Shrigley, Master Potter of Burslem, did well in his association with the Adams family and built himself a substantial house on the north side of Burslem Town Hall, together with an attached potworks. But not everything went according to plan for John, as in 1765 he is said to have attempted to build the largest hovel (a chimney around the oven) of his day, but as the last bricks were placed into position, catastrophe: the whole thing collapsed!

In his later years Ralph seems to have concentrated on property rather than potteries, having built up a considerable portfolio around Burslem. Among the inns he owned was The Leopard, Burslem's famous 18th-century coaching inn.

Ralph Adams died in Burslem on 23rd August 1766 and, like his father, left no will. However, it is clear

66. below: Artist's impression of the Brick House works in the 18th century by Bethan Wiffen (2021)

68. right: Portrait of Charles Edward Stuart (1720-1788) (Bonnie Prince Charlie) by Louis Gabriel Blanchet, signed and dated 1739

that he attended to the transfer of assets to his son John through a conveyance he had made in 1747, when it is likely that he transferred ownership of much property, including The Brick House, to his talented and industrious son.

JOHN ADAMS OF BRICK HOUSE, CELEBRATED SALT-GLAZE MANUFACTURER (1716-1757)

On 25th August 1747 John married Dorothy, eldest daughter of William Murhall of Bagnall Hall, co. Stafford, a Justice of the Peace for the County of Stafford and High Sheriff of the County in 1742. The Murhalls were of ancient stock, tracing their ancestry back to the 13th century. Their marriage settlement, dated 4th June 1747, was made between Ralph Adams, yeoman, and William Murhall, Esquire, and required William to find £200 as a marriage portion on certain lands in Staffordshire while Ralph granted various lands in trust for the future married couple.

Their marriage in 1747 followed closely in the wake of possibly the greatest upheaval ever witnessed by the country folk of Bagnall. In 1745 the Jacobite Army swept through their tranquil village with Bagnall Hall taking centre stage at this terrifying time.

A RELIC OF THE JACOBITE REBELLION

Generations of the Adams family have clung on rigidly to the belief that during the Jacobite Rebellion of 1745, Prince Charles Edward Stuart, the Young Pretender, colourfully nicknamed Bonnie Prince Charlie, received hospitality from the Adams family at Bagnall.

A memento of this somewhat unbelievable historic event was preserved by the family in the form of a mundane teapot, which allegedly was used to serve the Pretender with tea on that auspicious occasion. This bruised and battered relic of distant times was passed down through the family and eventually deposited in the museum at Tunstall. On reorganisation of museums in the Potteries, it migrated to Hanley, forming part of its heritage collection of Adams ceramics.

67. left: Salt-glaze teapot with white ornamental relief, 3.25 inches high by John Adams (1716-1757). Thought to have been used by the Adams family to serve tea to Bonnie Prince Charlie during the Jacobite Rebellion of 1745

Many thoughts flashed through my mind:

Did this unremarkable, commonplace object really form part of a lavish breakfast spread before Bonnie Prince Charlie himself?

Is there any evidence that could corroborate this rather incredulous and possibly far-fetched belief?

Or conceivably:

Is this 'relic' indicative of a deeper sympathy that the family might have held with regards to the Jacobite cause?

Jacobitism was a treasonable offence, as its underlying intention was the overthrow of the government and the replacement of the Hanover dynasty with a Stuart successor.

Openly and willingly entertaining the Young Pretender within one's own household would be a dangerous, if not seditious, act!

Family memorabilia were often preserved in order to bring family history alive. Certainly this artefact instilled a powerful reaction in me and set me on a course of investigation into the veracity of the story that would hopefully enable assertion to emerge from the mists of folklore.

THE JACOBITE REBELLION OF 1745

On 24th July 1745, Prince Charles Edward Stuart landed at Eriksay on the Outer Hebrides with only seven supporters (two Scots, five Irish) and his faithful valet Michael–hardly a convincing start to a campaign to regain the British crown for his father, James III, the Old Pretender.

Charles launched his rebellion on 19th August 1745 at Glenfinnan in the Scottish Highlands, gathering support and moving swiftly to capture Edinburgh. His army later routed the English at the Battle of Prestonpans on 21st September, a battle that was over in less than thirty minutes–an encounter which saw the British Army, under Sir John Cope, crumble in the face of a frighteningly fearsome Highland Charge!

69. below: **The Field of Prestonpans, 1745** – *coloured lithograph by Mouilleron after Sir William Allan*

70. Jacobite Rebellion of 1745

Such a decisive victory in the first significant engagement of the Jacobite rising was a huge morale booster, coming in the wake of his father's abortive invasion thirty years earlier in 1715.

The invasion was rapidly gathering force. In response to this imminent threat to the kingdom, George II recalled his son, the Duke of Cumberland, from Flanders, along with 10,000 battle-hardened troops.

The French, who had promised Charles that they would support the rebellion, sent two ships with money and weapons to Montrose.

It was on the basis of the assured support from English Jacobites, and the promise of a substantial French invasionary force, that the Jacobite army's Council of War agreed to invade England. Their carefully chosen route south, progressing through territories known to be strongly Jacobite, would, they hoped, swell the number of recruits to the cause.

On 8th November the invading army entered England unopposed, reaching the weakly defended Carlisle and immediately instigating a siege. In the desperation of impending doom, the elderly garrison submitted to the overwhelming Jacobite force, surrendering on 15th November. The invaders were quick to secure the arms of the garrison's militia in addition to 200 good horses that were 'requisitioned'.

A few days later saw a formidable British force under Marshall Wade, based at Newcastle upon Tyne, begin their march to relieve Carlisle, an expedition that would later be abandoned due to heavy snow, forcing them to return to Newcastle five days later.

Arriving at Preston the Scots were greeted by bells ringing and cheers from a reception party, but with the memory of defeat at the Battle of Preston in the failed rebellion of 1715, the suspicious Highlanders were apprehensive and strangely disturbed. With renewed assurances of significant anticipated support, the invading army of 7,000 marched to Manchester, a well-known centre of Jacobite leaning. Some would undoubtedly have seen it as a worrying omen that the sum total of recruits generated at Preston was only three!

71. above: **Bonnie Prince Charlie's statue at Derby, the southern-most limit of the Jacobite Rebellion of 1745**

The vanguard of the Princes' army, which consisted of about 100 horsemen, arrived at Manchester about 9pm on 28th November, followed the next day by the entire army. As if orchestrated in the theatrical sense, Charles Stuart made his entrance surrounded by a select band of Highlanders, with his dress of tartan plaid belted with a blue sash and topped with a grey wig and blue velvet bonnet, very much the dashing prince. This was in stark contrast to a significant proportion of his force, as one eye witness recalled:

At their first visit I was in the town and saw them come in, they appeared to be about 7,000; perhaps 4 or 5000 of them may be soldiers; the rest are a mere rabble; they are in general ill clothed, hosed and armed; the blind and lame are among them and the very aged and children bear arms.

(*History of Leek,* p.124)

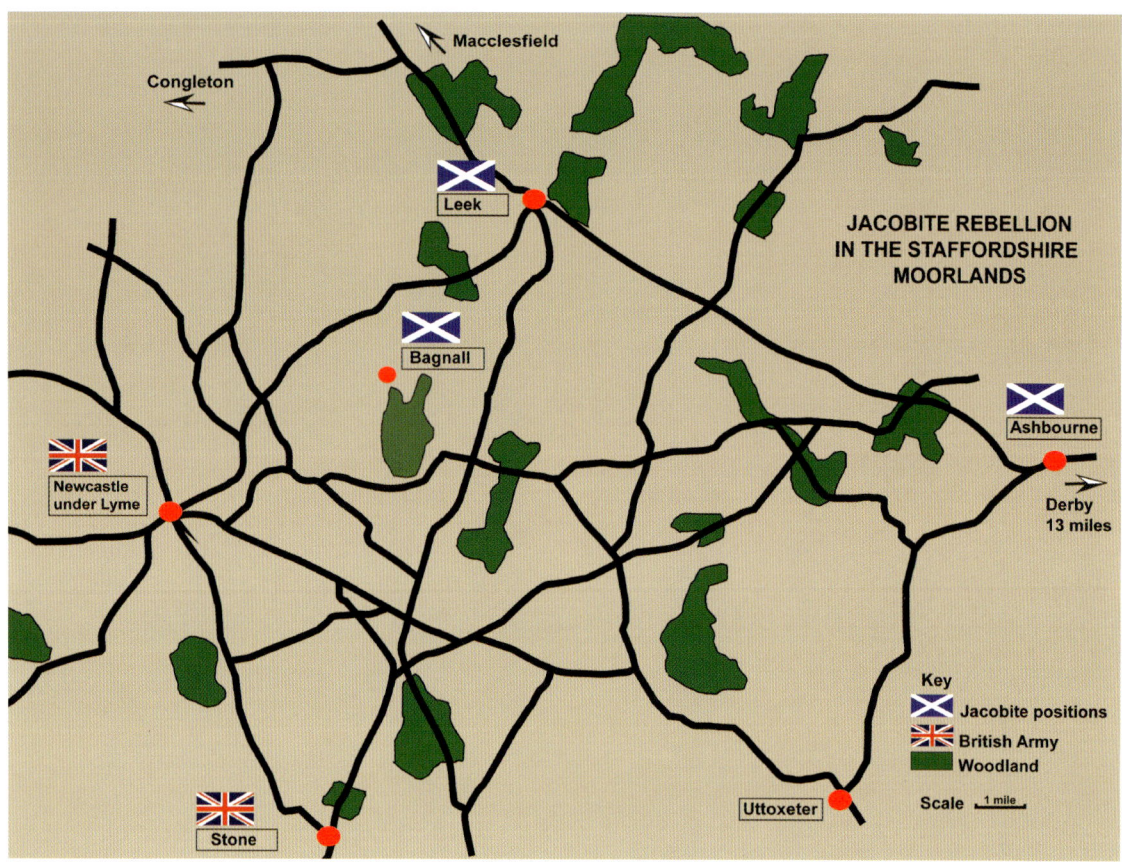

72. above: Jacobite Rebellion in the Staffordshire Moorlands

Meanwhile, formidable forces aimed at crushing the fledgling rebellion in its tracks were being deployed. George II had taken personal command of an army set up to defend London. His son, the Duke of Cumberland, had landed a force of 10,000 experienced soldiers in London with the intention of intercepting the Jacobite army in Staffordshire. Marshall Wade stood poised to act when needed in Newcastle upon Tyne.

The Pretender's army left Manchester heading south on 1st December, bolstered by 300 new recruits. The news of invasion spread like wildfire through the country, causing alarm and panic in the population.

Contrary to the expected carnage and brutality of the invasion, the Highlanders treated the population with a degree of civility, but let it be known that wherever they went they required the 'obedience' of the population, clearly stating that denying 'polite' requests for provisions would result in houses being plundered!

The extent of terror experienced by the population was evidently demonstrated by the actions of one poor old woman whose house was requisitioned to provide lodging for one of the Jacobite officers, a certain Cameron of Locheil, who

entered the lodgings and his 'landlady' threw herself at his feet, and with uplifted hands and tears in her eyes, supplicated him to take her life, but to spare her two little children. He asked her if she was in her senses, and told her to explain herself; when she answered, that everybody said the Highlanders ate children, and made them their common food. Cameron having assured her that they would not injure either her or her little children, or any person whatsoever, she looked at him for some moments with an air of surprise, and then opened a press calling out with a loud voice, Come out, children, the gentleman will not eat you! The children immediately left the press where she had concealed them, and threw themselves at his feet.

Robert Chambers, *Select writings of History of the Rebellion of 1745-46* (Edinburgh, 1840)

It was thought that the Highland army might march to Wales to garner support, but to deter this from happening bridges over the Mersey were quickly destroyed.

Some canny Staffordshire people, fearing their valuables would be seized, buried them in the ground; one even stashed silver plate in a mixen! Worried farmers hid their stock in remote forests and an air of quiet contempt for the invaders spread over the Staffordshire Moorlands.

Spirits were high among the invaders; their Prince had every cause to be jubilant as he had won the Battle of Prestonpans, taken Edinburgh, then Carlisle, and avoided Marshall Wade, and his illustrious General Lord George Murray would shortly outflank the Duke of Cumberland's forces waiting to cut them off in Staffordshire.

On leaving Macclesfield on 30th November, Lord George Murray split from the main force with a detachment of 2,000 men and made haste in the direction of Congleton. It was a cunning ruse aimed at drawing Cumberland's army from Newcastle-under-Lyme; Cumberland reacted by deploying forces to block the perceived move to Wales.

The main Jacobite army marched unobstructed to Macclesfield and then to Leek the 3rd December, closely followed by Murray, who had doubled back to join the main army.

The Jacobite army needed billeting. Early on in the rebellion they had lost thirty of their baggage waggons that had carried their tents. Owing to the severity of the weather and the lack of shelter, it was necessary to arrange quarters for the troops along the route. Soldiers were often billeted in barns etc., but officers were quartered in local gentry houses where they expected to be waited on hand and foot, often by the gentry family themselves.

It is recounted that Charles Stuart knocked on the door of St. Edward's vicarage at Leek to 'request' lodgings for the night. The vicar's wife, Mary Daintry, recognised the Prince and immediately slammed the door in his face and promptly collapsed. She is said to have died some two weeks later, presumably of shock.

An attack from Cumberland's forces was imminently expected and the Highland troops, in anticipation, sharpened their swords in readiness and, it is said, used the old preaching cross at St. Edwards's churchyard for target practice.

73. below: **Saxon cross in the churchyard of St. Edward the Confessor at Leek, Staffordshire– believed to have been used for target practice by the Jacobite Army**

74. left: Portrait of Charles Edward Stuart (Bonnie Prince Charlie) by Allan Ramsay, thought to have been painted in the palace of Holyrood while Charles prepared to march to London in 1745

On Wednesday 4th December, at about 11 o'clock, the vanguard of the Jacobite army entered Derby. They immediately inquired as to the whereabouts of the magistrates and demanded billeting for 9,000 men or more!

Bells were rung and a number of bonfires lit in celebration of the imminent arrival of Prince Charles Edward. The town crier was ordered to publicly proclaim the arrival of his Majesty and the magistrates were instructed to appear in their gowns to add to the occasion.

The rebels demanded money on pain of military execution and sent the town crier to announce a tax levy to be paid by 5pm on Thursday night. Finding that little money was forthcoming, they plundered houses in the town and 'requisitioned' horses from all around the area. The Prince arrived at dusk that evening on foot, attended by a large number of his men, who ceremonially conducted him to his lodgings.

The occupation of Derby caused a wave of panic throughout the country, nowhere more than in London. News had arrived at the capital on Friday 6th December, henceforth known as Black Friday. There was an unprecedented run on the Bank, and collapse was only avoided by the paying out of monies in sixpences, some of which had been heated up so that they were too hot to handle! Shops were for the most part shut and the King himself placed some of his most precious effects on board his Royal yachts under the protection of the guns of the Tower of London. Some Jacobite sympathisers openly displayed posters welcoming Prince Charles Stuart and his army to the capital.

Thursday 5th December was a period of reflection for the Prince's War Council. It was overwhelmingly decided to retreat, much to the vociferous objections of the Prince himself. Retreat was understandable, as a huge number of British soldiers were now encircling the rebel army. The rebels had penetrated deep into the heart of England and were only 127 miles from the capital, and realistically it looked unlikely that the French would be launching an invasion.

One of Cumberland's spies, a certain Joshua Ball, was captured and questioned to discover the location and strength of Cumberland's forces. He was plied with alcohol until he was totally drunk and thus unable to divulge any information to the enemy. It is acknowledged that the Jacobites had accurate intelligence of the British forces' deployment, thus enabling them to successfully evade confrontation with the much stronger force.

At 2 o'clock the following morning of 4th December, the Jacobites marched out of Leek, taking advantage of moonlight to escape the threat of an English attack. They marched through the night to Derby, by way of Ashbourne, under the noses of Cumberland's forces, who were also encamped at Stone and Stafford.

A Jacobite spy had been captured in Stone while on reconnaissance, and was taken to the Crown Hotel to be interrogated. Incredulously, having been given permission to use the toilet, he facilitated his escape, making his way back to inform the Prince. No doubt the intelligence he provided had a bearing on their hasty evacuation of Leek and deployment to Derby.

Morale was high among the Highlanders, no doubt encouraged by the knowledge that they were soon to be reinforced by Jacobite sympathisers and a host of invading French troops.

75. right: Portrait of Sir Watkin Williams-Wynn, the most prominent member of the Welsh Jacobites and a Tory MP, by Thomas Hudson

The Welsh Jacobites, most notably in the guise of Sir Watkin Williams-Wynn, the powerful North Wales squire, had openly stated that they would only come to the fray in the wake of a French army invasion; retreat seemed the only option on the table.

Prince Charles Stuart was mortified and ultimately felt that his council had betrayed him. He is said to have uttered,

Rather than go back, I would wish to be twenty feet underground. [adding later] in future I shall summon no more councils, since I am accountable to nobody for my actions but to God and my father, and therefore I shall no longer either ask or accept advice.

Alex Charles Ewald, *The Life and Times of Prince Charles Stuart* (London, 1883)

A ragged and disillusioned army retreated from Derby on 6th December, beginning its long and weary trek home and reaching Leek on the 8th. The Duke of Cumberland's army was three days behind them and determined to cut the rebels off before they reached Scotland.

In contrast to the jubilant march south, the dejected and disillusioned Jacobites spread over the country plundering houses in their wake. It was at this stage of the rebellion that the wayward army reached the village of Bagnall, seven miles from Leek.

The most intriguing evidence of the Jacobite's visit to Bagnall comes from a contemporary letter by James Middleton, whose brother, Reverend John Middleton, curate of Henley, visited Leek during this troubled time. The curate, it is thought, was commissioned by his friend Lord Gower, a cabinet minister, to 'make observations of the rebel forces'. James's letter to a friend in London dated 28th December 1745 states:

As to the rebels you were speaking of, they were no further than Darby, and returned back to Leek on Sat. … About 30 of their horse came to Bagnall, and took Justice Murhall along with them, and kept him two or three days: it's said he gave them £300 to be released.

J. Ward, *History of the Borough of Stoke-upon-Trent* (London, 1843)

An earlier account of a conversation between a John Telwright and Ralph Leigh in Burslem marketplace in 1810 gives us further information (written in Burslem dialogue):

Leigh – Whey, sartin sure it wur o' th' furst o' April, jist two year arter th' Scotch rebels coomn as fur as Baygna', (Bagnall), t' th' oud Justice Murhall's.

Telwright – Oi queit weel remember th' twak abait that; bu oi wur only 5 or 6 year oud. Th' Justice did no' loike em, oi've yeard.

Leigh – Oi think no'. Th' yung Pretender wi' his officers stedn to breakfast at the' squeirs; and afterwards th' Scotch sojers robt his hahis of his foire-arms an money, an maeydn him shew 'em th' road to 'art Darby.

76: William Hogarth's painting *The March of the Guards to Finchley,* depicting the fictional mustering of the British Army on the Tottenham Court Road

77. below: Bagnall Hall, home of Justice Murhall, whose eldest daughter Dorothy married John Adams of the Brick House, Burslem

The date of this dialogue establishes it took place some sixty-five years after the Jacobite rebellion, which, as Telwright states, happened within living memory, when he was 5 or 6 years old.

Justice Murhall lived at Bagnall Hall in the centre of the village and he has a clear link to the Adams family: as previously stated, his eldest daughter, Dorothy, married John Adams of the Brick House, Burslem, in 1747, two years after the rebellion. Dorothy was aged 27 on that ill-fated day when the rebels entered Bagnall.

A few yards from Bagnall Hall we find another member of the Adams family, namely William Adams of Bagnall Bank House. Williams' son Richard married Elizabeth, the eldest daughter of John Jackson of Greenwood Hall, Bagnall. Elizabeth was born one year before the Jacobite rebellion of 1745, and family tradition asserts that she often told stories about the rebels who visited Bagnall, these stories having been handed down to her through family connections.

There is ample evidence that robbing and plundering took place on the march from Leek to Derby, but in retreat the rebels became increasingly belligerent. In the village of Mayfield, the population barricaded themselves inside the village church of St. John the Baptist. The church door to this day is peppered with bullet marks probably fired by the rampaging Highlanders.

Sensing victory, the local population increasingly became more aggressive towards the Highlanders. Woe betide any Clansman who was left behind unable to keep up with the retreat; they would be at the mercy of aggrieved locals armed with pitchforks and scythes!

A gruesome reminder of the barbaric times occurred as a direct result of the mistreatment of Justice Murhall. It is stated that a wretched Highlander–an injured drummer boy–was captured, and the Justice in revenge had the poor unfortunate hung on a signpost at Leek and his skin sent to be tanned for a drumhead–not before he was dead, it is hoped.

So rushed and disorganised was the Jacobite retreat from Leek that it was stated that the Prince left behind a barrel of money, which was his war chest used to pay the troops. Certainly as the last dying embers of the rebellion burnt itself out it is evident that the Prince was literally spent out.

Cumberland's army, in hot pursuit, were unable to overtake the insurgents as they marched north to freedom, reaching Glasgow by Christmas Day.

The British forces caught up with the Highland army on the field of Culloden on April 16th 1746, when the Jacobite army of Charles Edward Stuart was decisively defeated by the British government forces under William Augustus, Duke of Cumberland. It was the last pitched battle fought on British soil, and a brutal aftermath followed in its wake.

Revisiting the Adams teapot, the long-treasured relic made by John Adams of the Brick House pottery, standing some 3 inches high and ornamented with decorated relief, it is no longer in my view a joyous memento of a gracious genteel breakfast, but a stark reminder of a turbulent time, when the sleepy village of Bagnall became the epicentre of an invasion that shook the country to its very core, and one that could well have changed the course of British history.

It is thought that the 'Jacobite teapot' heirloom was manufactured by a cousin of John Adams (b.1716) in the Holden Lane Pottery and kept by that branch of the family to eventually descend to P.W.L. Adams, who is

78. above: The church of St. John the Baptist in Mayfield on the outskirts of Ashbourne in Derbyshire, where, on the 7th December 1745, the local population took refuge when terrorised by the Jacobite Army

79. inset: Musket ball holes in the door of the tower of Mayfield Church, made by the retreating Jacobite army

80. above: **Painting of a scene from the Battle of Culloden by David Morier**

known to have deposited it in the museum in the early 20th century.

Forging further links to important potting familes, John Adams' daughter Lucy married James Daniel, Master Potter of Cobridge, whose uncle, Ralph Daniel, had been fundamental in introducing plaster-mould making into Staffordshire after witnessing the process during a visit he paid to France. In common with Adams, the Daniels stood out as one of the oldest local potting families: a John Daniel of Burslem was described as a potter in his will of 4th April 1587, thus symbolically uniting two of Staffordshire's most historic potting dynasties. It must also be noted that John's 2x great-grandfather, Robert, had previously forged the Daniels link, marrying Catherine, the daughter of Thomas Danyell of Burslem, in the early 17th century.

In 1757, at the young age of 41, John Adams died, leaving son and heir William fatherless at the age of 7. On 27th August 1758, John's widow Dorothy married John Hales, a potter of Cobridge, who would become an important influence on young William in his formative years. The Brick House pottery, the flagship of the Adams family potting business, was left vacant until the tenancy was taken over by an enterprising young potter by the name of Josiah Wedgwood in 1764.

THE BRICK HOUSE POTTERY UNDER JOSIAH WEDGWOOD

In 1759 Josiah Wedgwood commenced his own business, operating from the Ivy House Works, a small pottery owned by Josiah's cousins John and Thomas Wedgwood of the Big House, Burslem. Ivy House works was of modest size, comprising only two ovens,

81. right: *Portrait of Josiah Wedgwood from* The Scientific Correspondence of Joseph Priestley, 1892

a range of workshops and a small ivy-clad house fronting the road. Its location in the middle of the town would have put him in close contact with a number of other local potters and with a small workforce; it amply served his needs at this early stage of his career.

By 1762, no doubt finding the Ivy House works too cramped for his expanding business, he took up the lease of the larger Brick House works at a rent of £21 a year, relinquishing the Ivy House a year later. The Brick House works rent was paid to John Shrigley, the young William Adams II's legal guardian at the time.

The Brick House works stood on an extensive piece of ground and provided considerably more scope for the resourceful young master potter. Meteyard, in her *The Life of Josiah Wedgwood*, 1866, describes the scene:

> *The house was a tolerably roomy dwelling, with a small forecourt or garden in the front, and a somewhat larger strip of garden extending in the rear. One gable looked out on to a great open highway or plot of ground, yet broken by patches of common, holes from whence clay had been dug, and sherds of pottery; and on it, congregated to their play, the children from the neighbouring cottages, as also the potters' beasts of burden. The other gable of the dwelling overlooked the works, which occupied a considerable space of ground; the shops, such as the modellers, moulders, turners, throwers, and others, being all low two-storied tenements connected with each other, the upper chambers being generally approached by ladder-stairs from the outside.*

It was to this elegant and substantial house that Josiah brought his bride Sarah after their marriage on 25th January 1764, and soon the house would ring to the sound of a happy bustling family, with the first three children born at the Brick House before finally moving to Etruria Hall in 1769.

One of the first executive orders issued by Josiah on taking up the Brick House lease was the installation of a bell, housed in a cupola on the works roof. The bell was rung every morning at quarter to six to summon his employees to work. Prior to this 'alarm bell', an ox horn had been utilised for the same purpose, but confusingly most other works also employed an ear-cracking horn to awaken the workforce, making it difficult to distinguish between the rival potteries. With works following different schedules, it must have been total chaos. Josiah's elegant solution can be seen as part of a strategy designed to create a well-disciplined workforce, an essential component of the immensely successful business he later created.

Remarkably, the bell in question is now preserved in the manner of Lloyd's of London's Lutine Bell in the Wedgwood Museum.

Inevitably, the Brick House works became known as the Bell Works, a nickname no doubt devised by the workforce, but it is interesting to note that in all of Josiah's correspondence covering his tenure at the Brick House he never refers to it as the Bell Works.

82. left: *Black basalt ware by Wedgwood and Bentley, produced* 1769-80

Marlborough, Lord Spencer and Earl Gower, the latter often bringing his aristocratic guests from nearby Trentham to visit the acclaimed potter's works.

It was at the Brick House pottery between 1766-9 that Josiah perfected his world famous Black Etruscan ware, developed after years of experimentation from a crude form of the ware produced in Staffordshire called Egyptian Black, which he later called black porcelain.

July 26th 1766 was an important date in the history of Staffordshire. In Burslem it was a day of celebration and a public holiday, as the townsfolk marked the cutting of the first sod for the Trent and Mersey Canal:

The 'works' were nearly all closed, and from an early hour of the summer's morning, the population poured in. At noon, on a low level beneath the Brownhills, on the old ancestral land of the Burslems and Wedgwoods, and on the portion yet belonging to Thomas Wedgwood of the Overhouse, a dense throng gathered. Amongst it were to be seen noblemen, gentry, ladies, masters, and their workmen, all in holiday attire.

The centre of the group was composed of those officially connected with the canal. After some excellent speech-making, in which the veterans, the promoters of the scheme recounted their toils and dangers in the battle won, and like the prophets foretold the commercial and individual well-being the undertaking would insure, Mr Wedgwood, amidst enthusiastic cheers, dug up the first sod and soil, which, when placed in a barrow at hand, were wheeled away by Brindley, amidst reiterated plaudits.

Fresh speech-making followed. A barrel of old Staffordshire ale was broached on the spot; the healths of Earl Gower, Lord Anson, Lord Grey, the county members, the Committee, and other officers were drunk; and Mr Wedgwood was especially thanked, in the name of the whole assembly, for his indefatigable services in this good cause. Succeeding to this were luncheons and dinners at the Leopard and other inns. The

It was a time when superior French pottery was being imported in large quantities to the country. Josiah, no doubt sensing the need to improve the quality of his own wares to capitalise on this growing market, totally immersed himself in the task of producing fine and delicate earthenware. This he successfully achieved in 1763, with the introduction of his Queen's Ware– delicate cream-coloured items formed from the whitest clays from Devon and Dorset mixed with ground flint and exquisitely glazed. Years of meticulous experimentation had paid off and he was rewarded with the accolade of being appointed Queen's Potter by Royal Warrant to Queen Charlotte, Consort to George III.

Orders from the nobility and gentry flowed in for Josiah's beautiful creamware and he began to turn his attention to exporting his wares to the continent, reversing the trend of French imports with his superior pottery. Eventually a point was reached where French demands for Wedgwood's fine pottery became so great that the Royal factory at Sèvres began to imitate Wedgwood's work–a remarkable compliment to the great master.

Many distinguished visitors are known to have visited Josiah's now famous works to view the wares and be entertained: foremost among them were the Duke of

83. *below:* *A view of the Brick House works, circa* 1750

master-potters entertained their friends at home and regaled the men in the open spaces about the 'works'. A sheep was roasted for the benefit of the poorer potters, and at sunset bonfires were lighted in various parts of the town; a feu de joie was fired in front of Mr Wegdwood's house [Brick House] *and within a very large company assembled to partake of the bounteous hospitality which Mrs Wedgwood's skill as a housewife had prepared.*

(Eliza Meteyard, *The Life of Josiah Wedgwood*, 1866)

In April 1769, William Adams II married Mary Bourne, daughter and heir of John Bourne of Newcastle-under-Lyme, a prosperous cordwainer who ran a boot factory and owned a great deal of property in Newcastle, Sneyd Green and Cobridge. William, having achieved his minority, succeeded to the Brick House works and other properties under his father's will, and it comes as little surprise that he wanted to branch out as a potter in his own right. Operating from the family's most important potwork would have been foremost in his mind. He notified his most distinguished tenant of his intention through a letter, and Josiah Wedgwood communicated the news to his business partner Bentley in November 1769, stating:

84. left: Brick House Lane, Burslem (2021)

I have notice to leave the Brick House works next year. My landlord is married and will come to them himself. Here is a fine piece of work cut out for me!

The situation was not as disastrous as Wedgwood implied; he had already purchased the Ridge House estate–the intended site of his ambitious new works at Etruria–which was some 3 miles from Burslem and comprised of about 150 acres. Later in 1769, the first phase of Wedgwood's Etruria works opened to produce his black basalts and other luxury goods, which he identified as ornamental ware. The Brick House works continued under Wedgwood's management until 1773, when the works were finally closed.

By 1770 William Adams II had built a new factory at Sneyd Green on the site of one worked by his ancestors, and, interestingly, he had not pressured Wedgwood to leave the Brick House until 1773, when, four years after giving notice to quit, he finally took possession, working it in conjunction with his Cobridge works.

It seems fitting to give the final epitaph of the historic Brick House works to Eliza Meteyard, who, in 1866, stated

the 'Brick House and Works' stood on what now forms proportionally the site of the Wedgwood Institute; and, as associated with some of the most remarkable as also most touching events in the life of the great potter, one more fitting could not be found.

The Brick House was prepared and received his bride; and here it was, as he confides to Bentley, months after the marriage, he and his wife were still 'married lovers' ... here he teaches her the curious cipher or short-hand in which he preserves the precious and self discovered secret of his art ... Here his first three children are born; the eldest daughter whose noble destiny it is to become the mother of an eminently gifted man [Charles Darwin]. Here he buries his second-born son Richard; suffers the amputation of his long-diseased limb with fortitude and courage inherent in the highest natures. Here he welcomes the great Erasmus Darwin, and confers with him on many topics of philosophic interest ... In short, here Josiah Wedgwood unravels, like all of us, much of the mingled web of Fate; its hopes and joys, its pains and sorrows ... The Wedgwood Institute could have no more fitting site than the ground hallowed by associations so eminently characteristic of the great artist and generous Englishman it is raised to commemorate and honour.

WILLIAM ADAMS II OF COBRIDGE HALL

After the death of his father in 1757, William and his family continued to reside at the Brick House until 1762 when it was let out to Josiah Wedgwood. Shortly after, we find the bereaved family living at Bagnall Hall, the family seat of William's mother Dorothy née Murhall. Dorothy's father, the prominent Squire of Bagnall, had relocated to Moreton Saye Hall in Shropshire in 1747, no doubt traumatised by the Jacobite incursion he so graphically witnessed at first hand.

William must have received a good education as it is noted that he was able to keep his own accounts at the early age of 15. Commensurate with other master potters' sons, he was set on a course that would enable him to ultimately manage the family potting business.

In 1769, William entered into partnership with his stepfather John Hales, working a family potwork in Cobridge under the business name of Hales & Adams. John Hales, twelve years older than William, was a seasoned entrepreneur who forged a number of successful business ventures in the locality and it was he who undoubtedly sparked the spirit of enterprise that would be the hallmark of William's future business endeavours.

By 1774 William had let out the Brick House works to William Bourne, preferring to concentrate on his larger works in Cobridge, where he was experimenting with

*85. below: **William Adams II** (1750-1831) of the Brick House and Cobridge Hall*

86. below: *Layout plan of Cobridge Hall circa 1900*

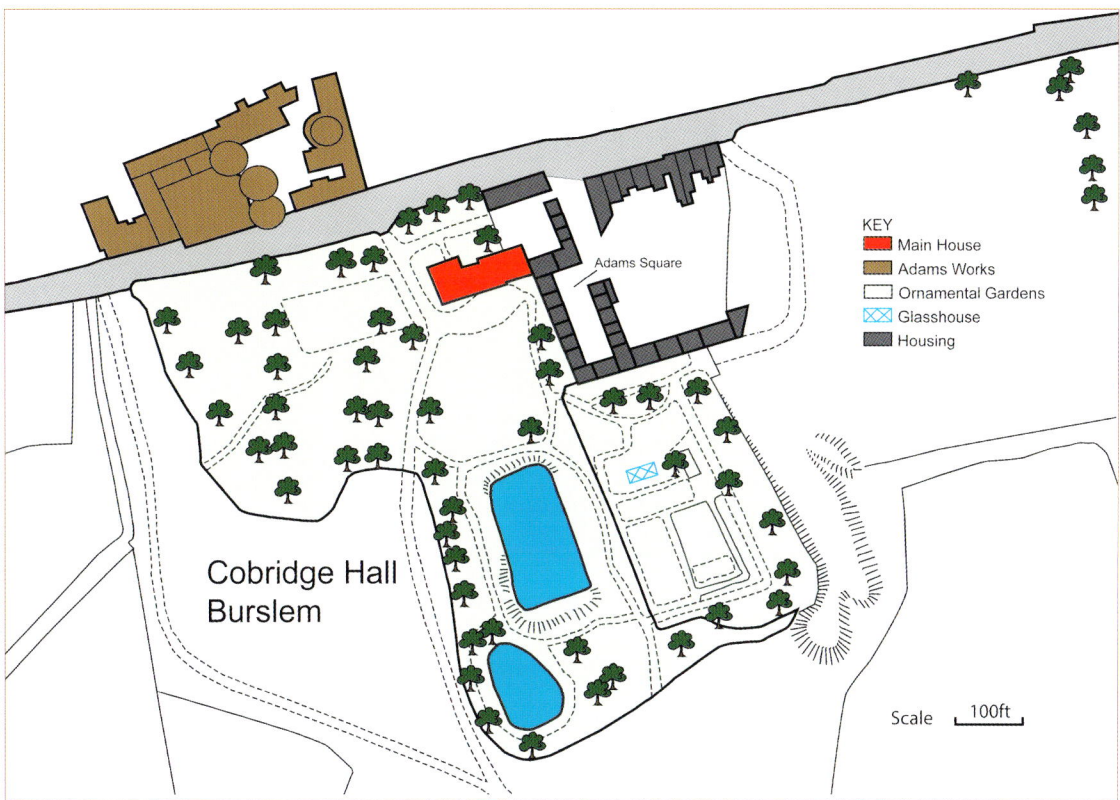

the very latest emerging pottery innovation, that of transfer-printing, and of course dabbling with a myriad of other potentially lucrative business ventures.

William continued his incessant land purchases to the point that, by 1806, he literally owned most of Cobridge. In 1777 he bought the Cobridge Gate estate and by 1780 had built his mansion of Cobridge Hall. Its situation was idyllic:

> *The extensive gardens were surrounded by a small park, the drive leading to the hall was a quarter of a mile long, and the front gates opened into what is known as Vale Place, Waterloo Road. The lodge was occupied by the coachman and the gamekeeper had a cottage half-way up the drive. Altogether it formed a very pleasant country house, and up to 1850 the situation was undoubtedly charming.*

(P.W.L. Adams, *A History of the Adams Family of North Staffordshire*, 1914)

This distinguished residence would become the seat of this branch of the Adams family for almost a century and, together with their summer residence–a country house called Wall Lane in Cheddleton– it provided an ideal haven for William's extensive family of thirteen children, sadly all of whom were to die childless.

While aggressively expanding his property portfolio, William had not ignored his potting heritage and by 1820 he owned five potteries in the area and was a highly regarded master potter. Undoubtedly, William had learnt the skills of potting from his stepfather, John Hales of Cobridge. It was at one of his Cobridge works that William Adams successfully experimented with copperplate printing, possibly under the auspices of his mentor.

The process of copperplate printing on pottery was initially carried out at Battersea in and around 1753. By 1756, Sadler & Green of Liverpool had perfected the technique to such a high level that even Wedgwood

87. below: Potteries with connections to the Adams families (William Adams I to V)

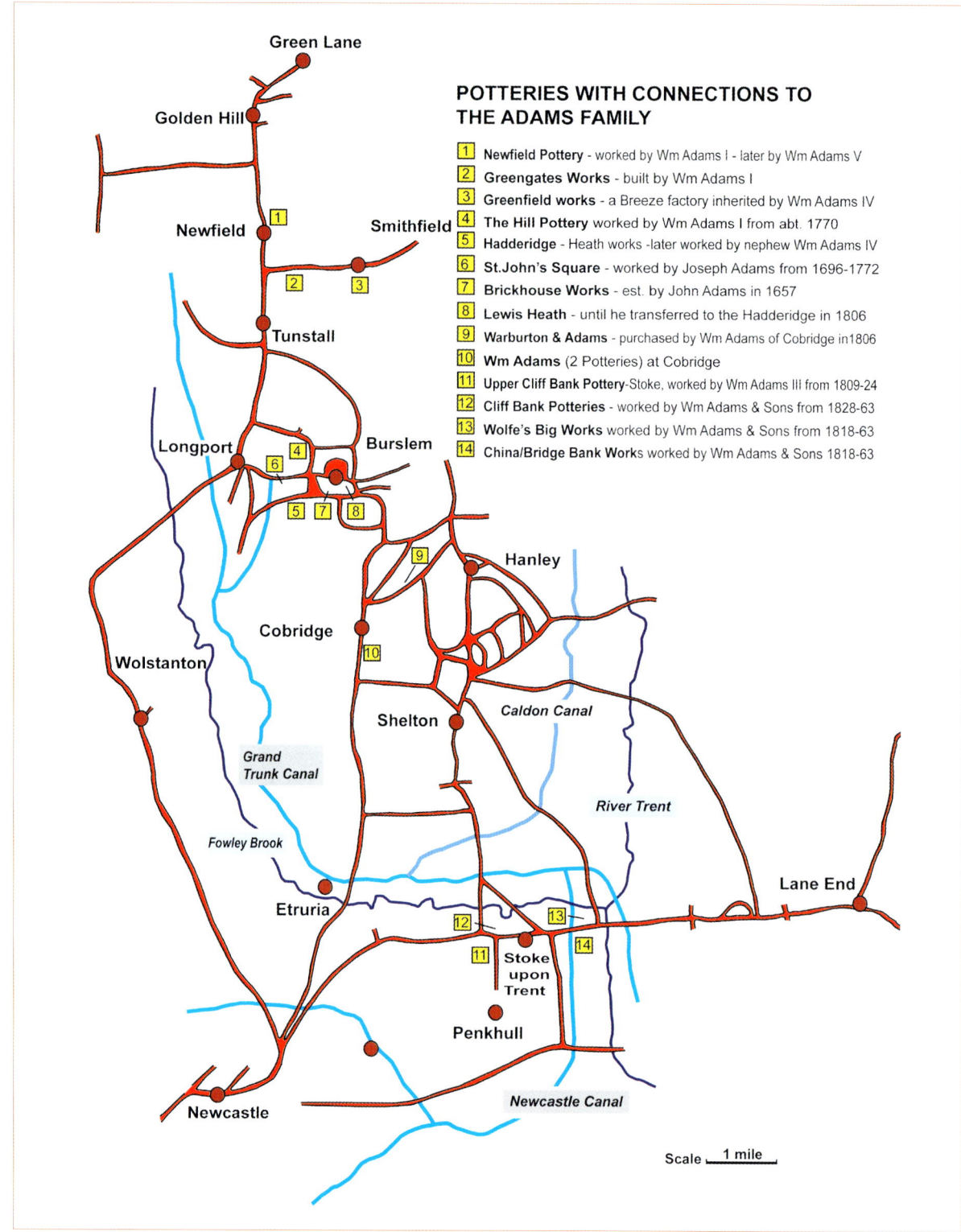

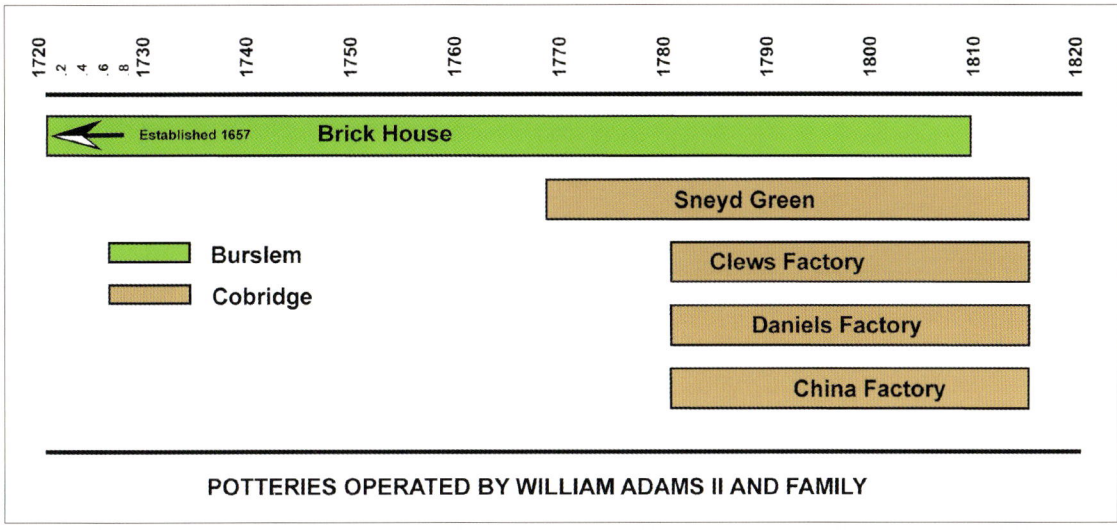

88. *above:* *Potteries operated by William Adams II and family*

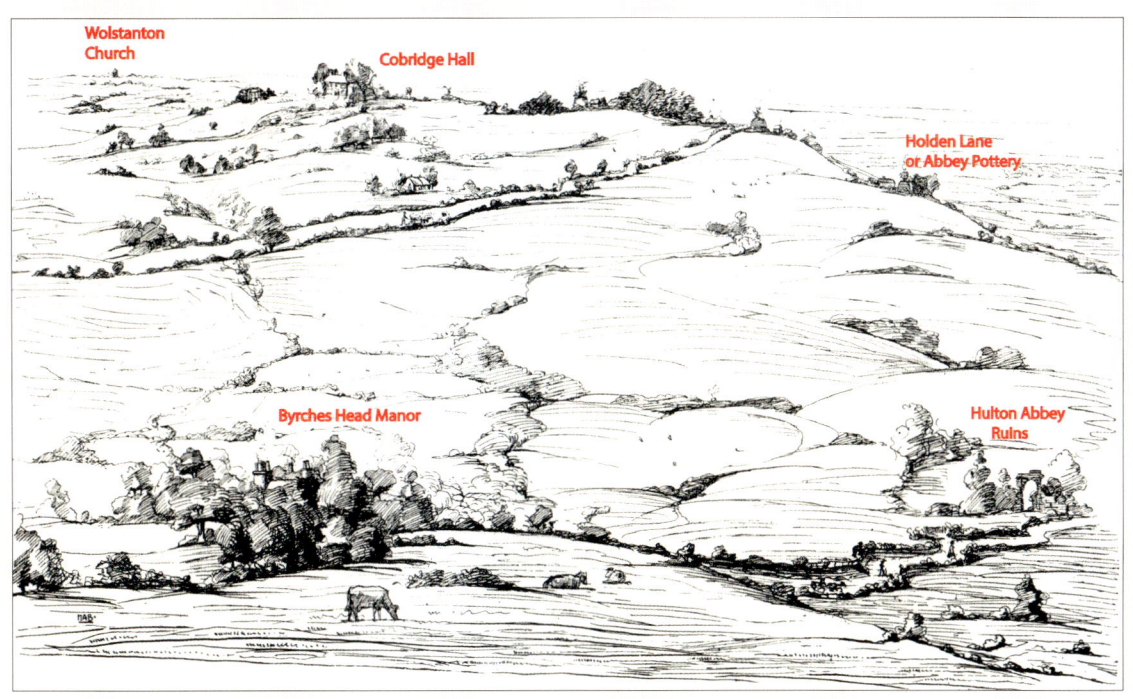

89. *above:* *Cobridge Hall - the seat of William Adams II and family from* 1780

90. *Adam's Tile works, circa 1840-1890, artist unknown*

84 ADAMS Britain's Oldest Potting Dynasty

1563-1869 Adams of Longcroft, Brick House & Cobridge Hall

91. below: **The Liberty of Cobridge** 1775

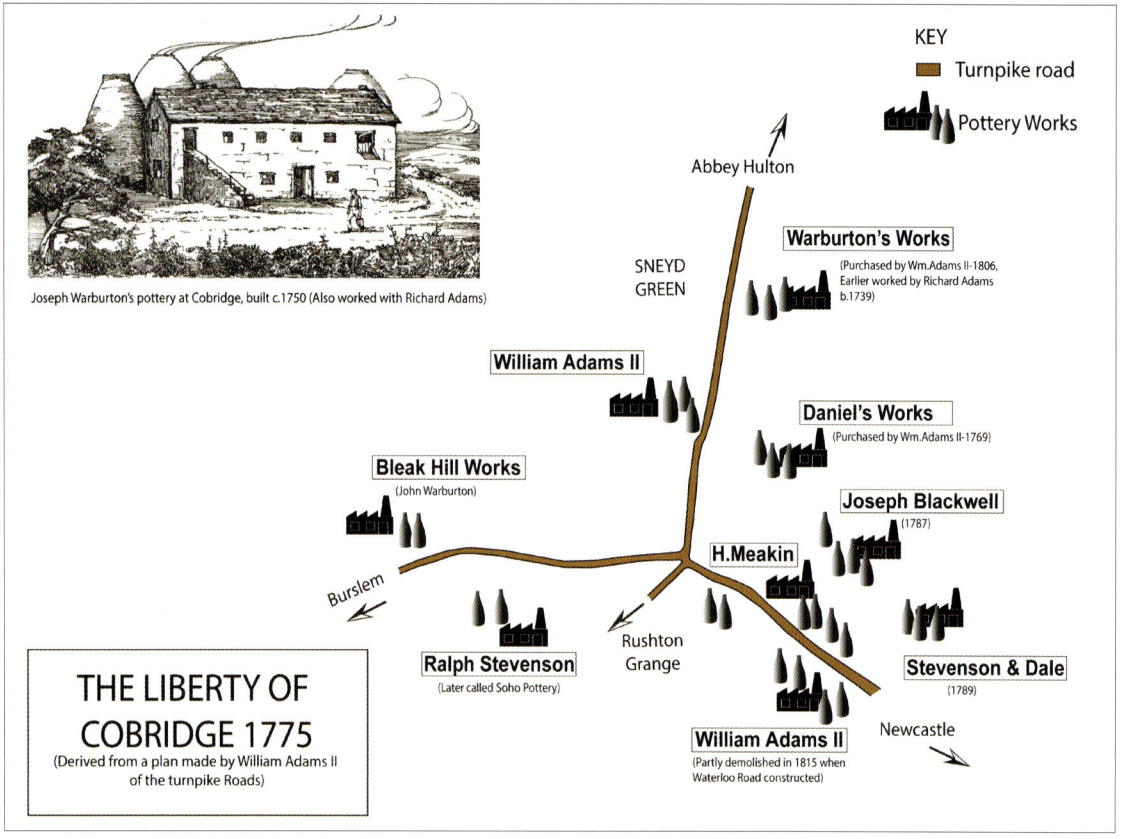

sent his wares to the Liverpool Company to have the transfers printed on them.

A concise description of the transfer-printing process is found in Arthur Hayden, *Chats on Old Earthenware*, 1909:

> *The copper-plate is inked, and a sheet of tough tissue paper, wetted with a mixture of soap, is applied to its surface and printed in a press. The paper is taken off, showing an impression or print, which is carefully laid on the surface of the piece of earthenware to be decorated. The design on the paper transfers itself to the earthenware.*

By 1775, William Adams was working on this innovative process at his own potworks, having employed an expert in the field, a William Davies of Worcester, to ultimately achieve perfection. So secret was the transfer-printing process that William Adams is known to have locked up the workers away from the prying eyes of rival potters, and was ultimately conferred with the accolade of being the first to introduce transfer printing to Staffordshire.

Demonstrating huge business acumen, William systematically acquired flint mills, coal mines, brickworks and forests, cutting out the middleman by supplying a great deal of the raw materials required by his potting works and indeed branching out to supply other manufacturers. The purchase of Knowl Wood in the parish of Market Drayton was driven by the need to supply his potteries with wood for producing the crates used to transport his wares. The coalmines he acquired supplied the ever-increasing demands of his red-hot furnaces. Acquiring paper mills at Cheddleton allowed for self-sufficiency in the fine rolls of transfer tissue so vital to the transfer-printing process and also

92 Below: *Map of Burslem circa 1850, showing the location of The Leopard Inn in relation to the Brick House works*

opened up further opportunities to wholesale the product to his competitors. The procuring of flint mills similarly not only cut overheads but also added to revenues and his ever-increasing bank balance.

An acquired tile works in Tunstall, rather than adding to Adams' portfolio of subsidiary works, was rented out, a strategy that would increasingly be used by William in the early years of the 19th century. A corn mill owned by the family called Wilberstones–now famously called Middleport–likely ended up as a rental asset.

On 21st October 1783, William Adams purchased James Daniel's estate at Cobridge, having successfully outbid the master potter Enoch Wood, offering £6,700 against Enoch's £6,000, a significant sum in the region of a million pounds in today's money. It is an interesting coincidence that William's purchase of the Daniel's estate occurred almost to the date of the Treaty of Paris, a treaty that ended the American Revolutionary War.

William had built up a strong export trade and was poised to capitalise on the boom that followed the ending of the war with America, and the purchase of Daniel's works was a component part of meeting the anticipated demand for pottery that would inevitably follow.

The boom years of the 1790's must have been exceptionally busy for our entrepreneur, and it comes as no surprise that he seized the opportunity for a break, enlisting his brother-in-law James Daniels to accompany him on an extended tour of the Baltic States.

A TOUR OF THE BALTIC

In 1797, aged 49, William Adams embarked on what can tentatively be described as his 'Grand Tour', choosing the rarely visited and inhospitable Baltic area as the focus for his intrepid expedition of more than twelve months duration.

The classic Grand Tour was a 17th and 18th century custom, whereby upper class young gentlemen of sufficient means toured Europe in search of art and culture; the Tour was was considered essential to broadening a young man's mind and finishing off his classical education.

The outbreak of the Napoleonic War at the end of the 18th century made travel to the popular Grand Tour destinations of France and Italy precarious to say the least and resulted in a growing trend of visits to safer alternatives such as Wales, the Scottish Highlands, and even more exotic locations such as South America, India and China.

Baltic travel in the later 18th century was very difficult; roads, where they existed, were

a perfect misery, axle-deep in mud or wet sand

(*Traveller's Guide to Germany*)

Sea routes, although poorly developed, were the best option for the adventurous traveller in the closing years of the 18th century.

93. below: **Kirkstall Abbey, a well-preserved Cistercian Abbey near Leeds**

94. below: William Adams II – Tour of the Baltic 1797-8

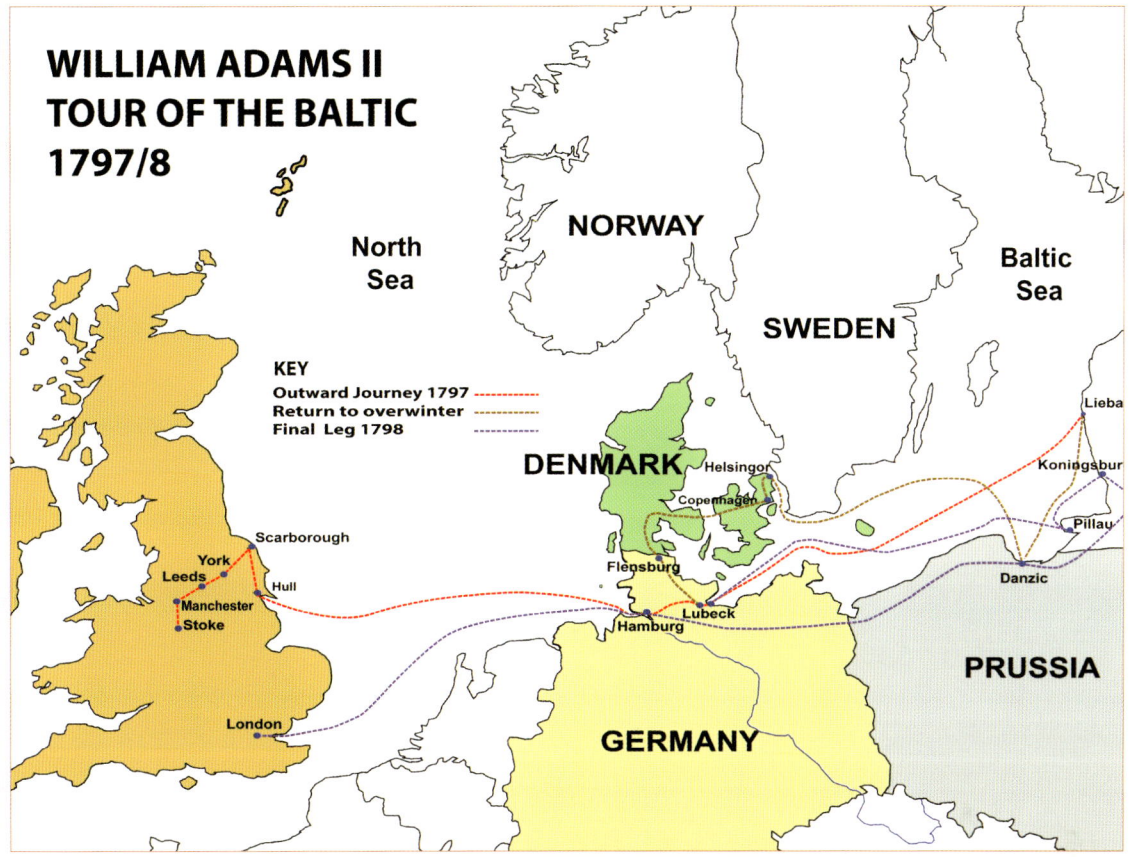

William Adams was an avid reader, known to have been fond of travelling abroad, and he might well have been inspired to undertake this gruelling adventure after discovering Sir Nathaniel William Wraxhall's publication *A Tour round the Baltic thro' the Nordic countries of Europe*, published in 1775–a book which no doubt contributed to the expansion of the Grand Tour towards the Baltic Sea and Russia.

Travel literature of the 18th century, commonly referred to as 'books of travel', were often in the form of maritime diaries, and in writing a record of his Northern adventure in this format, William might have been emulating the style of Captain James Cook, who published his diary in 1784.

It is unlikely that the wealthy and successful potter William Adams embarked on his tour with the overriding intentions of improving his business connections; he had already expanded his horizons in the business sense and had become a significant property developer in his locality, renting out his potting works to others.

William's diary entries commence on 18th June 1797, when he began his tour, travelling from Staffordshire with his brother-in-law James Daniel, reaching Manchester the next day.

95. above: The whaling ship Diana, *a slightly larger and later namesake of the ship William Adams II sailed on from Hull on his outward journey in* 1797

The following is a glimpse of their itinerary and impressions:

JUNE 19TH MANCHESTER

Having taken lodgings at the Swan Inn, Market Street Lane, they took in the sights of the city. Later, visiting a clothing manufactory, he was fascinated by the means used to cut the fustians (heavy cloth woven from cotton).

JUNE 20TH ROCHDALE–HALIFAX–BRADFORD–LEEDS

They visited Kirkstall Abbey, a ruined Cistercian monastery four miles from Leeds, whose picturesque ruins attracted artists of the 18th-century Romantic Movement, including J.M.W. Turner.
William's fascination for steam engines naturally drew him to visit the factories of Leeds that had utilized steam power in their manufacturing, eventually rendering it one of the richest towns in Yorkshire.

JUNE 22ND YORK

William was impressed with the Gothic cathedral, noting that it was more extensive than St. Paul's Cathedral in London. With regards to York as a place of trade, he remained unimpressed.

JUNE 24TH MARKET WEIGHTON–BEVERLEY–HULL

He commented on Hull's growing trade with the Baltic and the docks being noteworthy but not as extensive as Liverpool's, perhaps a tentative signal that he might have been evaluating potential business from the burgeoning Baltic trade?

JUNE 29TH HULL–BEVERLEY–DRIFFIELD–SCARBOROUGH

Scarborough Castle impressed him as did the fashionable resort with its elegant buildings and medicinal waters. The sea view from the castle he considered

one of the grandest in nature ... frequently is exhibited to the view of the astonished beholder from one to two hundred sail of vessels, gliding triumphantly on the ocean to their different destinations, which cannot fail to excite a wonderful sensation of the invention of man.

96. below: A view of Hull docks as represented in the early 19th century by William Henry Bartlett

JULY 3RD RETURNED TO HULL

JULY 12TH EMBARKED ON BOARD THE *DIANA* AT HULL

The *Diana* was built in 1774 and had a carrying capacity of 288 tons. Between 1785 and 1794 she had been a British whaling ship, based in Hull, subsequently becoming a transport and Baltic trader. This Hamburg-bound vessel carried cargo and, in addition to William and James, had only four other passengers. For two days he was inflicted with sea-sickness and on July 14th, off the Dutch coast, he

heard much firing from the celebration of the French Revolution at Texel.

It was a worrying sign of the turbulent events that were unfolding over the horizon and a grim reminder, if that were needed, that they were entering a potential war zone, the army of the French Republic having overrun the Dutch State in 1795.

JULY 19TH DISEMBARKED HAMBURG

Here reference is made to the

unpleasing reception they were given and the unaccustomed manners to which they were introduced.

Having spent the best part of two weeks exploring the locality, they departed Hamburg in one of the German stool waggons bound for Lübeck, some 40 miles hence.

AUGUST 2ND ARRIVED LÜBECK 6 O'CLOCK IN THE EVENING

The journey from Hamburg had been extremely unpleasant; for the most part they had travelled

1563-1869 Adams of Longcroft, Brick House & Cobridge Hall

97. below: The port of Danzig by Johann Karl Schultz, oil on canvas, 1837

through deplorable conditions, but hopefully it was not as disastrous a journey as the one experienced by another 18th-century traveller who was

thrown into a ditch when the springs of her carriage broke, then, after rattling and screeching over such roads or rocks that she felt she would never survive the journey, she was flung out of the vehicle again as one of the wheels flew off. She arrived at her destination, more dead than alive, without the strength to take off her clothes.

(*The Grand Tour*, Christopher Hibbart, 1987)

The town of Lübeck seemingly made a more favourable impression on our intrepid travellers and they found the *'bracing sea air most agreeable'*. Visits to numerous superbly decorated churches were noted. The horary or clock found in the Great Church particularly entertained: striking 12 o'clock, twelve figures representing the apostles came out to pay their respects to a representation of Christ.

Lübeck's central position on the Baltic resulted in considerable trade with all the ports in the vicinity– Danzig, Köninsburg, Pillau and St. Petersburg–most of which would form part of their onward itinerary.

AUGUST 15TH DEPARTED SHIP *GOOD INTENT* BOUND FOR LIEBAU

High winds and violent storms made the six-day voyage a dismal experience for all five passengers; William noted that he had spent six days on board without ever changing his clothes and had had numerous sleepless nights.

AUGUST 24TH ARRIVAL LIEBAU

Liebau formed part of the Duchy of Courland, which in 1795 had passed to the control of the Russian Empire as a result of the third partition of Poland. Today it is a city in western Latvia. The travellers found the Russian customs officials extremely tedious and irritating, commenting that Liebau was

98. above: **Kronborg Castle in Helsingør, Denmark–immortalized as Elsinore Castle in William Shakespeare's** Hamlet

protected or rather enslaved by about 2,000 soldiers of Russia whose pay is about 10 shillings annually…. Of Liebau I may say I found it to be a place of persecution, from officers – from fleas, which are abundant – and from sand on its shores.

AUGUST 25TH DEPARTED LIEBAU BOUND FOR DANZIG

Embarking on board the small sloop *Hoffnung* at 6 o'clock in the morning, the expectation was for a leisurely three-day voyage, but this was shattered by a lack of prevailing wind, which postponed their arrival until eight days later. Provisions ran out on the fourth day, swiftly followed by water a couple of days later. Hoped-for provisions in the form of fish from Cossacks likewise resulted in disappointment. It was with great relief that the weary group vacated the flea-ridden ship and embarked on the short walk ashore at Danzig to enjoy a simple but wholesome meal. (Tragically, nautical records indicate that the ship *Hoffnung*, of unknown flag, was at a later date lost in the Baltic on a voyage from London.)

SEPTEMBER 1ST DANZIG

The huge grain stores of Danzig housed produce destined for the English market. Large quantities of timber likewise passed to Britain through the busy port. Fish was astonishingly plentiful, fruit abundant and cheap. The town was defended by a garrison and was in the possession of the King of Prussia after a four-year-long struggle.

SEPTEMBER 11TH DEPARTED FOR THE PORT OF HELSINGØR, DENMARK

They sailed on board *Wilhelmina,* a 1,000-ton vessel under the command of Capt. John George Kinder in the company of five other passengers.

SEPTEMBER 19TH ARRIVED ELSINORE, DENMARK

Helsingør is a port in eastern Denmark whose main attraction was Kronborg Castle, said to be where Shakespeare's *Hamlet* was set. Suitably impressed with the literary connection, the companions set off for Copenhagen in a waggon, a pleasant journey of some 20 miles with

very agreeable views of the sea.

In 1795 a fire had seriously damaged part of the city of Copenhagen and, arriving only some two years later, they would have witnessed the ravaging effect of a destructive blaze that had destroyed the Palace, seven churches and some 1,400 houses.

99. above: **The Splenitive Englishmen travelling in Germany** – *a satirical print of Englishmen on tour in Germany*

OCTOBER 7TH

Travelling overland through Denmark, they arrived back at the town of Lübeck in northern Germany, where they leisurely overwintered some eight months before embarking on the last leg of their tour.

It might seem surprising that they chose to overwinter for such an extended period while only a few days' sailing from Britain, but a closer scrutiny of the developing situation in the North Sea could possibly explain their decision.

Studying the return route through Denmark and south to Germany, it would be logical to assume that they were headed for Hamburg and, as such, retracing their way home through the port of Hull.

Disturbing reports would no doubt be circulating in the area of the imminence of a major conflict between the British Navy and the Batavian (Dutch) Fleet.

During September the Dutch Fleet, under Vice-Admiral Jan De Winter, were blockaded within their harbour at Texel by the British Fleet commanded by Admiral Duncan. Early in October, Duncan was forced to return to Yarmouth for supplies; this action enabled De Winter to carry out a brief raid into the North Sea. When the Dutch fleet attempted to return to their safe haven, Duncan was waiting to intercept them off the Dutch coast. The result was the battle of Camperdown on 11th October 1797, when the British Fleet won a decisive victory.

William's 'forced' wintering in Lübeck was probably a consequence of this unfolding conflict on his doorstep, together with the onset of harsh winter conditions. The latter would result in the build up of sea ice in the Baltic, which would put paid to sea travel until the expected thaw of late April or early May the following year.

MAY 15TH 1798 EMBARKED ON BOARD *SECHS GESCHWISTER*

Bound for Pillau, a port where large vessels discharged their cargoes to be transported to Köningsburg.

100. right: **Auf der Mottlau in Danzig** *by Hermann Meyerheim*

MAY 20TH ARRIVED PILLAU

Expecting the onwards journey to be three or four hours, they took no provisions, but the actual connection took overnight, spent in a very filthy cabin, devoid of any food.

MAY 21ST ARRIVED AT KÖNINGSBURG

It was noted that the whole town consisted of very old buildings and narrow streets with the castle being the most prominent building. The environs of the town were deemed extremely pleasant. Departing Köningsburg they journeyed by road through prime agricultural land that had formerly belonged to Poland.

MAY 28TH ARRIVED AT DANZIG

Their arrival coincided with three days of festivities to celebrate the arrival of the King of Prussia, whose intention it was to

receive the homage of his subjects.

Through making the acquaintance of one of the 'most opulent' merchants of the town, a certain Mr Francis, they were able to get a ring-side view of the whole proceedings on board the generous host's barge.

JUNE 17TH DEPARTED DANZIG

They continued their journey in an old Russian carriage through north German towns en route for Hamburg. While stopping at some very elegant inns, it is equally possible that they might have experienced less salubrious hostelries, as some were

frequently little better than barns in which the traveller was tumbled pell-mell to sleep with the landlord and landlady, men and servants, and passengers of both sexes, cows, sheep and horses ... [and in some inns] broken shutters served the purpose of windows, straw took the place of beds, and, where beds were provided, these were likely to be little wooden boxes or troughs, as cold as they were uncomfortable.

(*The Grand Tour*, p.197)

JUNE 28TH ARRIVED AT HAMBURG

Few details are given of the return voyage, which, it is thought was made via London. The companions arrived safely back in Staffordshire in July of 1798 after a truly remarkable tour of just over a year.

William came back to a very different country from the one he had left a year before. Widespread alarm and panic had spread through the kingdom, and wild rumours were circulating of an imminent invasion from France. As early as 1793, with the fear of invasion from revolutionary France, parliament had empowered counties to raise a volunteer force to combat any likely attack. The formation of the Staffordshire Volunteer Cavalry on 4th July 1794 was part of this initiative.

STAFFORDSHIRE VOLUNTEER CAVALRY

Volunteers were required to provide their own horse and were recruited mostly from landholders and tenant farmers, while the officers were mostly drawn from the nobility and landed gentry.

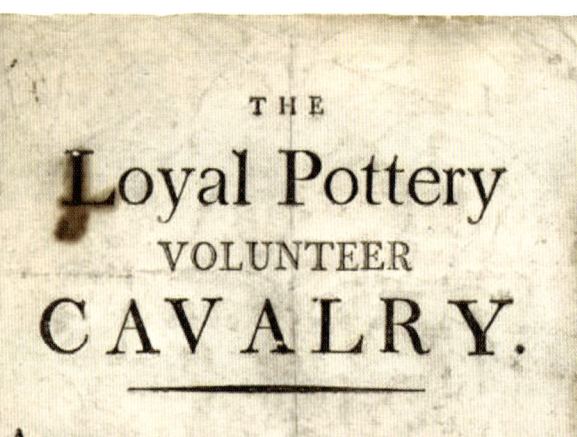

101. left: Printed notice announcing the outcome of a meeting held to discuss arrangements for the Pottery Volunteer Cavalry

102. below: William Adams junior, third son of William Adams II of Cobridge Hall

A sword belonging to William Adams junior of Tunstall, inscribed with the following verses, aptly expresses the Volunteer Cavalry's beliefs:

> Leagu'd with my friends the glittering sword I wave,
> Not to extend an Empire, but to save.
> To guard with steady front my native land,
> From foreign foes & factions desperate band.
>
> To stop the march of democratic rage,
> And shield the forms of innocence & age,
> To bid distrust & fear & discord cease,
> And shelter Virtue in the arms of Peace.
>
> Wm. Adams, Tunstall.

On formation, the troop had been under the command of Captain Commandant Sir John Edenson Heathcote of Longton. Sir John later

On 27th April 1798, just days before William's arrival back from his Baltic excursion, his second son William, together with a cousin–William Adams junior of Tunstall–enlisted as officers in the Staffordshire Volunteer Cavalry, together with 41 other recruits. A surviving document records their oaths of allegiance:

> We engage and pledge ourselves to bear true allegiance to the King, and to act on all occasions in aid of the Civil Power; and when called out to be under Military discipline, but will not be liable in any case to go out of the limits of the Potteries and Newcastle, within which district only we agree to act, the express objects of this Association being local defence.

VOLUNTEER CAVALRY SWORD OF WILLIAM ADAMS JUNIOR OF GREENGATES

Inscribed:

Leagu'd with my friends the glittering sword I wave
Not to extend an Empire, but to save
To guard with steady front my native land
From foreign foes and factions desperate band

To stop the march of democratic rage
And shield the forms of innocence and age
To bid distrust and fear and discord cease
and shelter Virtue in the arms of Peace

Wm. Adams Tunstall

A Staffordshire Volunteer Cavalry Officer in review order in 1794

103: *A light cavalry sword owned by William Adams junior, son of William Adams I of Tunstall – an officer in the Staffordshire Cavalry Volunteers*

104. left: **William Adams junior of Tunstall (1777-1805)** *bronze plaque on the Adams Clock Tower, Tunstall Park*

relinquished the command to the well-known potter Josiah Spode, by which time the troop had risen to seventy strong. Recruits came from all parts of the Borough and were mounted and equipped at their own expense, although it is known that local subscriptions bolstered the organisation financially.

The Birmingham Mail of Friday 2nd January 1914 gave further details of the Staffordshire Volunteer Cavalry, who were

to receive no pay unless when embodied or called out, but to attend mounted on a serviceable horse, not less than fourteen and a half hands high, for the purpose of exercise. When embodied to receive pay as cavalry and to be subject to military discipline. Each person attending on the day of exercise to wear a uniform provided at the expense of county subscriptions, together with arms and accoutrements provided by the Government ... each troop was to consist of not less than fifty men, including officers, and at that time the uniform consisted of a short scarlet cotee, very much like an open tunic, turned back at the bottom with yellow cloth, which was also the colour of the cuffs and collars. The breeches were of white leather, and were worn with military knee boots. The helmet, which was of the bearskin (Light Dragoon) pattern, had a black cloth turban with silver chain work, and a white-over-red feather on the side. The waistcoat, gloves, and belt were white, the officers wearing a crimson sash over their waistcoats.

Their sword was slightly curved and their hair was queued rather than clubbed.

For their motto, the regiment adopted:

Pro aris et focia (For our altars and our hearths)

And for its badge, it adopted the county emblem – the Staffordshire Knot – the heraldic symbol of the ancient Norman Barons de Stafford, the first of whom was a companion to William the Conqueror in 1066.

The Yeomanry cavalry was used to support local authorities to suppress civil unrest as witnessed in the food riots of 1795. The only occasion a Voluntary Cavalry troop was ever called up in national defence occurred when the Castlemartin Yeomanry was mobilised to help in the defeat of a small French invasion in the Battle of Fishguard in 1797, often referred to as the last invasion of mainland Britain. Following the defeat of Napoleon in 1815, all the Volunteer Cavalry Corps were disbanded.

105. above: **Badge of the Staffordshire Yeomary**

MINES AND MINERALS

By 1820, William Adams II had relinquished all aspects of the potting trade and rented out his numerous works to different potters, and his potting career came to an end. In 1817 one of his Cobridge potteries had been let to Ralph and James Clews, potters who had developed an enormous export trade with America, principally selling traditional blue and white transfer ware.

At the age of 70, one would think that William would have considered retirement, but seemingly this was the last thing on his mind as he actively switched his attention to mining, purchasing a slew of mines in the locality and renewing his interest in steam engines. As early as 1786 he had installed the first steam engine for the grinding of potters glaze at Milton; it was described as a small, atmospheric steam engine, with a cylinder of only 12 inches in diameter. In 1792 he entered into an agreement with the celebrated partnership of Boulton and Watt for the erection of a steam engine in one of the collieries he was involved with as an executor under his stepfather's will. Boulton and Watt's business plan required the mine owners to enter into a comprehensive agreement with their company whereby they assisted with the construction of the engines, providing the workforce and specialised parts, but they charged a yearly licence fee for the use of their patent; in the latter installation this amounted to £135.

In common with many of his ancestors, William had avidly supported the local church and, bolstered by his considerable fortune, extended his patronage to encompass schools and hospitals. He was a trustee of Cobridge School and contributed personally to the running of the school throughout his life, augmenting public subscriptions when required; he likewise supported other such ventures in Hanley and Sneyd Green. He was a liberal benefactor of the North Staffordshire Infirmary, actively serving on the organisation's committee and being noted as its vice-president in 1806.

106. above left: Portrait of Matthew Boulton, a prominent Birmingham manufacturer and business partner of the Scottish engineer, James Watt by Carl Frederik von Breda

107. above right: Portrait of James Watt–scientist, inventor and engineer who contributed to the development of the steam engine by Carl Frederik von Breda, 1792

108. top: Cobridge Free School– built by subscription in 1766 as a grammar school. From a drawing by Charles Lynam F.S.A.

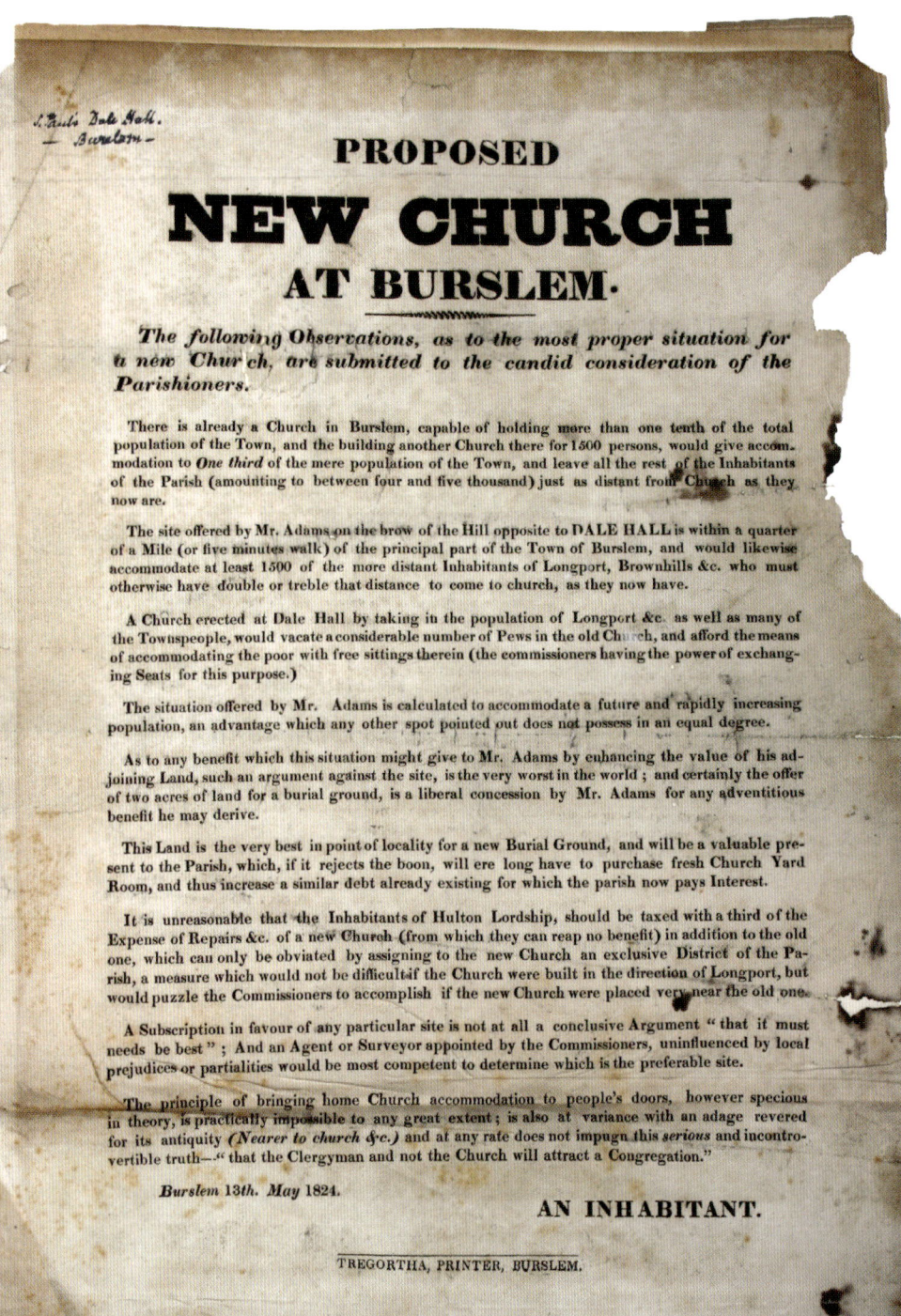
109. Poster of 1824 eliciting the comments of Burslem parishioners regarding a proposed new church in the town

110. above: Etching of the magnificent St. Paul's Church, Burslem, 1831

In his later years he is known to have developed a form of religious mania and could be heard talking to himself, alarmingly uttering tales of hellfire and damnation. It is at this tragic phase in his life that William predictably makes his greatest benefaction in 1827, donating land to build a new church in Burslem and contributing a substantial sum towards its erection.

The population of Burslem had increased considerably by the early 19th century, to a point where St. John's Church, Burslem, could not physically facilitate the needs of the parishioners. William Adams gave an acre of land from his Dale Hall estate to build the new church of St. Paul's Dale Hall and another acre for a vicarage, a quarter of a mile from the centre of Burslem.

Arrangements were made for the laying of the foundation stone on the 24th June 1828 and was organised on the scale of a royal visit. It was propitious that the day dawned with the sun shining on the righteous. The procession started from the Market Square and already at eight o'clock in the morning, a crowd of spectators had gathered to witness the arrival of those taking part in the ceremony. At nine o'clock, the Bishop of Lichfield and Coventry arrived, and the parade started down Newcastle Street.

Heading the procession were two constables followed by the Town Crier; then two men carrying flags, preceding the Longport Band. These were followed by the Parish Clerk, behind him Boys and Girls (students and choristers

111. Above: **St. Paul's Church, Burslem** *(Built in 1828 and demolished in* 1974)

carrying the flag of the National School), and flanked by two constables. Next came the Band of the Freemasons of St. Martins Lodge; then the Chief Constable, flanked by the Churchwardens, in turn followed by the Lord Bishop with the Rector of St. John's, also with a constable on either side. Next came the patron, William Adams, and behind him the Architect and the Contractor, again with a constable escort; and towards the rear, the Church Committee, followed by Subscribers, Another Band, Invited Visitors, and Clergy from other parishes. The whole procession moved forward in an impressive display of sight and sound, with the first bodies well into Newcastle Street before the rear had left the Market Square. Newcastle Street was lined with spectators, the Staffordshire Advertiser said there were quite 15,000 to witness the ceremony, while the bells of St. John's made their debut filling the air with joyful peals, being newly cast and hung.

One of the principal Free Masons offered the silver trowel to the Bishop. The Bishop duly performed his duty as the stone was lowered into position. In its hollow centre he placed a glass case made by Davenport's containing a few coins and other valuables. A brass plate on the stone engraved in Latin recorded the occasion. Translated this read:

The foundation stone of this Parochial Chapel,
dedicated to St. Paul,
erected partly by National Grant and partly by
Private Contributions, was laid by The
honourable and Right Reverend
Henry Ryder D.D.
Lord Bishop of Lichfield & Coventry
In the auspicious reign of George the Fourth
On the twenty fourth day of June In the year of
Redemption 1828
Glory be to God. The Honour to our Country
W. Whieldon. Rector

112. right: *St. Paul's Church, Burslem, while being demolished in 1974*

E. Wood. Chief Constable
W. Adams. Patron
Churchwardens L.H. Rhead. J. Clews.
T. Weatherby.   T.Hancock
L. Vulliamy. Architect

At the conclusion of the ceremony the procession reformed to make its way back to the Town Hall, there to partake of a most sumptuous public breakfast, prepared by Mr Pepper of the Leopard Inn. His Lordship sat down to the meal accompanied by thirty clergy from nearby parishes, a number of neighbouring gentry, and most of the respectable inhabitants of the town. So full was the spacious room that upwards of seventy gentlemen were obliged to seek accommodation in the inn. Revd. Edward Whieldon, on proposing the health of the Bishop, thanked His Lordship for his condescension in acceding to the wishes of the inhabitants of the town. The company all standing raised their glasses and drank. His Lordship in reply, expressed his obligation to them for the honour and the high satisfaction he felt on this occasion, and hoped it would not be the last time he would have the pleasure of coming amongst them, while he would always be anxious for their welfare and prosperity.

(B. Hodgkiss, *Mother Burslem*, 2001)

There was huge excitement in the locality for the new church. The finished building did not disappoint, its distinguished features being more akin to a small cathedral than a parish church. A contemporary commentator stated that it was built

of fine grained stone, from the quarries of Hollington, and is of a beautiful structure, of the plain Ecclesiastical style of the twelfth century, with a tower 115 feet in height, a lofty nave, and embattled side-aisles; the angles of the tower have octagonal turrets with ribbed pinnacles, and the extremities of the side-aisles are similarly ornamented ... The Churchyard, including the site of the edifice, contains exactly three acres, and the figure would be that of an oblong square, but that the eastern end answers to three sides of an octagon; it is fenced in all round with a breast-wall and handsome iron railings, with four entrance folding gates.

(John Ward, *The Borough of Stoke on Trent*, 1842)

True to his word, the Bishop accepted the invitation to consecrate the church on 20th January 1831. Tragically, in less than a month of the consecration, William Adams II had died; whether or not he attended the ceremony is unknown. I would like to imagine he did, with a well-deserved sense of pride in the truly imposing church that he had been so pivotally involved in procuring for the town.

Sadly, by 1974 the church had begun to subside and as it had become dangerous was demolished. The toppled Gothic ruins revealed one last secret: a prized collection of Enoch Wood's pottery buried in the foundation, now housed at the Potteries museum. Nothing remains of St. Paul's church today, with the exception of the stone wall which surrounded the churchyard, but which is stripped of its metal railings– a casualty of WW2 when they were removed to be recycled for the war effort.

113. Drawing of John Adams (1772-1847), eldest son of William Adams II

William was laid to rest in St. John's Churchyard, alongside his wife Mary, who had predeceased him in 1792. The first recorded burial in the new St. Paul's churchyard did not occur until 15th June 1831, and was of a Mr. Pointon, earthenware manufacturer of Burslem.

William Adams II had also been patron of the Rectory of St. John's Burslem, having purchased the glebe land, which amounted to some 57 acres, the patronage of which, worth an estimated £4,000, passed on his death to his son. As far back as 1809 William Adams II had been keen to ensure Burslem Church had a good Rectory, personally paying £250 of the £1,200 building costs.

William Adams II's will, dated 10th January 1831, left his extensive estate in trust for all his surviving children. The eldest son John is credited with having sold the family's Brick House works and other properties before he died in 1847 aged 76 (his two brothers, Thomas and William, having predeceased him by dying in 1834, aged 60 and 55 respectively). The last two survivors of William's extensive family were Anne and Mary Adams. The two unmarried sisters lived out their lives in Cobridge Hall exceedingly well-provided for by family legacies, and are remembered by S.B. Furnival of Cobridge as

driving out most days in an old-fashioned but rather dashing yellow coach and pair of horses (with rumble behind). Anne wore a rather large golden wig and was very stately.

The last survivor of the family, Mary, died in 1869. She had inherited a considerable fortune during her solitary life but tragically became insane in her later years. The fact that none of this extensive family ever married is no doubt due to their father's influence: he on occasions actively impeded access to suitors, as was clearly evident when Mary's engagement was broken off by her father for seemingly no apparent reason. Mary's estate was the subject of much litigation and the contents of Cobridge Hall were put up for sale in 1870:

COBRIDGE HALL, near Hanley and Burslem - Attractive sale of elegant and substantial HOUSEHOLD FURNITURE, splendid GOOSE-FEATHER BEDS, SILVER PLATE, richly-cut GLASS, CHINA, EARTHENWARE, LINEN, Library of BOOKS, WINES, CARRIAGES, SADDLERY, and MISCELLANEOUS EFFECTS.

(*Staffordshire Sentinel,* Saturday 5 March 1870)

(The wine cellar was noted to have comprised of 150 bottles of port and 120 bottles of sherry, all known to have been in bottles upwards of thirty years.)

Tragically, this branch of the Adams family came to an end and the demise of their family home followed all too swiftly in 1913, when Cobridge Hall was demolished, leaving the Bagnall Adamses as senior representatives of this illustrious family.

114. above: Part of the Daniel's estate purchased by William Adams II in 1783

116. right: William Adams I of Greengates, Tunstall (1746-1805): a bronze medallion at the Whitworth Art Galleries, Manchester

6

1746-1821
ADAMS OF GREENGATES

The latter part of the 18th century was truly the golden age of English potting, elevated in no small measure through the efforts of the legendary Josiah Wedgwood, the 'father of English potters', whose influence did so much to transform what had been a peasant craft into a beautiful art form.

Many Adams family members have been associated with Josiah Wedgwood but few, if any, developed such a close association with the great master as did William Adams I of Greengates, the family's most gifted potter, a fact acknowledged by N. Hudson More who states that

> *Next to that of Wedgwood, the most important name among English potters of the last quarter of the 18th century is that of Adams.*

(*Wedgwood and his Imitators*, 1909)

The ceramic authority William Turner, F.S.S., further notes that

> *William Adams flourished at a period when the Potteries attained the apex of that reputation which had made the district famous the world over. He helped considerably to brighten & extend that fair reputation.*

William Adams I was born in Burslem within weeks of his father's death and sadly was deprived of his mother, who died before he had even reached his first birthday. Fortunately for the young William, his maternal grandfather Joseph Adams was at hand to raise the boy until he achieved his majority and inherited the family potworks at St. John's Square, Burslem. Joseph Adams, described as a master potter/blacksmith, was comparatively well off financially, owning two inns and a private house in addition to his other business ventures.

117. above: Corner of St. John's Square Burslem with Hanover Street beyond. Twigg's old colour works in the middle of the row was previously a pottery owned by Joseph Adams (grandfather of William Adams I)

115. left: A depiction of Tunstall marketplace with the old town hall, built in 1816, now the site of the clock tower erected in memory of Sir Smith Child, Bart

118. above: **Photograph of Twigg's colour works in Hanover Square, Burslem**

William's uncle, also a Joseph Adams, was likewise described as a master potter and undoubtedly influenced young William, attending to his education and possibly, through his role as church warden, signing the potter's apprenticeship document for the boy, binding him to master potter John Brindley.

Residing at Bagnall, William would have probably received his elementary education at the Adams Free School in Hanley, but the exact means by which he achieved such a high level of mastery in chemistry and art, which served him well during his life, is somewhat perplexing.

The family's potworks at St. John's Square, and no doubt John Brindley's works, were a stone's throw away from Josiah Wedgwood's pottery at the Brick House, which he leased in 1762, when William Adams I was 16 years of age. Assuming William had been apprenticed to John Brindley at the age of 10, he would be nearing the completion of his apprenticeship in 1762.

John Brindley's elder brother James, the great canal engineer, was a close confidant of Josiah Wedgwood and, possibly through these connections, Josiah became aware of the talented young William and took him on as an assistant, rather than as apprentice, to help with the experimental side of his jasper work.

There certainly seems to be a window of opportunity for this cooperative venture from 1762 to 1769, after which time William, at the age of 23, tentatively took on his own works at St. John's Square. Further proof that William Adams I was moving in these illustrious circles is revealed through his marriage in 1771 to Mary Cole of Turnhurst.

119. below: *Sites of Historic Potteries in Burslem*

TURNHURST HALL

Undoubtedly the most notable occupant of Turnhurst Hall was no less than James Brindley, the celebrated pioneer of canal building, one of the greatest men of 18th-century England, whose work on developing a network of some 360 miles of canal fundamentally helped to hasten the Industrial Revolution.

Mary's parents had moved into Turnhurst Hall in the wake of the Jacobite Rebellion of 1745, occupying half of the substantial gentry house that had been rebuilt around 1700. Never ostentatious, this comfortable and roomy house achieved notoriety for being thought to be the last house in England in which a family fool was maintained. In the Coles' era, the house was sub-divided into two under the ownership of the Alsager family.

It was to this ancient edifice that James Brindley brought his young bride Ann Henshall in 1765. Taking out a 21-year lease, they were to live there until James's death aged only 56 in 1772.

Growing up at Turnhurst, Mary Cole would have witnessed the comings and goings of many of the finest minds in England. Foremost among the frequent visitors were Brindley's lifelong friends Josiah Wedgwood and Erasmus Darwin and other illustrious members of the famed Birmingham Lunar Society.

Contemporary accounts describe the setting of the house: it had a rear garden and pleasure ground and a small lake to the front. A seemingly unremarkable summerhouse, located in the outer courtyard, takes on an alluring aura when one discovers it was Brindley's office and the place where he sketched far-reaching plans that ultimately transformed the country, and made him a national hero.

Did the youthful Mary wonder what the great engineer was doing as he dug up his garden, constructing a working model of the first canal lock, the remains of which were evident up until the early 20th century.

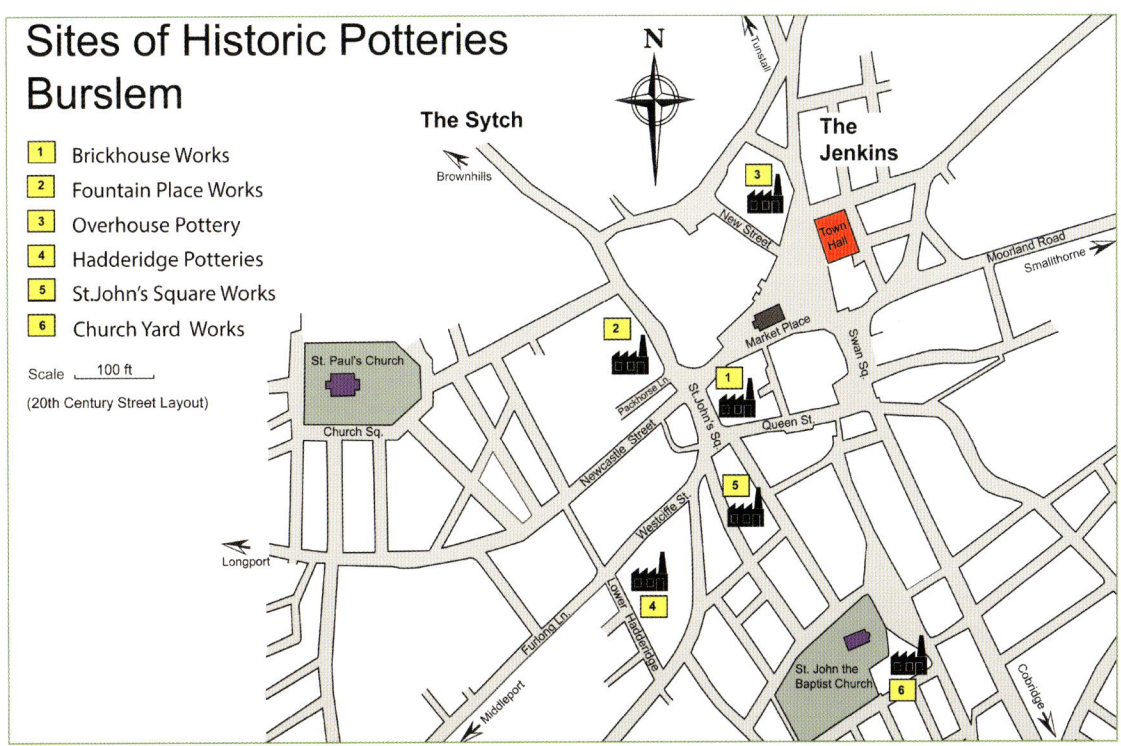

Adams of Greengates

TURNHURST HALL

A lead rainwater hopper dated 1718 records a period of occupation by John Bowyer

Photographs circa 1920s by Percy W. L. Adams

Residence of the pioneering canal engineer James Brindley who leased it from 1765 until his death in 1772. The Cole family, parents of William Adams I's wife, leased one part of the sub-divided property from 1766 until 1856.

Adams of Greengates

122. above: **An 18th-century plan for the Trent and Mersey Canal (marked in red)**

Mary's marriage to William Adams I in 1771 reveals an intriguing web of connections, with James Brindley seemingly at the core. William had been apprenticed to James's younger brother, master potter John Brindley, and, likewise, James was a mutual friend of Josiah Wedgwood.

As a master potter of note, William was actively involved in Brindley's ambitious Trent Mersey canal project, The Grand Trunk, which was to be so vitally important to the development of the pottery industry.

121. left: **James Brindley, the noted canal engineer, painted by Francis Parson in** 1770

On 27th September 1772, James Brindley died. A poignant epitaph appeared in the Chester Courant on 1st December that year:

James Brindley lies amongst these Rocks,
He made Canals, Bridges and Locks,
To convey Water; he made Tunnels
For Barges, Boats, and Air-Vessels;
He erected several Banks,
Mills, Pumps, Machines, with Wheels and
Cranks;

Adams of Greengates   113

123. above: Engraving of Etruria by H. Warren (1794-1879)

*He was famous t'invent Engines,
Calculated for working Mines;
He knew Water, its Weight and Strength,
Turn'd Brooks, made Sloughs to a great Length;
While he used the Miners' Blast,
He stopp'd Currents from running too fast;
There ne'er was paid such Attention
As he did to Navigation.
But while busy with Pit or Well,
His spirits sunk below Level;
And, when too late, his Doctor found,
Water sent him to the Ground.*

WEDGWOOD'S PROTÉGÉ?

In her *Life of Josiah Wedgwood*, Miss Meteyard clearly shows Josiah's great interest in William Adams I, explaining that Wedgwood thought he was *one really clever pupil,* one who was entrusted with materials to carry out experiments on the developing of his jasper body. Operating in such a dynamic, cutting edge environment, the young entrepreneur would have acquired the chemical and experimental skills that he later employed throughout his life.

Josiah left the Brick House in 1769 and continued his jasper experiments at Etruria and, according to Meteyard, William Adams continued assisting his mentor. This is highly probable, as William was not wholeheartedly involved in his own potting venture until 1775, the precise year that Wedgwood is thought to have perfected his solid jasper, a product that would be hailed as a triumph in the art of pottery.

It is highly likely that William Adams I and Wedgwood continued as friendly rivals after their initial cooperative ventures, comparing notes with each other, as was evident in Miss Meteyard's book:

When the pupil [William Adams] made a success of his experiments first known to his great master, Wedgwood remarked ... I have hitherto put too much butter in my paste.

124. above: Print of the Greengates works, dated 1787

This is a clear indication of continued cooperation, and a conversation that might have occurred on the clay-hunting exploits they often carried out together with master potter John Turner.

The strong bond that developed between Wedgwood and his young associate was to stand the test of time, even continuing when William Adams I set up his own extensive Greengates works, marketing similar products to Wedgwood.

It is important to note that Adams developed his own distinct style of jasper, different in composition, colour and ornamentation, all contributing to the concept that he was a follower of Wedgwood rather than a copyist – a legitimate stance if, as it seems, he assisted experimentally with the work.

By the time of his marriage in 1771, William had come into his inheritance together with a significant sum that had accrued in a trust established to enable him to start his own pottery works. True to form he began his first tentative steps in business, renting a pottery in Tunstall in 1779, which by 1784 he had purchased outright. He then began building his new and prestigious Greengates works, which he completed two years later.

The continued cooperation between William Adams and Wedgwood is also evident in the many invoices that exist for purchases he made from William Adams for ceramic wares. It was common practice for manufacturers to purchase earthenware from each other to assist in fulfilling shipments at times when they were particularly busy. Twelve such invoices exist, the largest amounting to £43 12s 6d, detailing, among other items, Queen's pattern plates, salad dishes and toilet ware, mostly destined for export, all carefully packed in crates.

William and Mary Adams had seven children, three of whom died in infancy. The birth of their eldest son, William, was commemorated in a surviving christening jug, dated 1777. This cream-ware jug, finely painted in black and red, is attributed to William Adams I, and was produced at the family's St. John's Square works. It is now in the Wedgwood Museum Collection at Barlaston.

125. above: A 1906 photograph showing one of the jasper warehouses at Greengates, the shelving and woodwork having not been altered since they were installed by William Adams I in 1780

Greengates, the first important pottery in Tunstall flourished and soon other new factories sprang up, swelling the population of Tunstall enormously and making it unrecognisable in a description from 1795:

The pleasantest village in the pottery.
(J. Akin, *The Country around Manchester*, 1795)

As the demand for Greengates' high-quality products increased, jaspers, basalts and cream stoneware flowed out of the works, which, in common with Etruria, became a celebrated factory serving the lucrative Cheshire carriage trade. The enlargement of Greengates in 1786 hardly kept pace with the demands for the wares. The leasing of the recently extended Newfields pottery, owned by Admiral Child, allowed for further expansion, which replaced Burslem as a centre of production of 'useful' wares while Greengates concentrated on 'ornamental' wares.

Much of the output of Greengates had been exported to Europe, with the French trade being particularly buoyant until this came to a grinding halt with the onset of the Revolutionary Wars. William, demonstrating his innate entrepreneurial skills, switched his focus to the London market, aggressively promoting his wares to the fashionable set and establishing a showroom in the capital while expanding his retail outlet at Greengates. It is probable that the prestigious order for George III's jasper buttons came via the London showroom located in Fleet Street. From this important venue orders flowed in from wealthy and aristocratic customers eager to purchase Adams' ornamental and tablewares to grace their elegant drawing rooms and salons.

Other competitors were not so successful in these tumultuous times. The noted Staffordshire potter John Turner had built up a large trade with France, but sadly the French Revolution wreaked havoc on his business. He was left with no orders and unable to collect outstanding accounts. In desperation he travelled to France in an attempt to recoup some money owed, only to be thrown into a Parisian prison, narrowly escaping the guillotine. Turner's once flourishing business struggled on until 1803, when it was sold,

126. above: Greengates House, Tunstall – the home of William Adams I (drawn by W. Scarratt for P.W.L. Adams in 1906)

with William Adams purchasing some of the moulds and patterns.

Adams' early financial success can be mostly attributed to the sales of a singular product–his extremely popular blue printed ware–as opposed to Wedgwood, who capitalised on huge sales of his beautiful Queen's Ware. Both employed identical strategies, but with entirely different products.

Josiah Wedgwood's influence on the aspiring Adams was broad and extensive, ranging from business strategies to architectural design. There can be little doubt that the ultimate inspiration for Adams' Greengates Works was Etruria, the first large industrial complex in the Potteries.

The façade of Etruria was very influential, variations on it being the most common works frontage in the Potteries for more than a hundred years. One of the few surviving street elevations for a potworks of this period is that of William Adams's Greengates Pottery in Tunstall. This works, dating from the 1780s has now partly subsided and is hidden from the road by a wall and more recent building. An early nineteenth-century print, however, shows the works as originally built, depicting a central block of nine bays in length and three storeys in height, flanked by a pair of wings of four bays and two storeys.

The three central bays of the main block project and are surmounted by a pediment. Like Etruria, there is a tall cupola in which hung the works bell.

(Diane Baker, *Potworks*, 1991)

William Adams probably continued to reside in Burslem, until his new house, Greengates, was completed in 1787. It was located a respectable

127. above: Layout plan of Greengates Hall and Works circa 1900

Adams of Greengates   117

128. below: Potteries operated by William Adams I and Family (1720-1805)

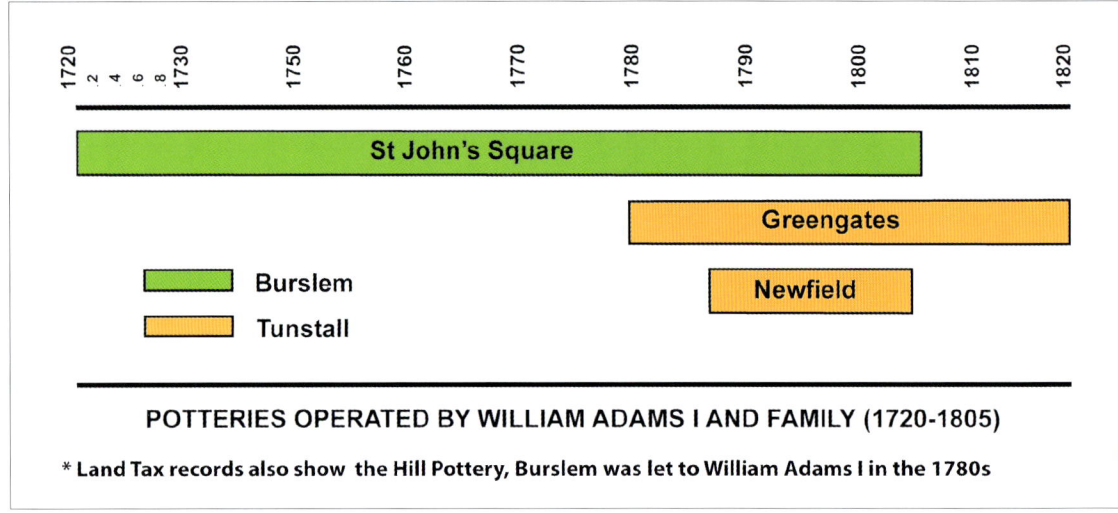

POTTERIES OPERATED BY WILLIAM ADAMS I AND FAMILY (1720-1805)

* Land Tax records also show the Hill Pottery, Burslem was let to William Adams I in the 1780s

distance from his works, in a secluded area known to locals as Botany Bay. Set in its own land and screened by trees from the works beyond, it provided the up-and-coming master potter with a residence commensurate to his wealth and status.

Idyllically situated down a narrow lane overhung with laburnum trees, Greengates was described as a comfortable house, substantially built, with

a neat oak staircase leading up to a third storey; the chimney pieces are of wood and plaster, carved and moulded in the Adam style with wreaths and medallions – so fashionable towards the close of the eighteenth century. They were painted white. Some of the designs (medallions) are the same as those used on the jasper ware. They are now oak-grained and varnished, but well preserved.

(William Turner, *William Adams: An Old English Potter*, 1904)

Omitted from the above description was the unique facility enjoyed by William Adams: an in-house laboratory, according to contemporary accounts, was located at the back of the mansion where the master potter spent endless hours experimenting. His goal was that of Wedgwood's–to ultimately improve his art–and it was in this hallowed spot that he successfully developed his own unique jasper ware, many original pieces of which are preserved in great houses throughout the kingdom and indeed beyond.

ADAMS JASPER WARE

William Adams I was a true master potter, skilled and knowledgeable in so many aspects of his chosen art, a gifted ceramic chemist and an exceptional modeller with huge artistic aptitude.

129. above: Business card of William Adams I of Greengates

130. left: **William Adams I of Greengates** *– a sketch of him in later life*

131. below: **Diana resting after the chase,** *a William Adams I plaque in the Lady Tweedmouth's drawing room*

Unquestionably, his association with Josiah Wedgwood had been the cornerstone of his rise to pottery prominence, but his innate skills and dogged determination to succeed are what ultimately led him to produce such exquisite work, the quality of which remains unsurpassed.

A close scrutiny of William Adams work reveals much of the uniqueness of his productions, however, it must be stated that similarity of designs employed by different manufacturers were often a result of using the same reference materials. In William Adams' era, all had access to Sir William Hamilton's book the *Collection of Etruscan, Greek, and Roman Antiquities,* and other volumes that provided inspiration for creating figures from antiquity. Likewise, the exhibits seen in the British Museum were open to all and could be referred to for inspiration.

Adams jasper ware is unique with respects to:

Colour - Metallic oxide dips were used and when fired produced beautiful and delicate colours. Oxide of cobalt yielded blue, and both Wedgwood and Adams employed such blue decoration, with 'Adams Blue' being distinguished by its faint shade of violet, a quality of tone that is highly prized among collectors.

Hayden, in his *Chats on English Earthenware,* elaborates:

> *The beautiful Adams Blue, which is of a violet tint, is much admired.*

Jasper mix – Adams used an entirely unique recipe to formulate his jasper.

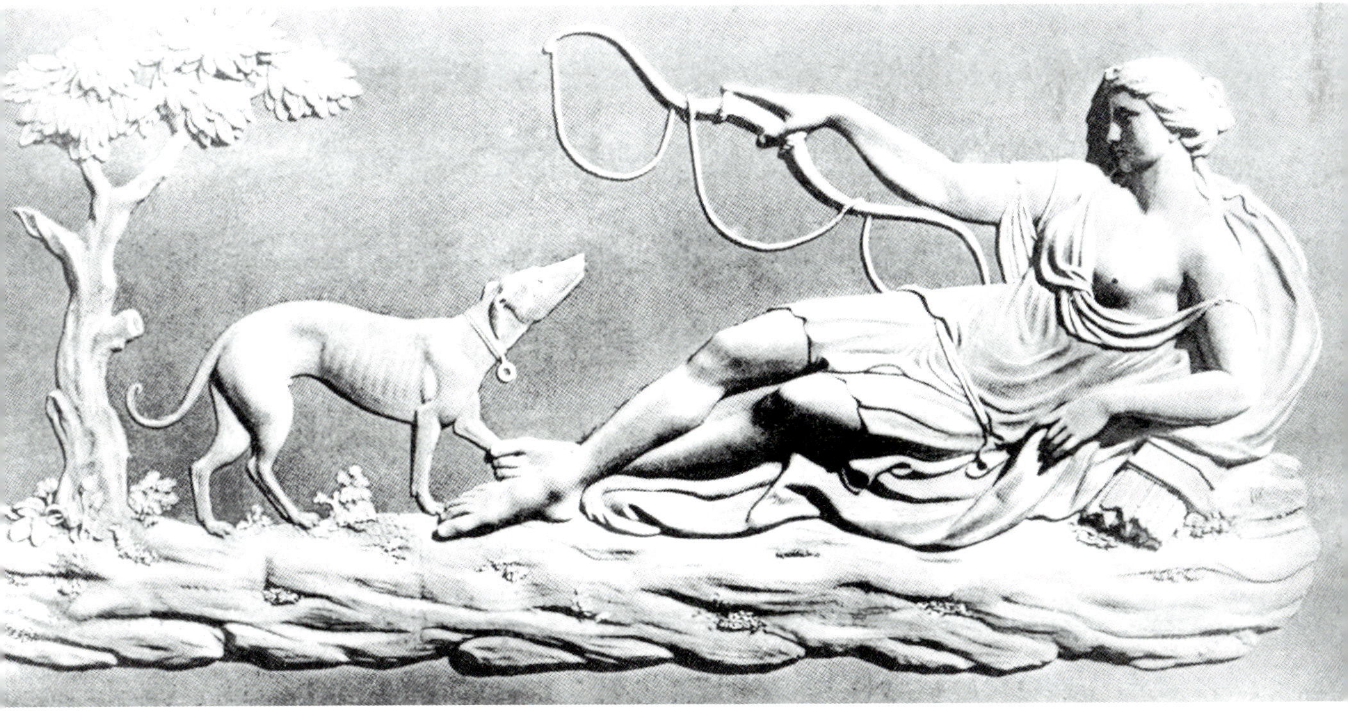

120 ADAMS Britain's Oldest Potting Dynasty

133. below: **Staircase installed by William Adams I leading to the Long Warehouse in the west front of Greengates**

134. below: **Window of old jasper mixing room at Greengates, circa 1900**

Ornamentation – Close scrutiny of the modelling applied to the jasper bodies, such as the treatment of the figures and drapery etc., reveal intricate differences of technique. William Adams was a skilled modeller in his own right and is known to have personally carried out work on some of the company's finest work. He was not averse to employing experts to assist; most notable among William's modellers was the highly skilled Joseph Monglott, a Swiss artist of

132. left: **A blue jasper dip vase with white reliefs depicting Apollo crowning a kneeling girl made by William Adams I circa 1787-1805**

considerable repute who settled in England in 1785. William had enticed Monglott to work at Greengates, and he eventually became his chief working modeller at the factory. Joseph Monglott's father was an officer in the French service, prior to the Revolution, but sadly was guillotined at Montpellier during the reign of Robespierre. It is stated in William Turner's book, on the subject of William Adams, that

> *it might be said, if Wedgwood had his Flaxman, that Adams had his Monglott.*

Notably, both artists were among the finest working in the 18th-century ceramic industry.

Hayden, in his *Chats on English Earthenware*, 1909, aptly summarises Adams jasper compared with Wedgwood:

> *The beautiful Adams Blue ... is much admired, and in the finely-modelled classic relief the style is less frigid than Wedgwood, as William Adams drew his inspiration more from Latin than Greek models. As a rule his jasper is a trifle more waxen than that of Wedgwood, but never glossy.*

135. right: A woodcut of the blue and white jasper vase given to William Adams I by Josiah Wedgwood, later known as The Keepsake Vase

Adams' reputation for fine work spread, as did his patronage, and there was an ever-increasing demand for his wares as he seemingly competed in the very market that Wedgwood had so dominated for years.

However, it is pleasing to note that, according to Meteyard, Adams and Wedgwood remained friends, it seems, to the bitter end: as a dying wish, she recounts, Josiah bestowed a precious gift on his friend.

THE KEEPSAKE VASE

Preserved in the Adams family archive is an intriguing poem. Written in an anonymous 19th-century copper-plate hand, it passionately relates the story of a vase gifted to William Adams by Josiah Wedgwood as the great potter lay on his deathbed:

The Keepsake Vase

A fragile vase of elegance and beauty,
Cleverly fashioned by the potter's art
Token of friendship and rewarded duty
Memento of a true and faithful heart.

Within his chamber lay the master, dying
Nearing the haven where all stirrings cease
Behind him life of strenuous effort lying,
Lived in the interest of Art and Peace.

His wandering thoughts, e'er prone to loving action,
Reviewing scenes of the departed years,
Recalled to mind with tender recollection
His favourite pupil – who stood by, in tears.

According to Meteyard, in her *Life of Josiah Wedgwood*, the vase in question had been presented to William Adams of the Greengates Pottery, Tunstall, who had been a favourite pupil of the master. The vase had been treasured by Wedgwood as the one that

they had arranged together for the last time at Etruria.

Meteyard, realising the significance of the vase, tracked it through the Adams family, finding it had descended to Helen Adams, a granddaughter of Williams Adams I, who had married Reverend William Avery in 1849, and stated that it

now adorns, with other choice specimens of Wedgwood ware, a quiet parsonage in Cornwall.

Meteyard was able to obtain a photograph of the elusive vase around 1855. This was used to make a woodcut, which was included in her book, giving us a rare glimpse of this treasured possession. It appears that Meteyard negotiated with Reverend Avery for its purchase, but with little success. In a letter dated 23rd November 1867, shortly after the death of his wife Helen, we are informed that a Mr Barlow of Auburn

136. right: William Adams I, leaning against the fireplace at Greengates examining a vase with his cousin William Adams III of Stoke. The Wedgwood Keepsake Vase is clearly visible on the mantlepiece

Adams of Greengates

137. above: **Upper High Street and Christ Church Tunstall in 1848** *drawn by William Scarratt (Greengates Hall shown on the right)*

Lodge, South Kensington, had offered £50 for it, but it does not seem to have been accepted. Since then, the whereabouts of the treasured heirloom has remained a mystery.

A fascinating illustration exists of William Adams' drawing room at Greengates, seemingly commissioned for William Turner's book *William Adams: An Old English Potter* in 1904. William Adams I is portrayed leaning against his jasper-adorned mantelpiece, discussing the finer points of a vase being carefully held by his cousin, William Adams III of Fenton Hall.

Turner further elucidates that the room was carefully portrayed as it would have been in William Adams I's time, with the likeness taken from a bust portrait of William Adams I, and the cousin's image from a portrait by Keeling.

Michael Keeling was an English portrait painter who exhibited at the Royal Academy between 1782 and 1809; he was thought to have trained under Sir Thomas Lawrence and is known to have worked mainly in Staffordshire. In 1819, a year before his death, he was commissioned to paint William Adams III and his wife Sarah, née Heath.

Remarkably, a close scrutiny of the painting reveals an image of *The Keepsake Vase*, in pride of place on the mantelpiece. A note on the drawing explains that the picture was drawn from the room itself and that the cousin's meeting took place in 1804, a year before William Adams I died.

Given all the circumstantial evidence regarding *The Keepsake Vase* and its perceived importance to the Adams family, there is no reason to disregard Meteyard's account of the gift of the vase as a memento of the close cooperation between the two friends.

HARMONIOUS FAMILY LIFE

Revealing insights into William Adams' character are to be found in the reminiscences of Mrs Boott of Derby, a regular visitor to Greengates who considered William Adams to be

138. above: **Elizabeth Adams** (born 1779), *youngest daughter of William Adams I*

139. above: **Mary Adams** (born 1772), *eldest daughter of William Adams I*

a true type of English gentleman – benevolent, generous, and a singular attractive personage ... (additionally) that his wife was a loveable character, and that the children were examples of obedience, affection, and all that makes a home harmonious and happy.

(William Turner, *William Adams: An Old English Potter*, 1904)

This was a picture of marital bliss that was to be shaken to the core with the deaths of some of his children, tragically taken by consumption, a deadly disease that so cruelly visited many familes in the 18th century.

Boott's description of Greengates House states that

it was elegantly furnished and stood in its own grounds. Many specimens of his exquisite work in jasper adorned the walls ... and many a walk did my sister and myself take with this admirable man through those nicely stocked rooms of vases, plaques, and everything of possible description in this beautiful fabric; and I could sigh now, as I call to mind the number and variety of these costly articles he bestowed on my mother, who was a special favourite with him, and the many articles in the way of smelling bottles and other pretty mementos given to my sister and myself ... [as Turner summarizes] *... a pleasing reminiscence of a good man.*

(William Turner, 1904)

William Adams had many health issues throughout his life, and was described by P.W.L. Adams as *never being a very robust man*. He sadly died in January 1805 at the relatively young age of 59 and was buried in St. John's Church Burslem. Adding to the excruciating anguish, his eldest son William had also passed away within a month of his father, most probably after contracting cholera.

His will shows that he provided well for his family, leaving £2,000 to each of his daughters, Mary and Elizabeth, and a comfortable yearly allowance to his wife Mary, who tragically died before the end of 1805 and was laid to rest beside her husband.

The family business was left under the control of trustees, with eldest daughter Mary taking charge of

the accounts. Younger son and heir Benjamin was only seventeen at the death of both his father and elder brother, and woefully the manufacture of jasper stopped abruptly, and precious recipes so carefully formulated were securely locked away and never divulged to anyone.

In 1809, aged 21, Benjamin took charge of the once-thriving Greengates works, although we are left with the distinct impression that business concerns hardly

140. left: Benjamin Adams of Greengates and Congleton (1788-1828), 5th and youngest son of William Adams I

141. right: Reverend Benjamin Adams (1826-1909) with his wife Lucy

142. top: Fritton Church Suffolk, where Reverend Benjamin Adams was rector until 1907

Adams of Greengates 127

143. Family tree of Adams of Greengates

ADAMS
OF GREENGATES

Edward Adams of Bagnall
Bank House, Bagnall
Heir to his brother Wm Adams
bap. 12 Feb. 1660/1
bur. Norton 22 Apr. 1727

=¹⁶⁸⁷ **Elizabeth,** only dau. of John Meare of Handley Green
bur. Norton 3 July 1733

Dorothy Meare =1st **William Adams** of Bagnall =2nd **Sarah Braddock**
of Norton Green Bank House, Bagnall dau. of William
Hall bap. Burslem 5 Nov 1702 Whieldon of Ipstones
(1710-1735) bur. Norton 20 Dec. 1775 and Kingsley
d. Apr. 1787

Edward Adams = **Martha,** 2nd dau. of Joseph
b. 1709 Adams, **Master potter**
bur. 1745? bap. Burslem 15 Sept 1723

DESCENT TO
ADAMS OF FENTON HALL
AND GREENFIELD

William Adams I of Burslem =¹⁷⁷¹ **Mary,** eld. dau. of John Cole
Greengates, **Master Potter** Turnhurst Hall
of Tunstall near Tunstall
bap. Burslem 15 June 1746 bap. 31 Aug. 1747
Founded the Greengates bur. Burslem 5 Nov. 1805
Pottery
bur. 10 Jan. 1805

Mary, bap. St. John's **William Adams** of **Elizabeth,** **John Adams** **Joseph Adams** **John Adams** **Benjamin Adams** of =¹⁸¹³ **Sarah,** dau. of John = **Rev. Wm Sutcliffe**
Burslem 25 Oct. 1772 Greengates, Tunstall bap. St. John's bap. 22 July 1781 bap. 1 Jan. 1785 ob. infans, 1786 Greengates, Tunstall Hilditch of Sandbach, Rector of Bosley
d. 6 Nov. 1835 bap. St. John's Burslem Burslem 26 May 1779 bur. 2 Jan. 1783 bur. 9 Sep. 1788 bap. St. John's Burslem co. Chester co. Chester
bur. Burslem 6 Nov. 1777 d. 9 Jan 1820 19 Mar. 1788 d. 24 Jan. 1858
d. Feb. 1805 d. 1828
bur. Burslem

Rev. Wm. Avery = **Helen,** b. 1815 **William Hilditch** **Margaret,** **John Hilditch Adams** **Rev. Benjamin Adams** =¹⁸⁶⁴ **Lucy Bloss,** youngest dau.
Rector of Manaccan **Adams** bap. St John's Burslem bap. St. John's Burslem Rector of Fritton, Suffolk of James Webster, of Milton,
Cornwall b. 1817 10 Jan. 1818 22 Apr. 1819 b. 1826 co. Cambs.
d. 1836 unm. d. unm.1839 d. 11 Dec. 1850 d. 18 July 1909

ADAMS BRITAIN'S OLDEST POTTERY DYNASTY

occupied much of his time, and that he preferred to indulge himself in sporting activities, to the detriment of his pottery business.

Ample inheritances allowed him to live an extravagant lifestyle, with leisure pursuits high on the agenda. He hunted with the North Staffordshire Hounds and slavishly followed the racing calendar. He often fished with his Adams cousins of Stoke and with the Breezes of nearby Greenfields, associates who also enjoyed the lives of sporting country squires, but crucially, unlike Benjamin, when times were hard they were able to live frugally.

The early years of the 19th century heralded a slump in the potting trade, with the onset of the French Revolution, as previously mentioned, having wreaked havoc on many of Staffordshire's potters.

At this crucial time, Greengate's output appears to have been focussed mainly on stoneware and blue printed pottery, but lacking his father's flair and entrepreneurial skill, Benjamin responded to the downturn and the lack of demand by making cheaper products in order to compete. The damage to Greengates' reputation was immense, and together with the heavy losses sustained in exports to the USA, contributed to the dire financial situation Benjamin found himself in by 1820.

Plagued with ill health and weary with business life, Benjamin ceased trading and put his family business up for sale, withdrawing to live in Cheshire with his wife Sarah, a daughter of John Hilditch of Sandbach.

Benjamin died in 1828 when his only son was only two years old, having enjoyed a merry if rather short life. His widow remarried Reverend William Sutcliffe, rector of Bosely, co. Chester. Their son Benjamin Adams followed his stepfather's calling and took up Holy Orders, becoming far removed from the potting connections of their illustrious forefathers.

Greengates works was sold to John Meir, a small pottery owner in Tunstall in 1820. The adjacent land and the Greengates House was also purchased by him a year later. It would remain in the Meir family till 1896, when, in a shrewd move, a branch of the Adams family, the Adams of Greenfields, bought the historic works. Back under Adams control, the factory re-introduced jasper-ware production, using many of the moulds and patterns that had sat in the dusty cupboards for nearly a century.

With hindsight, it is evident that had Benjamin been able to hold out against selling Greengates for a few years, he would have undoubtedly benefitted from the huge growth of trade in earthenware exports to the USA that occurred from the 1820s to the 1850s. This is especially poignant, as his previous unsuccessful thrust into the American market had contributed to his downfall.

On 5th March 1821, a local newspaper announced the sale of the contents of Greengates House. Listed for sale was a book entitled *Herculaneum and Etruscan Antiques*. This might be a reference to William Hamilton's book – *Collection of Etruscan, Greek and Roman Antiquities* – one of the most influential art publications of the 18th century, known to have been used by Wedgwood in developing his style and no doubt found in the Greengates library. It is tempting to reflect that this learned manuscript might once have been studied, analysed and highly prized by William Adams himself, and heartening to think that a branch of the family might just have rescued it for posterity.

145. right: *Bronze plaque to William Adams III in St. Peter's Church, Stoke-on-Trent*

7

1660-1829
ADAMS OF BAGNALL AND FENTON HALL

The last of the three contemporary cousins, William Adams III, descended from the same branch as his famous cousin, William Adams I, this being the Adams of Bucknall Hall and Bagnall. Born into the era of the rapidly expanding potting industry, William Adams III was to mastermind the meteoric growth of his family business, which rose to become one of the largest businesses in the country by the middle of the 19th century.

Potting was in his blood: William's great grandfather's elder brother, William Adams of Holden, born 1642, is credited with having been the first to produce salt-glaze ware in Staffordshire, a process that was later perfected by Astbury, Wedgwood and Whieldon. This groundbreaking innovation was to make Staffordshire famous in the late 17th and early 18th century, until it was superseded by the more durable cream ware, so superbly perfected by Josiah Wedgwood.

The earliest known Adams item, a slipware salt cradle circa 1700, now located in the Wedgwood Museum, is attributed to William Adams of Holden and for many years was proudly displayed at the Adams Greenfield works.

EDWARD ADAMS OF BAGNALL BANK HOUSE (1660-1727)

Edward Adams was still a youth at the death of his father, but fortunately he was well provided for under

144. left: *Edward Adams (1660-1727) of Holden, Burslem and Bagnall, master potter, youngest son of William Adams (1599-1677)*

146. right: *Side view of Bagnall Bank House (photographed in 1913)*

Adams of Bagnall and Fenton Hall   131

148. below: **Carved detail on an Adams' family sideboard, dated 1709, probably commemorating the birth of Edward, second son of Edward and Elizabeth Adams of Holden**

149. below: **Norton Green Hall, the seat of Francis Meare, where Dorothy Meare, 1st wife of William Adams, was born on 7th June 1710**

his father's will, receiving a good education. He is assumed to have joined his elder brother William's potting business at Holden, residing in the family home at Sneyd Green until his marriage to Elizabeth, only daughter of John Meare, master potter of Handley Green. The Meares were an ancient and distinguished family who, in the early 14th century, had held the manor of Norton. During the English Civil War they were staunch Royalists and were apparently rewarded by Charles II for services rendered in the Battle of

147. left: **Elizabeth, wife of Edward Adams of Holden, daughter of John Meare of Handley Green**

150. right: Rev. Humphrey Repton (1619-1695), incumbent of Norton-in-the-Moors and grandfather of Dorothy, 1st wife of William Adams of Bagnall. (A formidable cleric who routinely excommunicated parishioners for their various misdemeanours)

Worcester by the presentation of a Flemish cup or pitcher. After the restoration, Charles is known to have rewarded those who had helped him escape and this leads one to speculate that the Meares just might have played a part in Charles's flight from the battle.

It was into this fiercely Royalist family that Edward married on 5 May 1687, just over two years after the death of Charles II, dubbed by many 'The Merry Monarch'.

Edward's regular attendances at the Tunstall Manor Court, as both officer and juror, reveal a public-spirited individual who took his responsibilities seriously, probably only relinquishing these when he took on the demands of rearing a family.

His wife, Elizabeth Adams, is specifically mentioned in her father's will, dated 14th September 1693, not for

151. below: St. Bartholomew's Church, Norton-in-the-Moors (photograph 2021)

152. right: Thomas Whieldon (1719-1795), master potter of Fenton Low, High Sheriff of Staffordshire 1788

any financial legacy, but for a gift of a household item: a *joynt cheer* – a highly prized chair, hand-built by a joiner. Elizabeth's mother, Elizabeth Meare, inherited the remainder of the household goods. An interesting Adams sideboard dated 1709, with an intriguing Charles II era carving attached to the top, most probably commemorates the date of the birth of their second son, Edward, father of William Adams I.

Contemporary documents show that Edward continued to live at Sneyd Green after his marriage. In 1712, aged 52, he retired to Bagnall, having inherited his older brother's estate there, and lived the life of a gentleman until his death in 1727.

WILLIAM ADAMS OF BAGNALL BANK HOUSE (1702-1775)

William, the elder son of Edward and Elizabeth Adams, clearly combined potting with his farming activities, although it is evident from the *Sheriff's Great Roll of Staffordshire* in 1739 that he favoured country pursuits, being described as *William Adams of Bagnall, Gentleman.*

On 4th May 1730, William married Dorothy, elder daughter of Francis Meare, esquire of Norton Green Hall and they had two daughters. She died at the young age of 25 and was buried in the family vault at Norton-in-the Moors on 8 June 1735. Within six weeks, William was married again, taking Sarah, the widow of Samuel Braddock of Howard Park, Cheddleton, as his bride.

Sarah was the only daughter of William Whieldon of Ipstones. She came from an eminent potting family, her first cousin being Thomas Whieldon, master potter of Fenton Low, a potter of distinction, and one who played a leading role in the development of Staffordshire's potting industry.

William Adams had a pew in Norton Church, where his first wife's grandfather John Repton was incumbent, and there exists a brass nameplate that was originally attached to William's pew, still preserved in the church today.

THOMAS WHIELDON, MASTER POTTER OF FENTON LOW (1719-1795)

The Bagnall Adamses were indeed fortunate to count Thomas Whieldon among their close kin, one the most skillful and intelligent potters of the 18th-century, and a pivotal figure in the history of the potteries.

L. Jewitt, in his *Ceramic Art of Great Britain,* noted that

> *Thomas Whieldon's name is more intimately mixed up with the early development of the potter's art than that of almost any other man.*

Further accolades emanated from the pen of William Burton, the noted ceramic writer, who further elucidates that

> *for the post of honour no name could enter in competition with that of Thomas Whieldon, who between 1740 and 1780 improved all the older processes, and wrought with them new kinds of ware.*

Whieldon, like most of the potters of his day, started business from humble beginnings, operating from a small thatched potworks at Fenton Low. He initially

153. left: Dorothy, eldest daughter of Reverend John Repton, Rector of Stoke-on-Trent, wife of Francis Meare of Norton Green Hall and mother of Dorothy, 1st wife of William Adams of Bagnall (1702-1775)

manufactured snuffboxes and knife-handles and pedalled these around the country in a basket strapped to his back. Through relentless perseverance and a focus on improving his ware, his trade increased considerably, enabling him to purchase his rented potworks in Fenton and subsequently Fenton Hall, which he leased out, living a mile away in Penkhull.

By 1754, aged only 34, Whieldon was a highly successful businessman with extensive trade connections and a reputation for producing high quality wares.

His excellent reputation enabled him to attract some of the most skilled craftspeople of the area; foremost among them were Josiah Spode, the prominent modeller Aaron Wood, William Greatbatch and the young Josiah Wedgwood in 1754, aged 24.

Whieldon was quick to recognise Josiah Wedgwood's energy and aptitude and offered the dynamic young potter employment. He must have realised Josiah's immense potential because, on 30th December 1758, he offered Josiah an unbelievably generous agreement, one that allowed Josiah the full liberty to experiment with a view to improving ceramic wares and glazes without ever having to reveal his methodology!

Josiah immediately got down to work in Fenton Hall, in a room that was converted into a laboratory, writing in an experimental notebook:

Page 1... began at Fenton Hall ... February 13th 1759 – Experiment No: 1 ...

It was probably the beginning of Josiah's systematic experimentation, a methodology that would serve him so well in his lifetime and which allowed him to perfect his wares to the exquisite perfection that he ultimately achieved.

Some five decades on William Adams III would be in residence at Fenton Hall, singularly aware that he was following in the great master's footsteps, taking on the lease for a remarkable 24 years.

Whieldon's faith in Josiah's abilities were well founded and the young potter went on to vastly improve the quality and richness of the glazes. It was a relationship built on trust, which proved mutually beneficial to both parties, with Whieldon gaining vastly improved wares and the financial rewards that followed, and Josiah gaining the technical knowledge which enabled him to successfully launch his own business on the termination of the agreement that ended in 1759.

154. above: Fenton Hall, home of William Adams III (1772-1829). On the right, Whieldon Grove–the home of Thomas Whieldon (1719-1795)

Adams of Bagnall and Fenton Hall

155. below: Family tree showing the link between Thomas Whieldon and William Adams III
156. bottom: William Adams of Bagnall (1736-1802) – an oil portrait after Joseph Highmore

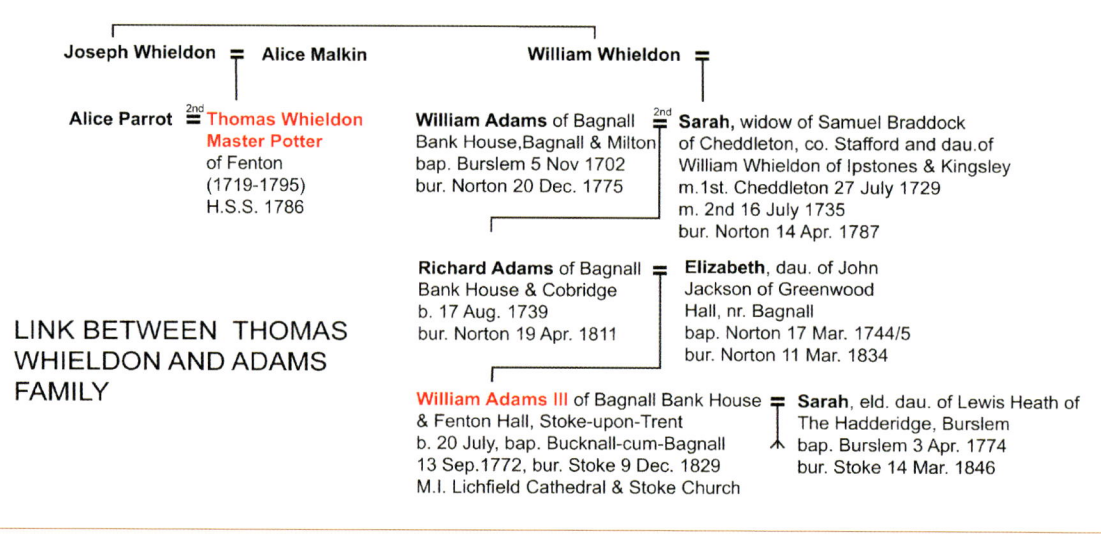

LINK BETWEEN THOMAS WHIELDON AND ADAMS FAMILY

The inevitable parting of their ways passed amicably, Whieldon realising that Josiah's ambitious ideas were at variance with his more cautious approach and, having amassed a considerable fortune from producing ordinary tableware, he was unwilling to enter into what he perceived as speculative ventures.

The pair remained friends throughout their lives and Josiah's reputation became legendary, but it is likely that Josiah learnt much from his time with Whieldon, successfully assimilating much of the master's business practices in later life. Josiah's eagerness to employ the best craftsmen, his care of the workforce and the building of housing for his workforce all hark back to the innovative practices he had witnessed at Fenton Low and cast a light on the impact that Whieldon's business habits might have had on the up-and-coming entrepreneur.

Thomas Whieldon had prospered throughout his business life and is reputed to have amassed a fortune of some £10,000. In 1780, at the age 61, he wisely decided to retire from trade and, taking drastic action, set about demolishing his pottery works and planting an ornamental garden on the site. He resided at his elegant mansion at Whieldon Grove until his death in 1795, only three months after the death of his friend Josiah Wedgwood.

His long retirement was taken up with local affairs, and in 1787 he held the office of High Sheriff of Staffordshire. He had achieved much in his long life and mentored a number of our most noted potters; they owed a considerable debt to the master potter, as is aptly summed up by A. Hayden in *Chats on Old Earthenware*, 1909:

It is rightly believed that Thomas Whieldon had a great and lasting influence on the potters of his generation.

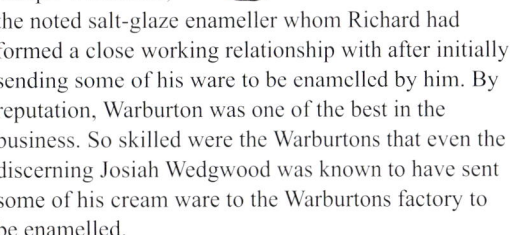

157. right: William Adams of Bagnall (1736-1802) modelled by Arnold Machin, A.R.A. (from a painting by Joseph Highmore)

His magnificent mansion, Whieldon Grove, was destined to be pulled down to make way for the Manchester to Birmingham Railway, but Fenton's greatest son–probably the first great master potter–is immortalised by the street that bears his name: Whieldon Road in Fenton.

Despite his family's prestigious potting connections, William Adams (b.1702) does not seem to have contributed a great deal to his family's potting ventures, preferring no doubt to focus on his farming concerns, a trend eventually followed by his two eldest sons, William and Edward. Nevertheless, he had the foresight in his lifetime to provide the necessary funds to establish his younger son Richard in his own pottery, ensuring the survival of his family's ancient craft.

RICHARD ADAMS, MASTER POTTER (1739-1811)

Richard learnt the 'mistery and art of potting' through an apprenticeship at the Holden Lane pottery, near Handley Green–a potworks which had once belonged to his great uncle William Adams–and he subsequently joined his elder brother at their Cobridge works producing salt-glaze ware.

In 1759, aged 20, we find the enthusiastic young potter Richard established in his own works at Cobridge, bolstered financially by his father, who had advanced him a share of his patrimony, and producing a range of salt-glaze ware which at that time were much in vogue.

Based in Cobridge, Richard Adams was a stone's throw away from his brother-in-law Joseph Warburton, the noted salt-glaze enameller whom Richard had formed a close working relationship with after initially sending some of his ware to be enamelled by him. By reputation, Warburton was one of the best in the business. So skilled were the Warburtons that even the discerning Josiah Wedgwood was known to have sent some of his cream ware to the Warburtons factory to be enamelled.

Trade was buoyant throughout the 1760s, with Richard Adams and his close associates benefitting greatly from the orders that flowed in–in particular from Holland. But change was in the air, and by the 1770s the demand for salt-glaze products waned, gradually to be replaced by the more durable fluid-glaze process recently invented by Enoch Booth of Tunstall.

Dynamic potters of the day such as Wedgwood embraced the new developments, but Richard Adams, in common with many well-established master potters, was more sceptical of the new processes that were coming to the fore. By 1787, no salt-glaze manufacturer is listed in Staffordshire and production of this fine ware, so particular to the county, came to an end. Richard Adams seized the downturn as an opportunity to retire, and in 1793, aged 56, he handed

158. left: The Cobridge manufactory of Joseph Warbuton and Richard Adams, circa 1759

Adams of Bagnall and Fenton Hall

159. below: Greenfields, near Bagnall, home of Richard Adams (1656-1724)

over the reins to his recently married son William Adams III and took up a more leisurely outdoor life.

Ironically, Richard Adams was to give up potting in favour of farming, while a generation later his one and only son was to do the opposite, relinquishing his farming activities to concentrate on building up his already thriving potting business.

Like his cousin Thomas Whieldon, Richard in later life put trade to the background in favour of country pursuits. He was particularly fond of shooting and was considered an excellent shot and dressed well in the Regency fashion of the day:

With powdered wig, brass-buttoned kersey-mere coat, long waistcoat, knee breeches, long stockings and buckle shoes.

P.W.L. Adams, *A History of the Adams family of North Staffordshire*, 1914

Richard was not of an ambitious nature, nor ever strove to make a large fortune, preferring to live a quiet unassuming life, in complete contrast to his fiercely ambitious son.

On retirement, Richard had moved to a modest house, Grange Lane in Cobridge, allowing his son with a growing family to occupy the family home, the Bagnall Bank House, while William also owned a small cottage nearby–probably the cottage identified as Greenfields, which figures in 19th-century family photographs.

Richard Adams died in 1811 aged 72 and was buried at St. Bartholomew's Church, Norton-in-the-Moors, and both he and his wife are commemorated on a monument in the mother church of St. Peter ad Vincula at Stoke. When Richard died, his widow Elizabeth went to live with her son William at Cliff Bank, Stoke, near to the pottery he was working at the time.

By all accounts, Elizabeth Adams was a formidable lady–small in stature but described as sharp tongued and not averse to making caustic comments whenever she saw fit. She was the daughter of John Jackson of Greenwood Hall near Bagnall, a large rambling old country house, once occupied by Judge Bradshaw, one

161. above: Inset–Detail of inscription on the base of the flagon

160. right: Hand-wrought silver flagon presented to Bagnall Church in memory of Elizabeth, widow of Richard Adams of Bagnall

of the regicides of Charles I. Elizabeth was born at Greenwood one year before the Jacobite Rebellion of 1745. It was old Mrs Richard Adams who passed down the family stories, told to her by her parents, regarding the rebels' visit to Bagnall Hall.

Richard's tenacious widow outlived her husband by twenty-three years and her only son by five years, dying aged ninety-one as a result of being knocked down by a cow whilst out walking!

Elizabeth died on 14th March 1834 and was buried at Norton-in-the-Moors beside her husband Richard Adams, Master Potter. The family presented to Bagnall Church a silver flagon in memory of Mrs Richard Adams; the inscription on the base, with lozenge-shaped impaled arms, stated the following:

To the Glory of God & in memory of ELIZABETH, widow of Richard Adams, Master-Potter of Cobridge & Bagnall, Staffordshire, born at Greenwood Hall A.D. 27th February, 1744: died at Fenton Hall, 11th March. 1834.

WILLIAM ADAMS III OF FENTON HALL (1772-1829)

William Adams III, while never achieving the fame of his celebrated cousin of Greengates, was arguably the most successful of the Adams potting businesses and ultimately the branch that endured the longest.

Under his management, the company rose to prominence by shrewdly identifying trends and markets, a stance aptly described by Josiah C. Wedgwood in *Staffordshire Pottery and its history*, 1913:

From 1790 onwards 'blue printed' seems to have superseded every other sort of earthenware. It was the first opportunity common folk had had of getting a decorative plate to eat off; and it made the fortunes of the Spodes, the Adamses, the Bournes, the Mintons, the Ridgeways, and many another master of the good old days ...

In the process it undoubtedly played a prominent role in establishing Staffordshire as the principal centre of pottery production at the dawn of the Industrial Revolution.

One wonders what William's unassuming father Richard would have thought as his dynamic young heir launched into a partnership with his father-in-law in a pottery at Burslem in 1793, at the age of 21. He was setting out at the very time when many master potters, Richard among them, thought that the pottery industry was waning; how wrong they were!

On 18th January 1793, William married Sarah Heath, the daughter of Lewis Heath, master potter and brewery owner. The partnership would oversee a successful potting venture for over ten years at Burslem, initially at Low Street, later moving to The Hadderidge works, which Lewis's son Thomas purchased outright in 1806. It is interesting to note that The Hadderidge, a Queen Anne style house, had been built by William Adams II of Cobridge Hall, but had been sold out of the family; a generation later it would revert back to William Adams IV by virtue of his mother.

Combining potting and brewing, Lewis would likely have had an inn attached to his pottery works, which

162. below: **St. Chad's Church Bagnall,** circa 1910

164. left: Upper Cliff Bank House at Stoke – the home of William Adams III from 1809-1819 (photograph 1941)

In 1804, William Adams III relinquished his share of The Hadderidge Pottery and took over the Cliff Bank Works at Stoke the same year. He was following in the wake of Josiah Wedgwood, who had also, early in his career, operated from the same pottery while in partnership with Alders and Harrison. It was a shrewd move to locate himself in Stoke, at the very heart of the burgeoning potting industry, where he made the well-known blue printed ware, figures, portrait busts and indeed general earthenware of every description.

He rode out every morning from Bagnall to his Cliff Bank Works at Stoke up until 1810, when, to facilitate easier access to his pottery, he took up residence in a substantial house nearby (Upper Cliff Bank House) which he rented from his great friend and kinsman John Davenport. With typical entrepreneurial flourish he acquired Wolfe's Big Works and the Bridge Bank Works in 1818 and a further factory, the Upper Cliff Bank Works, in 1828. So successful did he become that by 1829, the year of his death, he was working four large factories in Stoke together with three in Burslem, and Adams was one of the largest firms in the potteries.

On inheriting his share of his grandfather's estate at Bagnall in 1811, William sold it to his friend Thomas

was supplied from his nearby brewery, with all ventures adding grist to the mill.

Family tradition has it that Richard Adams had not entirely approved of William's engagement to Sarah Heath, but later acquiesced (perhaps after pressure from his wife Elizabeth who, interestingly, signed the marriage bond with Lewis Heath). Things must have settled down after the marriage as we find William and his new bride residing at the family home of Bagnall Bank House soon after the birth of their first child Anne in 1793.

Residing at Bagnall, William naturally took an interest in the affairs of the local church, taking on the post of churchwarden of St. Chad's, Bagnall, from 1801-1805. A page reproduced from the Parish Register, written in his own hand, demonstrates how meticulously he attended to the accounts. It must be remembered how potentially onerous the taking on of the warden's responsibilities could have been at this time. P.W.L. Adams states in his *Notes on some North Staffordshire Families*, 1930,

> *a rate was levied upon the parishioners to cover outgoings but there was seldom sufficient money to meet expenses, the incoming warden took over the debt or the outgoing made up the deficiency.*

An interesting sketch commissioned by P.W.L. Adams depicts the happy couple leaving Burslem church after the wedding, with Richard and his wife and guests all drawn from contemporary descriptions.

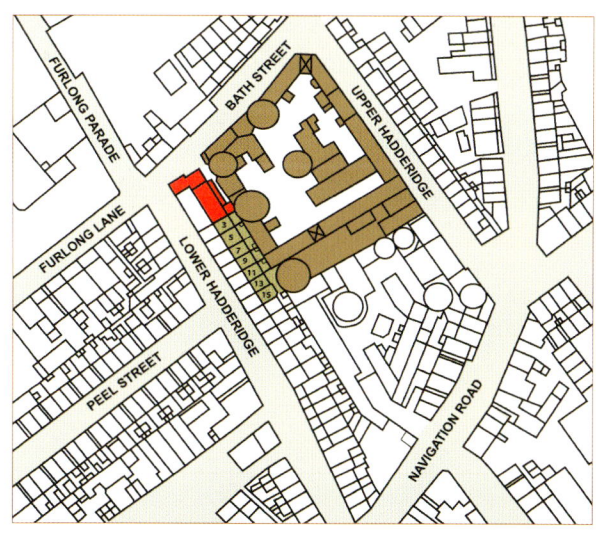

165. above: Layout plan of The Hadderidge Works, Burslem (1890)

163. Left: William Adams III of Fenton Hall, painted by Michael Keeling, 1819; photograph ©Jonathan Gray

Adams of Bagnall and Fenton Hall

166. left: *Thomas Heath of The Hadderidge, brother of Sarah Adams, wife of William Adams III, probably painted by Michael Keeling, 1819; photograph ©Jonathan Gray*

167. right: *Cliff Bank Pottery, Stoke-on-Trent, circa 1900*

168. left: *Part of Church Street, Stoke-on-Trent, in 1818, showing parts of Adams' Big Works on the left and the Bridge Bank Works on the right with an Adams canal barge loading wares*

Adams of Bagnall and Fenton Hall

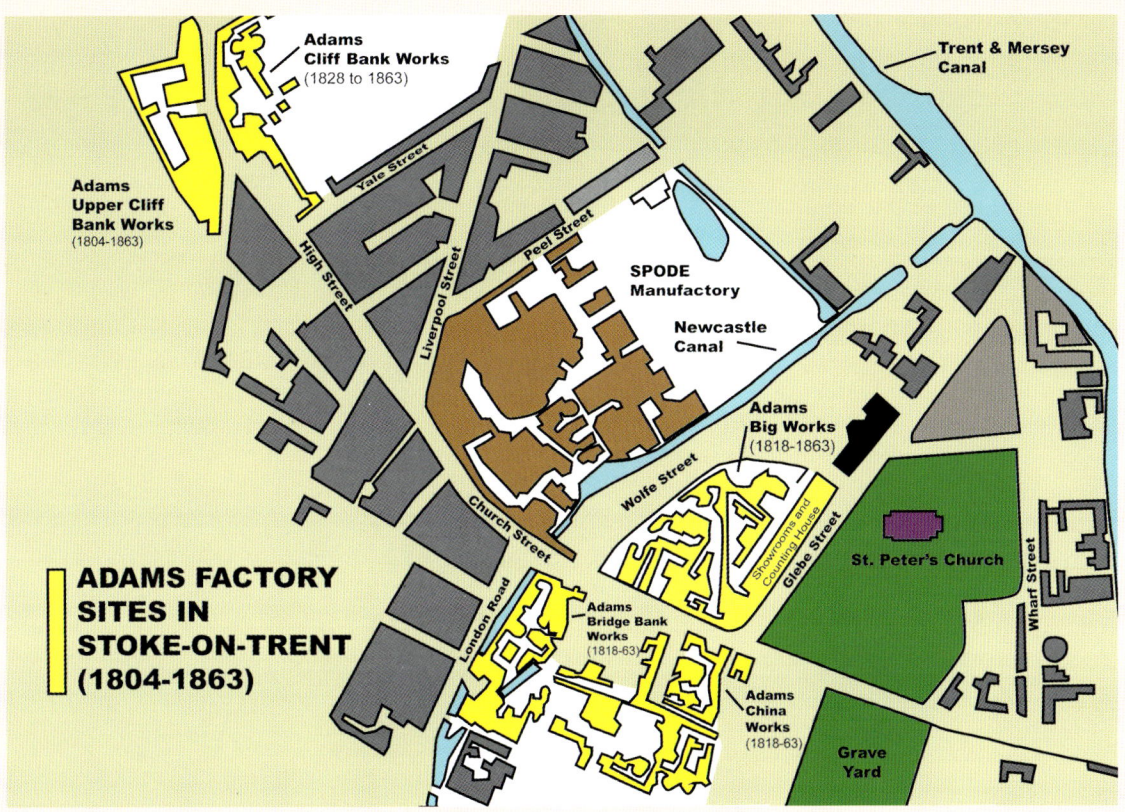

170. below: Plan of the extensive Adams factory sites in Stoke-on-Trent (1804-1863)

Wolfe of Bagnall, reinvesting the proceeds in his business. William's four sons were systematically brought into the partnership on their coming of age, beginning with his eldest son, William Adams IV, who became a partner in 1819.

By the 1820s William's potteries were buzzing with trade from all over the world. They had successfully negotiated the dire trading conditions caused by the war with France that had been so disastrous for Staffordshire's potteries (with at least thirty going bankrupt). They had survived bleak times in the early 19th-century, when sales to their main market of the USA fell by a staggering 75 per cent, but were well poised to capitalize on the boom that followed.

In 1818 William took up residence at Fenton Hall, leasing it from his Whieldon relatives. William's distant cousin Thomas Whieldon had died in 1787, and

it was with his son George that William signed the long lease, one that would extend for some 11 years to the death of William and provide a further 6 years of tenure for the widow and her family.

Fenton Hall was described by Ward in (1843)

as concealed by its low and woody situation near the Trent, and has extensive pleasure grounds, gardens, and fishponds attached.

This comfortable early Georgian-period house suited William admirably, being perfect to accommodate his growing family and entertain his wide range of friends and acquaintances.

Having successfully built up one of the largest businesses in the country, William wisely delegated much of the running to his four sons. His eldest son, William Adams IV, was given responsibility for the crucial Liverpool Shipping office, and the younger sons assisted their father in the running of seven factories which turned out a vast number of wares.

169. left: Sarah, eldest daughter of Lewis Heath of The Hadderidge and wife of William Adams III of Fenton Hall, painted by Michael Keeling, 1819; photograph ©Jonathan Gray

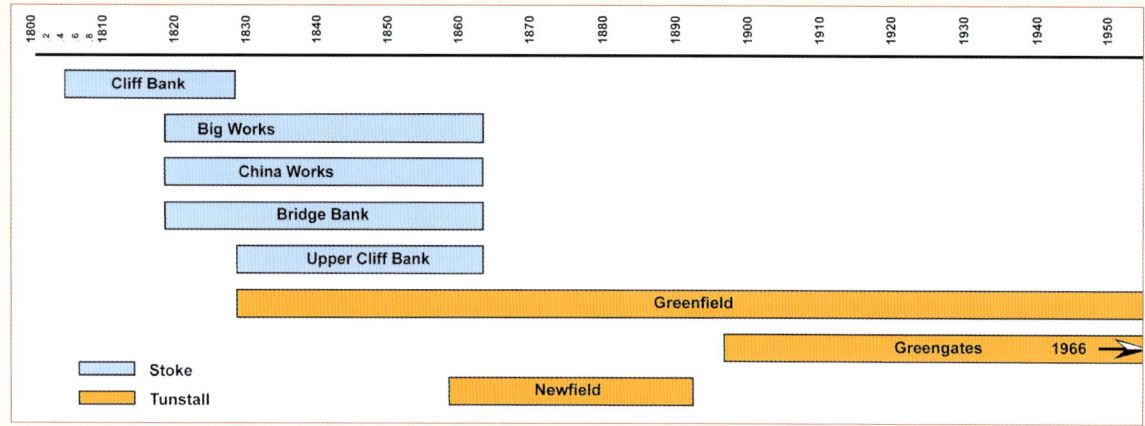

171. below: **Potteries operated by William Adams III and family (1804-1966)**

172. below: **Plan of Fenton Hall, sometimes referred to as 'Great Fenton House', circa 1900**

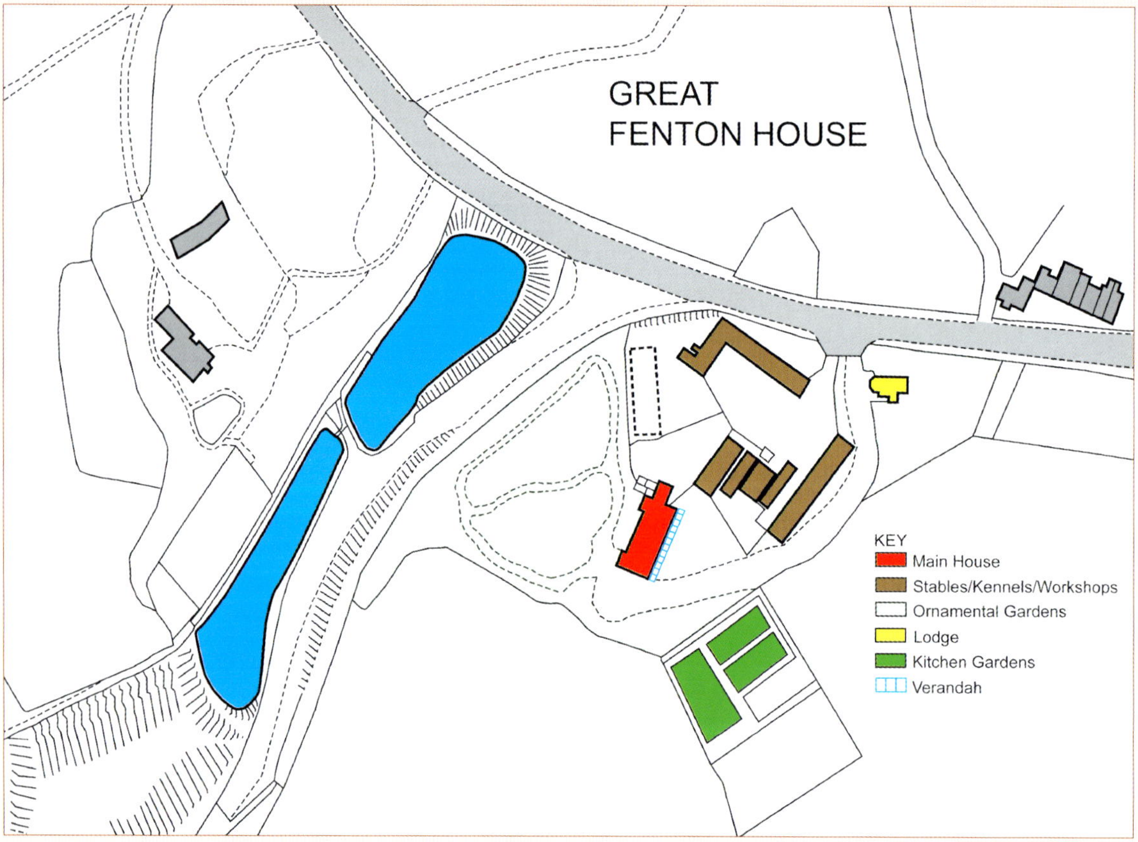

173. below: William Adams III's flute, preserved in the family collection. William was by all accounts proficient with both the flute and violin, often playing at family parties

174. middle: Josiah Spode I (1733-1797), a prominent English potter and founder of the Spode Pottery Works. Josiah was an accomplished violinist who often accompanied his friend William Adams III in local musical gatherings

William Adams III was noted for his keen sense of humour and genial sociable manner, this trait aptly reflected in his favourite saying:

*He that cannot see a joke
Is not fit to live in Stoke.*

He was also an accomplished musician, excelling at playing both the violin and flute, and in musical evenings he accompanied his friend Josiah Spode I, an accomplished violinist and potter of note. Generations of Adams and Spode families were intimate friends as were many of the noted Staffordshire potting families, a social link that was maintained through to the 20th century. The Adams family photograph albums of the early 1900s regularly show the family socialising with Wedgwoods and other noted pottery dynasties.

A charming account portraying family festivities at Fenton Hall on Christmas Day, 1824, is reproduced in Percy W.L. Adams *Notes on Some North Staffordshire Families*, 1930:

There assembled a family gathering in the dining room at Fenton Hall in north Staffordshire – that delightful room with its French windows opening on to the veranda and lawns. In December these windows were tightly closed and shuttered when the room would be cosy with its traditional Staffordshire fire blazing up the chimney with the good Staffordshire coal, and Yule logs. The portraits of the head of the family and his wife painted by Michael Keeling some five years earlier hung upon the wall. But it is the people we want to describe rather than the room or its furniture. At the head of the table is William Adams, then 52 years of age, Sarah, aged 49, buxom, smart, and comfortable, sits opposite. They had been married 32 years all but a few weeks. William's mother was there, it was her 80th Christmas and she was to see ten more. She was somewhat short in stature, but very erect, keenly

175. above: Drawing of Stoke from Penkhull, clearly showing the pottery works surrounding Stoke Parish Church

William Adams of Sneyd Green, of Bucknall Hall & of Milton, co. Stafford, 2nd surv. son of John Adams of Birches Head and Bucknall Hall.
b. 1599, bur. 25 Oct. 1676
═ **Catherine Hanson** of Stoke-upon-Trent
bur. 26 Mar. 1702

William Adams of Sneyd Green, Greenfields & Bagnall,
bapt. 20 Nov. 1642
bur. 15 May 1712
unm. Will proved Lichfield

John Adams
bap. 1644
d. 1717

Samuel Adams
bap. 1648
d. 1729

Katherine Adams
bap. 1657/8

Edward Adams of Bagnall Bank House Bagnall. Youngest son of Wm. Adams of Sneyd and Bucknall Hall.
Heir of his eldest brother Wm Adams of Sneyd. Bap. 12 Feb. 1660/1
bur. Norton-in-the-Moors 22 Apr. 1727

Dorothy eld. dau. of Francis Meare of Norton Green Hall, by Dorothy, dau. of John Repton, Rector of Stoke-upon-Trent
b. 6 June 1710, bur. 8 Jun. 1735
═1st **William Adams** of Bagnall Bank House, Bagnall & Milton
bap. Burslem 5 Nov 1702
bur. Norton 20 Dec. 1775
2nd═ **Sarah**, widow of Samuel Braddock of Cheddleton, co. Stafford and dau. of William Whieldon of Ipstones & Kingsley, m.1st. Cheddleton 27 Ju 1729, m. 2ndly. 16 July 1735
bur. Norton 14 Apr. 1787

Elizabeth, bap. Stoke 7 Feb. 1730/1
d. without issue
1st═ **Joseph Warburton** of Rushton Grange Cobridge

Dorothy, bap. Stoke 18 Feb. 1732/3
bur. Norton 1744

William Adams of Bagnall
b. 4 Oct. 1736
bur. Norton 21 Sept. 1802
d. unm.

Edward Adams
b. 13 Mar. 1737/8
d. unm.

Richard Adams of Bagnall Bank House & Cobridge
Master Potter
b. 17 Aug. 1739
bur. Norton 19 Apr. 18

William Adams III of Bagnall Bank House & Fenton Hall, Stoke-upon-Trent
Master Potter
b. 20 July, bap. Bucknall-cum-Bagnall 13 Sep. 1772, bur. Stoke 9 Dec. 1829
M.I. Lichfield Cathedral & Stoke Church
═1793 **Sarah**, eld. dau. of Lewis Heath of The Hadderidge, Burslem
bap. Burslem 3 Apr. 1774
bur. Stoke 14 Mar. 1846

Ann, b. 1793
bur. St. Paul's Burslem
12 Nov. 1856
═
Joseph Twigg of Bank House, Burslem

Sarah b. Bagnall 2 Sept. 1796
bur. 10 Feb. 1831 Chorlton-on-Medlock co. Lancaster
═ **James Guest** Medlock Cottage co. Lancaster

William Adams IV of Greenfield nr. Tunstall & Liverpool
Master Potter
b. 9 Nov. 1798
bur. Tunstall 30 Oct. 1865
M.I. Wolstanton Church
═1827 **Jane**, eld. dau. and coh. of Jesse Breeze of Greenfield co. Stafford & Little Chell
b. 3 Nov. 1804
bur. Tunstall 28 July 1864

Lettice, bap. St. Chad's Bagnall 2 Mar. 1801
bur. Stoke 18 Jan. 1827

Edward Adams of Basford Hall nr. Stoke-on-Trent
bap. Bagnall 16 Oct. 1803
bur. Wolstanton 5 Jan. 1872

ADAMS OF GREENFIELDS

ADAMS
OF BAGNALL & FENTON HALL

Elizabeth, only dau. of John Meare of Handley Green, co. Stafford
m. Dilhorne, co. Stafford
bur. Norton-in-the-Mooors 3 July 1733

Richard Adams
bur. Apr. 1724

Ralph Adams
bap. 1654
d. 1693

Jonathan Adams
bap. 1651
bur. Sept. 1719

Grace
bap. Burslem 1 Jun. 1691
bur. 30 Jun. 1701

Elizabeth = **Joseph Hulme** of Bagnall Grange

Edward Adams
b. 1709
bur. 1745?
= **Martha,** 2nd dau. of Joseph Adams, **Master potter**
bap. Burslem 15 Sept 1723

ADAMS OF GREENGATES

Elizabeth, dau. of John Jackson of Greenwood Hall, nr, Bagnall
bap. Norton 17 Mar. 1744/5
bur. Norton 11 Mar. 1834

Thomas Adams
b. Sept. 1741
d. young

Ralph Adams of Milton & Endon =1770 **Martha Ball** of Norton & Endon

Sarah
b. 1744
bur. 1769

Mary
b. 1746
= **Thomas Gee**

Richard Adams
bap. Bucknall-cum-Bagnall 6 Oct. 1774
bur. Norton 26 July 1778
d. unm.

Mary, youngest dau. and coh. of Jesse Breeze of Greenfield co. Stafford & Little Chell, b. 10 July 1811
bur. Wolstanton 3 Dec. 1863

Lewis Adams of The Watlands
bap. 14 July 1805
Master N.S. Harriers 1836-40
1st Chief Bailiff of Stoke 1839-42
bur. Stoke Sept. 1850
d. unm.

Thomas Adams of Liverpool
bap. Bagnall 31 May 1807
bur. Stoke 12 Mar. 1863

Samuel Adams
b. 19 May 1809
d. 4 July 1809

Elizabeth
b. 14 July 1810
d. 12 July 1862

Frances
bap. 8 Aug 1814
bur. Stoke 1 Mar. 1879
= **John Massey Morris,** co. Flint

Susanna
bap. Stoke 21 Sept. 1815
bur. Norton 17 Dec. 1815

177. left: East end of the Chancel of Stoke Parish Church of St. Peter-ad-Vincula, with William Adams III's bronze plaque beneath the flag

178. right: Parish Church of St. Peter-ad-Vincula, Stoke-on-Trent, with William Adams III's grave in the foreground

alive to all that was going on. A notable woman was Elizabeth, widow of Richard Adams, 1739-1811, Master Potter, of Cobridge. She was as usual dressed very plainly in black, with charming and beautifully coiffured white mob cap as befitted her age, and as usual slightly disapproving of her daughter-in-law, Sarah Adams, who she considered too fond of her taffetas, silk trimmed with her favourite Mechlin laces and other becoming fineries. She had also many 'fronts' and wigs of which her mother-in-law certainly disapproved and which her husband with a twinkle in his eye is known to have put under the pump (and soaked them). The table groaned with its fare. Indeed there were many mouths to feed for besides the family of nine children, there were the Heaths from the Hadderidge, and Joseph Twigg and his children from the Hamil, and James Guest, the cotton magnate from Manchester ... After dinner each person present signed his or her name in the book ...

After the wine in the afternoon, we can imagine there was music, for William delighted in it, he was himself very clever with the flute and violin, his sister-in-law Theodosia, was also a good violinist. There may have been others among the party to help in that way. Music at home was popular in those days and there were often musical parties given by the Woods at Brownhills, where Theodosia was in much request.

William was very fond of walking, regularly taking long strolls through the countryside. It has been suggested that a journey he made on foot from Liverpool to Stoke, some forty-five miles, contributed to his early death on 2nd December 1829, aged 57. This is, however, unlikely, as the legendary walk took place some 12 months before his demise; his 'aristocratic' gout was the most probable contributor to the possible fatal heart attack he experienced while playing his usual evening game of cards.

William Adams III was buried in the churchyard of St. Peter's ad Vincula Church, Stoke on Trent, his grave lying on the south-west side of the church, as close as it was possible to be to one of his potteries, Wolfe's Big Works, which at one time was adjacent to the churchyard. Nearby lie the tombs of fellow pottery magnates, John Hales of Cobridge and his musical associate and friend Josiah Spode.

A bronze portrait medallion and alabaster tablet was erected in William's memory on the south wall of the sanctuary of St. Peter's Stoke and, together with his cousin William Adams I, he is commemorated on a plaque in Lichfield Cathedral which has apparently been covered over as the result of building works during the construction of the cathedral gift shop.

William's wife and family continued to live at Fenton Hall and the business's succession was ensured as William Adams IV stepped up to head the thriving partnership, an arrangement that would endure a further 24 years until 1853, when the partnership was sadly dissolved.

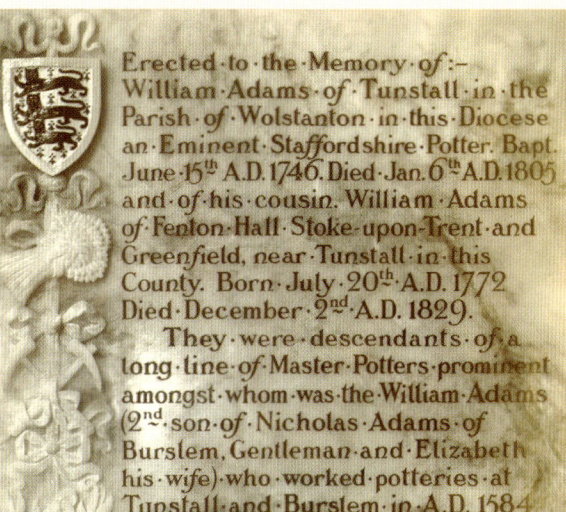

179. left: A memorial tablet to William Adams I and III in Lichfield Cathedral

Adams of Bagnall and Fenton Hall

181. right: *The arms of Adams of Greenfield quartered with Heath of The Hadderidge and Breeze of Greenfield*

8

ADAMS OF GREENFIELD
William Adams IV (1798-1865)

William, eldest son of the fiercely ambitious William Adams III, was of a totally different character to his outgoing father, being characterised as a thoughtful individual, a man of quiet tastes. On a cursory glance, perhaps that was not the most appropriate personality trait to help him cope with the hugely demanding business environment he would shortly be exposed to, when, in 1819 and aged 21, he was admitted as a partner into the family potting firm. He would have experienced the inevitable pressure entailed in running such a massive concern, which by then encompassed six factories in Stoke and an array of subsidiary ventures. But his baptism of fire was yet to come, as within a year the inexperienced young partner would find himself booked on a packet ship destined for America, with the daunting brief of expanding sales in this up-and-coming market.

DEVELOPING THE AMERICAN MARKET

A somewhat casual note, written obliquely in the Adams family Bible, records for posterity that

William Adams Junior took his passage on board ... 1st September 1822 for New York, United States of America.

Shipping documents add further detail, revealing that the ship he sailed on was the *Panthea*, a 370-ton American packet ship, the master being a Thomas Bennett.

The ship's manifest for the New York customs recorded an arrival date of October 5th 1822, making the voyage from Liverpool 35 days – a fairly typical

180. left: *William Adams IV of Greenfield Hall, Tunstall (1798-1865) – a recent copy of a portrait by William Scott of Liverpool in 1842*

182. right: *Entry in the Adams' family Bible stating that in 1821 William Adams IV sailed from Liverpool to New York on a two-year business trip*

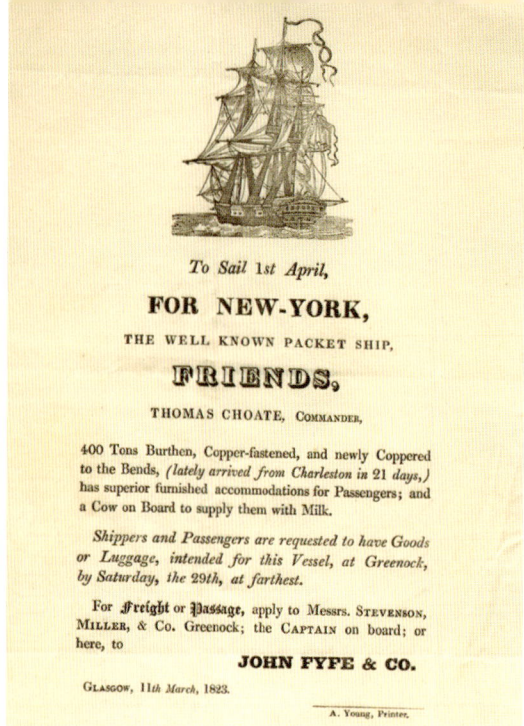

183. left: **Poster advertising a packet service from Scotland to New York,** 1823

184. below: **The Black Ball Line packet ship** New York **off Ailsa Craig,** dated 1836

sailing for a packet ship of the time, which usually made the westward journey (amusingly designated in sailor-slang as *uphill*) in an average of 40 days, while the eastwards, *downhill* leg could take half that amount, achieved by riding the prevailing winds and currents.

Under the passenger entry for William we find an H. Spooner, aged 27, likewise designated as an English merchant; whether or not he was a travelling companion for the young potter is unknown, but I would like to think that H. Spooner was a friend or trusted Adams employee.

It is possible that the ship *Panthea* was owned by the American Red Star shipping line, a competitor of the leading Atlantic packet company, the Black Ball Line.

The packet trade, which developed in the 18th century, consisted in ships carrying cargo, passengers and mail between Europe and America. Booking a passage on the early packets often involved tedious waiting around as they would only sail when their cargoes were full, for obvious economic reasons.

185. *A view of South Street from Maiden Lane, New York,* circa 1827

Realising the importance of the American trade, a group of New York merchants set up the Black Ball Line in 1818 to service the Atlantic packet trade, but uniquely they undertook to leave New York at fixed days each month, irrespective of cargo or passengers. The line took its name from its flag–a black ball on a red background–and for ease of identification their ships also displayed a large black ball painted on the front top sail.

The Black Ball Line and other rivals achieved a fearsome reputation for rigidly adhering to schedules whatever the weather, and the harsh treatment of the sailors, that was necessary to keep to the timetable, which earned the ships the nickname of the *Yankee bloodboats*.

A number of traditional sea shanties specifically refer to the brutal regime of the Black Ball Line; the lyrics of the 'New York Girls', a cautionary tale of a sailor being tricked by a pretty girl, only to be duped into spending his money or even robbed, refers to the infamous Yankee bloodboats:

As I walked down the Broadway
One evenin' in July
I met a maid who asked me trade
And a sailor John says I

To Tiffany's I took her
I did not mind expense
I bought her two gold earrings
And they cost me 50 cents
(Chorus)
And away, you Santee
My dear Annie
O, you New York Girls
Can't you dance the Polka?

Says she, 'You limejuice sailor
Now see me home you may'
But when we reached her cottage door
She this to me did say

'My flashman he's a Yankee
With his hair cut short behind
He wears a pair of long sea-boots
And he sails in the Blackball Line'

(Chorus)

'He's homeward bound this evenin
And with me he will stay
So get a move on, sailor-boy
Get crackin' on your way'

So I kissed her hand and proper
Afore her flash man came
And fare ye well, me Bowery gal
I know your little game

(Chorus)

I wrapped me glad rags round me
And to the docks did steer
I'll never court another maid
I'll stick to rum and beer

I joined a Yankee blood-boat
And sailed away next morn
Don't ever fool around with gals
You're safer off Cape Horn

(Chorus)

The sea shanty 'Blow the Man Down', with its many references to the Atlantic Trade, describes a potentially catastrophic situation that many sail boats experienced: being caught in a gale with the top sails fully set. It was a mishap that could, with an unbalanced cargo, capsize the ship, with devastating consequences.

(The title 'Blow the Man Down' is thought to refer to Man-o'-war).

Frequent allusions are made in this shanty to the harsh treatment of the packet ship sailors:

> *Twas devilish hard treatment of every degree*
> *To see these poor devils, how they will all 'scoot'*
> *Assisted along by the toe of a boot.*

So driven were the captains of the American packets to keep to time that it was reported that

> *a Yankee captain never takes off his clothes to go to bed during the whole voyage ... the consequence of this great watchfulness is that, advantage is taken of every puff of wind, while the risk from the squalls and sudden gusts is, in a great measure obviated.*

Crossing the Atlantic in the golden age of sail was hardly a pleasurable activity, nor was it free from danger. Only a few months prior to William's voyage from Liverpool, the Black Ball Line ship *Albion* had been wrecked off the coast of Ireland with the loss of forty lives.

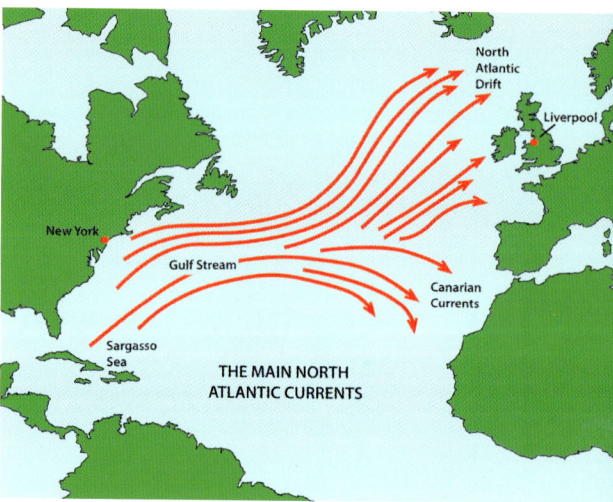

186. above. **Major North Atlantic currents**

187. above: Ship Superior – a three-masted ship of the Black Ball line battling an Atlantic storm

A typical packet ship of the early 1800s could accommodate ten to twenty well-off cabin passengers, while the poorer folks were forced to make the crossing in the dark, damp and often rat-infested steerage area.

From the onset it was supposed that William would tour the Southern States of the USA and Mexico before establishing an office in New York to handle imports, but through the diary of John Ridgway, a Staffordshire potter who was on a similar trade mission, we discover that the pair met up in New York of 21st November 1822, six weeks after William disembarked his ship.

The remainder of William's two-year visit is shrouded in mystery; he probably spent it touring the country, acquiring images and forming trade connections which would prove invaluable to the company in the coming years. By the time he left America he had established not only an office in New York but also a warehouse and showroom.

A tantalising reference to William's return sailing is found in Percy W. L. Adams' book *A History of the Adams family of North Staffordshire*, 1914:

His return passage on his first journey was a record one for speed at that time, long before the day when steamships began to ply across the Atlantic. It appears that he left Long Island in one of the finest crafts of the day, under the command of Captain Rogers. Half a gale was blowing from the west; and, with as much sail as she could carry, the good ship made the passage to Liverpool in 14 days.

In 1823, the record for the fastest passage from New York to Liverpool was held by the Black Ball Ship the *New York*–a crossing achieved in 15 days 16 hours!

By 1825, William Adams IV had established a profitable exporting business between Liverpool and New York, operating their American side of the business at 248 Pearl Street, at the very heart of New York's ceramic centre, where they marketed their hugely popular American Historical ware.

William Adams & Sons produced two very popular series of wares for the American market: the 'American Views' and the 'Columbus Views'.

Demand for their goods was high, fuelled by buyers from the growing middle and working classes who increasingly sought attractive dinnerware. The buoyant market was further enhanced by virtue of the imagery that Adams employed, which was perfectly matched to the growing interest in American Landscape Wares.

188. left: Jane Adams (1804-1864), wife of William Adams of Greenfield and eldest daughter and co-heiress of Jesse Breeze, from a painting by William Scott of Liverpool

Although William Adams IV is known to have brought back images himself from his tours of America, it is clearly evident that the inspiration for the 'American Views' series came directly from the engraved illustration in John Hinton's book *The History and Topography of the United States* (1830-1832).

Fuelled by the Industrial Revolution and the resulting growth of mass production, Staffordshire potters were able to produce inexpensive goods that quickly dominated the American market and William Adams & Sons were foremost players in this important market throughout most of the 19th century.

So attuned were the Staffordshire potters to the mood and swings of the American market that it was said that potters decorated their wares with any image certain to please the American market:

> *The scenes that decorated these included a vast array of subjects specific to American interests: prominent statesmen, cities and towns of note, landmarks of historical or political importance, and scenes of the American Landscape.*

(Nancy Siegel, *Along the Junita: Thomas Cole and the Dissemination of American Landscape Imagery*, 2003)

The influence of Staffordshire's potting industry on the everyday life of England and indeed America was graphically illustrated in a 1908 literary description:

> *You cannot drink tea out of a teacup without the aid of the Five Towns ... you cannot eat a meal in decency without the aid of the Five Towns ... that you may drink tea out of teacup or toy with a chop on a plate. All the everyday crockery used in the kingdom is made in the Five Towns ... wherever in all England a woman washes up, she washes up the product of the district; ... whenever and wherever in all England a plate is broken the fracture means new business for the district.*

(Taken from Arnold Bennett, *The Old Wives Tale*, 1908)

William Adams IV undertook a second tour of America in about 1825, certainly before his marriage, and it is thought that on this occasion he brought back the images that inspired the Adams 'Columbus series'.

On his return, his adventurous days over, he settled down, and on 9th May 1827, William married Jane, the elder daughter and co-heiress of Jesse Breeze of Greenfield near Tunstall, the ceremony being held at St. Margaret's Church, Wolstanton.

An entry in the Breeze family bible, preserved in the Adams archive, reveals that Jesse Breeze died on Thursday 26th October 1826 - some six months before his daughters marriage - at Greenfield, at about 6 o'clock in the morning. He was aged only 50 years.

THE BREEZE FAMILY OF GREENFIELD

Jesse Breeze was the eldest son and heir of John Breeze of Greenfield Hall, Tunstall. He received a good education, attending Repton School in Derbyshire, before joining his father in his colliery and potting ventures. Prior to living at Greenfield Hall, John Breeze had lived in Burslem, where he owned considerable property in addition to owning two potteries, one at Longport and the other, the Knowl Works, where they produced porcelain, black basalt, blue-printed ware and other high-class earthenware. In 1801 John purchased the Greenfield estate (then referred to as Smithfield) from the trustees of

189. The Breeze family coat of arms

190. *Greenfield Hall – Oil on canvas. 30 x 38 inches by J. Munday 1911, commissioned by P.W.L. Adams*

ADAMS OF GREENFIELD William Adams IV (1798-1865)

Theophilus Smith, whose life had come to a wretched end earlier that year when he was embroiled in a sensational murder case that rocked the normally peaceful rural community and made national headlines.

Theophilus Smith had purchased the estate in 1790 and renamed it Smithfield, building the Hall and some forty cottages, a shop and an inn, and a year later adding a manufactory to the enterprise.

Writing in 1829, Simeon Shaw described Greenfield Hall in glowing terms, stating that

the very elegant and commodious mansion, seen from the highroad, has a truly picturesque appearance in a pleasant hanging wood, fronted by a fine lawn.

This idyllic impression of the vicinity of the hall was further elaborated on by Henry Wedgwood in his *Romance of Staffordshire*, 1875, where he states,

The reader may have noticed on passing by train, between Tunstall and Pitts Hill station, a brick-built hall, situate on the summit of the hill ... few sites could have been more prepossessing or beautiful ... the hall overlooked the valley of the Chell and the rising heights above.
The view presented in those days was much different than now. It was woody and picturesque, where the squirrel delighted to play. It might have travelled a mile or more without forsaking the branches of trees, which to the south-west, even close to the hall door, was a straggling patch of brushwood running for miles in extent. Over this

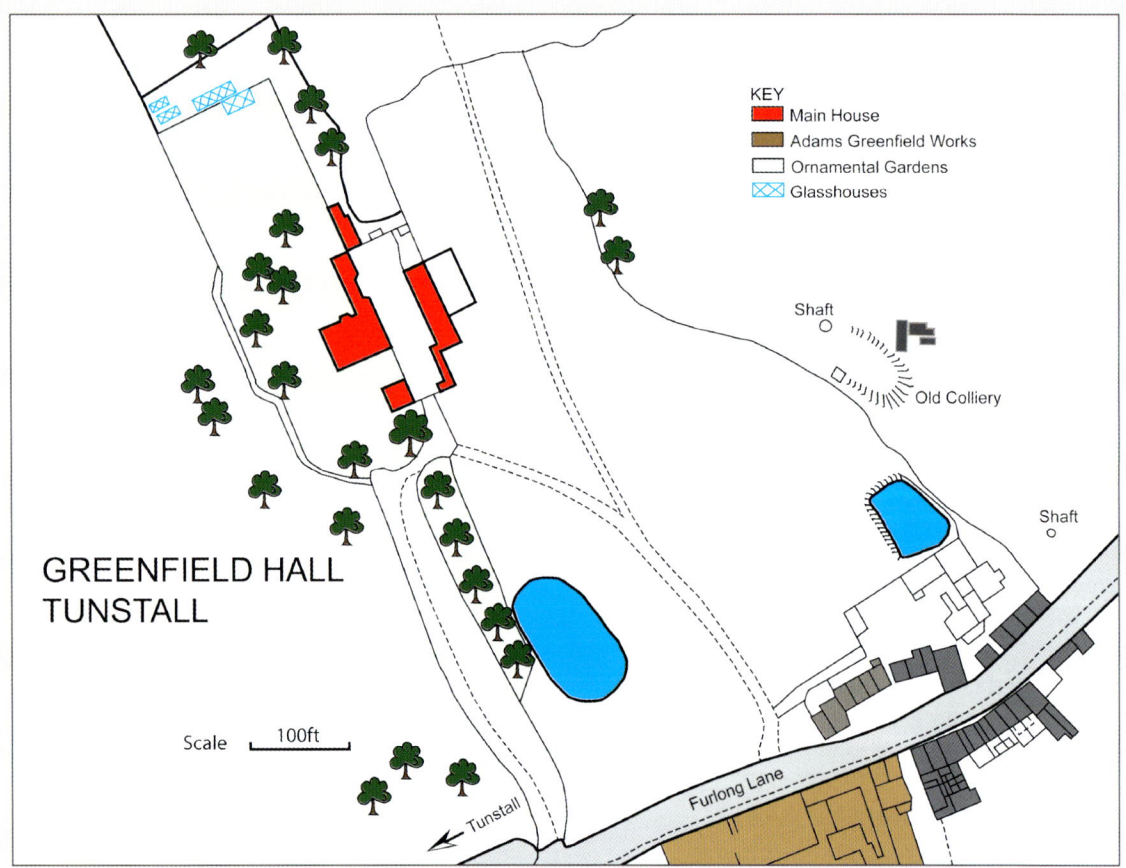

191. below: **Layout plan of Greenfield Hall, Tunstall,** circa 1900

192. View of Smith-Field from Forty Miles Around Manchester, 1794. Artist Edward Davies, engraved by W.C. Wilson

at a distance was Bradwell, brightening in no small degree the beauty of the scene. The hall was approached by a shady avenue that led out of an old winding road from Tunstall to Chell. As you passed down the road your ears would have been saluted by a colony of rooks that had made their home near the mansion. The little smoke that rose from the potters' ovens disturbed but in a small degree the purity of the atmosphere; and the cottages with their gardens, dotted here and there, rather enriched than otherwise the charming character of the neighbourhood.

ATTEMPTED MURDER AT SMITHFIELD HALL

On the evening of 28th June 1800, the Liverpool stagecoach was rapidly approaching Tunstall when the driver was abruptly asked to pull up. Two men clambered out and continued their journey on foot. One man was Peter Wainwright, a Liverpool merchant, and the other his friend and travelling companion Theophilus Smith, the well-known potter of nearby Smithfield Hall.

Smith was in dire financial straights, on the verge of bankruptcy and due to appear in court the very next day. He was worried he would be accosted by bailiffs and suggested to his friend Wainwright that an approach to his house over the fields would be appropriate.

But Smith had other motives; dark and brooding thoughts entered his mind as they awkwardly trudged over the fields towards Smithfield. Smith was aware that Wainwright was having an affair with his wife, and as they were crossing the field near the Hall, Smith pulled out a pistol and signalled that he was going to shoot himself. Wresting the gun from Smith's hand, Wainwright thought he had averted his friend's demise, but Smith apparently had another weapon on his person which he immediately discharged, aiming directly at his travelling companion, but fortunately he missed his mark.

A furious struggle ensued with Wainwright once more disarming his assailant. Smith outwardly seemed ashamed of his deadly actions but then pulled out yet another concealed pistol which, when fired, met its

193. above. Mary Adams (1772-1835), *eldest daughter of William Adams I of Greengates, Tunstall*

target, striking Wainwright at point-blank range. Wainwright let out an almighty scream while the crazed Smith unleashed a savage knife attack on his helpless companion.

Assistance came in the nick of time and the grievously wounded Wainwright was taken to nearby Greengates Hall, the residence of William Adams I, where the poor unfortunate received the best possible medical attention. A bullet was extracted from his back having passed within inches of his stomach.

Thanks to the care he received from the family at Greengates, Wainwright slowly regained his health and is known to have emigrated to America.

Smith, however, was a wanted man; the *London Evening Gazette* of 12th July 1800 printed the following front-page advertisement:

Fifty Guineas Reward *to anyone who should apprehend or give information about a Mr Theophilus Smith of Smithfield, near Tunstall in the county of Staffordshire. It appears that Mr Smith did maliciously cut with a knife and shoot through the body of Mr Wainwright of Liverpool, merchant, this morning about three o'clock at Smithfield, aforesaid, since which he has made his escape.*

It appears that Theophilus made his way to London, but was arrested by two Bow Street officers who found the wretched man hiding in a house in Pall Mall. Although armed with two loaded pistols, he offered no resistance. He was later transferred to Stafford jail where he committed suicide while awaiting trial.

The account of the deadly fight is known to have emanated from Wainwright while he was convalescing at Greengates. Smith apparently refused to discuss what some speculated might have been a failed attempt at a duel, which might account for the number of pistols that seem to have been brandished during the fracas.

An interesting letter in the Adams' family archive demonstrates the bond of affection that existed between the Adams and Wainwright families. The letter was written by Mary Adams; the daughter of William Adams I of Greengates, on 5th November 1800:

My dear Mrs Wainwright!

I take the liberty of addressing you in consequence of some conversation you and my brother had when he was in Liverpool, respecting Ben. My father thinks it necessary to send him from home and if Mr Leven will have a vacancy at Xmas, wishes to place him there. I hope Mr Wainwright is well and that this will find you and the dear children so. Bessy and I have been returned from Harrogate a fortnight – we were absent seven weeks.

I know it will give you pleasure to hear that my face is very much better, and I have very great hopes that with a little prudence this winter,

194. above. **Breeze of Greenfield's tomb in St. John's churchyard, Burslem**

I shall get rid of the complaint entirely. If you should chance to see Dr. Brandreth, will you think it too much trouble to inform him of this as he kindly expressed a wish to hear if I got better.

My father and mother as well as Willy and Bessy wish to join me in kind remembrance to you and Mr Wainwright.

Believe me my dear Mrs Wainwright to be Yours very affectionately

Mary Adams

It certainly appears that the Adams family held the Wainwrights in high regard–a sentiment that was no doubt reciprocated. It is likely that Wainwright was well known to William Adams of Greengates prior to the fateful attack as Percy Adams found references in old ledgers to the firm of Peter Wainwright and Company, American merchants with an office in Liverpool, who had dealings with his great-great grandfather John Breeze. This ultimately would help to explain Wainwright's emigration to America.

After purchasing the Smithfield estate in 1801, John Breeze, aware of the sad associations, renamed it Greenfield, and it later became, by virtue of his wife, the property of William Adams IV and once more the seat of a joyful, contented family.

After the death of Jesse Breeze in 1826, Greenfield works was let to Messrs. Wood & Challinor, but by 1834 it appears to have been assimilated into the Adams group of potteries by right of Jesse Breeze's co-heiresses, Jane and Mary, respectively by then the wives of William Adams IV and his brother Edward.

On his return from America, William Adams IV established offices and a warehouse in Liverpool to handle their expanding trade and acted as agents for other potting concerns. So successful did this venture become that William found it necessary to take up residence in Liverpool, while his father and brothers, Lewis, Edward and Thomas, managed the extensive Stoke factories.

195. left. Lewis Adams of The Watlands, Master of the North Staffordshire Harriers, and first Chief Bailiff of Stoke-upon-Trent

LEWIS ADAMS, FIRST CHIEF BAILIFF OF STOKE-ON-TRENT

Lewis, third son of William Adams III, was born on 11th July 1805 at the family home in Bagnall and baptized at the local church by William's friend the Reverend Thomas Wolfe three days later.

Emulating his older brothers, he was admitted as partner in the family potting business on achieving his age of majority in 1826 and helped to run the very extensive Stoke potteries. By all accounts he appears to have been a most able manager, universally respected by his large workforce.

After the death of his father in 1829, Lewis continued to live with his mother and unmarried sisters at Fenton Hall until 1835 when he moved with the family to The Mount at Penkhull, leasing it from the Spode family. Lewis's family had a long association with the Spode family and would have been regular visitors to the Mount over the years. It is also interesting to note that, before building The Mount, Josiah Spode II had previously rented Fenton Hall, the house which his friend William Adams III leased after him from the Whieldons.

Lewis was Master of the North Staffordshire Harriers from 1836 to 1842 and kept his hounds in kennels at Wolstanton. In 1842 he sold the pack to William Davenport, who later inaugurated the North Staffordshire Hunt, which Lewis hunted with until his death in 1850.

THE MOUNT

The Mount was considered one of the most prestigious mansions in the district–spacious, elegant and with extensive pleasure grounds. John Ward wrote:

Of the mansions within the Township of Penkhull, we may say, indeed within the compass of the Borough, The Mount erected by the late Josiah

196. *The Mount, Penkhull, Stoke-upon-Trent, the residence of Lewis Adams between* 1838-1842

197. below: Layout plan of The Mount, Penkhull, Stoke-on-Trent circa 1900

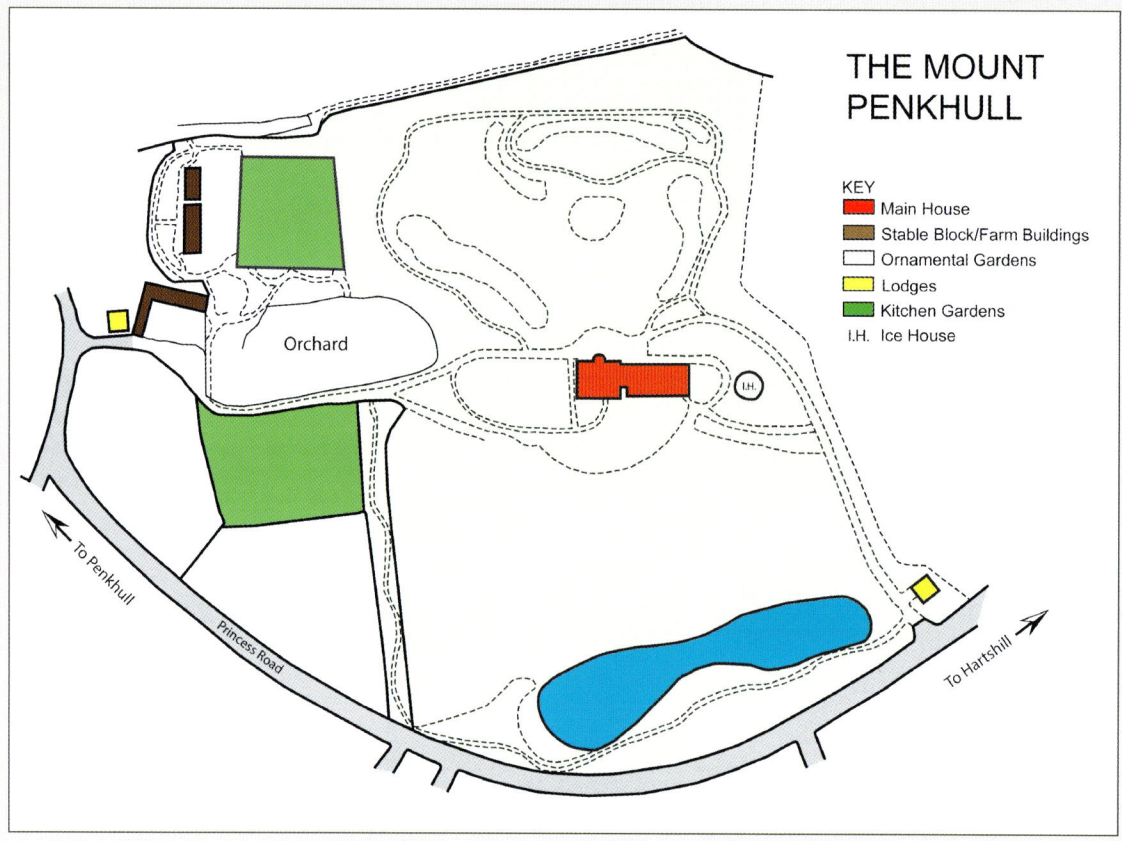

Spode, Esq., bears acknowledged pre-eminence. It stands near the village, and is surrounded by plantations and a highly ornamented domain. The house is an oblong building of brick and stone with a semi-circular entrance on the west front with an elegant and lofty dome, which lights the staircase and gives an exterior air of grandeur to the structure.

As a fortunate survivor to the present day, it still exudes an air of grandeur, a visible display of past wealth and status, perfectly suited to being a residence for Lewis, the shortly-to-be appointed first Chief Bailiff of Stoke-on-Trent.

CHIEF BAILIFF OF STOKE-UPON-TRENT

In 1839, at the young age of 34, Lewis was appointed as the first Chief Bailiff of Stoke-upon-Trent, an annual appointment that interestingly, he also held in 1840. As Chief Bailiff, Lewis's role was essentially concerned with the preservation of the peace through the deployment of constables and the appointment of the town crier.

By 1842, Lewis had bought The Watlands estate in Wolstanton, an elegant house that had been built by the wealthy Rogers family in 1816. No doubt adhering to the terms of a lease, we find Lewis still in residence at The Mount in 1844, as an auction of some of his household furniture is advertised in the local newspaper, listed as:

At the MOUNT, early in the ensuing month, without reserve:
A Portion of the HOUSEHOLD FURNITURE, and miscellaneous property, belonging to Lewis Adams Esq., (who is changing his residence)

Presumably the delayed move enabled Lewis to add a wing to The Watlands and other refurbishments, which included interior doors complete with the Adams' coat of arms.

Poor Lewis did not enjoy his salubrious mansion for long, dying in 1850 at the age of 45. The outpouring of grief during the public funeral demonstrated his popularity throughout the Potteries, among all classes of the population. The Staffordshire Advertiser reported the sadness that pervaded the locality:

> *Saturday, the 28th ult. Will long be remembered and no less regretted by the inhabitants of Stoke-upon-Trent, being the day on which the remains of the late Lewis Adams, Esq., of The Watlands, were consigned to their last resting place, and on which occasion the tradesmen and others in the line of the route in which the funeral had to pass closed their shops and drew down their blinds, thus manifesting a deep sense of regret for the loss of one whose kindness and urbanity had endeared him to all. The adult workmen in the employ of the firm in which the deceased took an active part, numbering nearly four hundred, assembled to pay the last tribute of respect in their power (to the memory of one who was ever kind and indulgent towards them) by walking in the procession to meet the funeral cortege, and afterwards accompanying it to the church. The concourse of spectators, which was large, evinced their respect also by their quiet and orderly demeanour, and many were the tears that were shed as the hearse containing the remains passed by. [We have received a communication from a committee of Messrs. Adams' workmen, intended as attribute of respect to the memory of the deceased. It expresses their deep sense of the uniform liberality of their employers, not only as to prices, working wages, &c., but also as to the complete freedom of conscience and liberty of thought in religion, politics, trades union, &c, which they have invariably enjoyed under the firm. The article, which is too long for publication, concludes with warmly eulogising the many excellent qualities of the deceased gentleman, and with expressions of deep regret at his unexpected removal.]*

Lewis's younger brother Thomas and unmarried sisters continued to live at The Watlands until 1862 when it was sold to Edward Thomas Wedgwood Wood,

198. below: **Coat of arms of Stoke-on-Trent**

ensuring the occupancy of the stately mansion by yet another potting family. The 1871 census reveals that the family enjoyed a privileged existence with an extensive household, including: a governess, lady's maid, cook, housemaid, kitchenmaid, footman, page, groom and coachman.

By 1881, Oliver Lodge, a merchant banker, was in occupation, but sadly by the 1940s the once-sophisticated mansion was reportedly in a tragic state of repair, and in 1950, presumably badly decayed, it was demolished to make way for a housing estate.

MERCANTILE LIFE IN LIVERPOOL

Life in Liverpool suited William Adams IV and his young bride, who were said to have been *the handsomest couple in Liverpool* and who revelled in the vibrant social life that existed at the time.

Three of William's children were baptised at St. Augustine's Church Liverpool: Lettice in 1831, William in 1833 and his youngest daughter Mary in 1835. All reveal the duration of his tenure at Liverpool, which extended significantly beyond the

199. The Watlands, Wolstanton – home of Lewis Adams from 1844 until his death in 1850. Photograph by Cecily Adams 1892

200. below: Layout plan of The Watlands circa 1900

death of his father in 1829, when William Adams IV became senior partner.

The journey from Stoke to Liverpool was made not on foot, as was his father's preferred mode of travel, but was now achieved through a combination of horse-drawn carriage and the railway. He would drive to Whitmore Station in an open barouche, as the railway line from Stafford to Crewe via Stoke was yet to be completed. At Whitmore, the carriage would be placed on an ordinary rail truck and the occupants would sit in the carriage until they reached their destination, no doubt benefitting from an admirable view, although rather vulnerably exposed to the elements!

When in residence at Greenfield, he was often seen driving around in a carriage pulled by a pair of almost black horses complete with gleaming, silver, mounted harnesses.

Individual portraits of the handsome couple, painted in 1842 by William Scott of Liverpool, were commissioned. Jane's portrait is particularly interesting as family tradition asserts that the amethyst brooch clearly evident in her portrait, and given as an engagement present, was at one time lost only to be miraculously found under the hoof of one of the horses at Greenfield soon after their marriage.

The couple were very fond of taking the air at Llandudno on the North Wales coast and often frequented Cheltenham where they would take up residence at 47 Montpellier Terrace. William's youngest daughter Mary at one time resided in the town where her husband William Simms Bull was a prominent Alderman and one time Deputy Mayor.

In 1839, Sarah Adams, the widow of William Adams III, had inherited The Hadderidge estate from her brother Thomas Heath who had died unmarried, and for a time her sons carried on The Hadderidge pottery in conjunction with their Stoke works, the ancient Hadderidge estate once more under the control of an Adams.

THE CONTENTIOUS ISSUE OF CHILD LABOUR IN THE POTTERIES

The Adams' factories, in common with other major manufacturers, were heavily reliant on child labour, with many hundreds of children employed, some as young as seven or eight years of age. It was noted that Wedgwood's Etruria works, in 1818, employed over one hundred children, a few of these under the age of ten.

The eagerly awaited Parliamentary Commission of 1840 into child labour in the Potteries, dubbed the Scriven Report, exposed the sad plight of many of the 1,500 children who were involved in the industry, bringing to public attention some of the dire conditions that existed for these exploited youngsters.

Dr. Samuel Scriven's brief had been to report on

the Employment of children and young persons in the District of the North Staffordshire Potteries and on the Actual State, Condition and Treatment of such children and young persons.

It must be said, the report makes for very uncomfortable reading.

Through the use of questionnaires, visits and interviews, undertaken in 173 different potteries, Scriven's findings cast a dark shadow over the contentious practice and resulted in legislation that aimed to improve the working conditions of children, some of whom worked up to 72 hours a week, often for as little as 1 shilling a week.

No individual works were specifically named and shamed in the legislation that ensued, as despite the arduous conditions, it was noted that the average pottery working conditions were better than the minimum required by law.

So numerous were the potteries that Scriven made the conscious decision to focus on the distinct factors which affected the quality of the physical working conditions in the factories.

The works that Adams rented in Stoke were described by Scriven as

the most ancient in the district, extending over 12 to 14 acres of ground, and situated in the lowest part of the town; the rooms throughout are in a very dilapidated condition, as well as close, damp, hot, dirty, and uncomfortable.

A reference to a Painting Room in one of the Stoke factories describes the workplace as

a close, dark dreary-looking apartment, with two windows that partially open; without ceiling, and having a hot stove. The children look pretty well and appear happy.

A typical working potter would require three child assistants:

1. To turn the potters wheel.
2. To cut the clay and form it into balls for throwing on the wheel.
3. To carry the wares to the oven.

Possibly the worst job in the factory carried out by child labourers was that of the mould-runner. Boys as young as eight or nine would take heavy plaster moulds filled with damp clay and run with them to a drying room and, having placed them on the shelves, immediately return for another mould. This arduous task would be repeated for up to fourteen hours a day, six days a week, with often catastrophic effects on the youngsters' health from the hot dusty environment.

The account of 11-year-old Jos Wilkinson of Messrs. Maddock & Seddons' earthenware factory, Burslem, is particularly poignant:

I run mould and wedge clay for Wm. Bentley; have been at work five years; I am sure I was six years old when I began; cannot read or write;

201. below: **Greengates' workers circa 1892** – *clearly showing the employment of young children at this time*

ADAMS OF GREENFIELD William Adams IV (1798-1865)

*202. right: **William Adams IV of Greenfields** (1798 – 1865)*
photographed in later life

never went to school; go to Sunday school ... have got a father; he's a collier, but has no work this good while; my mother is a baller (supplies the thrower with balls of clay); she is out of work; have three sisters and four brothers; one brother drives donkeys, another works in pit, another has nothing to do; one sister turns wheel, 'tother two canna work, them is little 'uns. I get 3s 3d a-week; come at half past six to work, go home at nine; work Mondays and every day. `Wm. Bentley licks me sometimes with his fist; he has knocked me the other side the pot-stove for being so long at breakfast; half an hour is allowed, but he makes me work before the half hour is up. I go home to dinner, but only stop half an hour, he won't let me bide an hour. I live quarter of a mile away, and have to run home and back out of it, and get my dinner too; I never get a bit of play, am very tired when I get home at night, get my supper and am glad to go to bed. I get milk-meat for breakfast, and taters and salt for dinner, sometimes a bit of bacon; would rather work 10 hours a-day than 15; should not care then if I had less wages. I should go to school then and have a bit of time for play.

Scriven's report also highlighted the fact that most children were employed by the skilled pottery worker, not by the factory owner; the latter, it was said, could easily turn a blind eye to cruel treatment.

Sending their children to work in such grim circumstances was often the only course of action for families on the breadline. Samuel Tams of Adams' Stoke works, voiced the sad irony of this situation:

I work three days a week, and earn to support my wife and family about 9s a week or less. My boy earns 2s or 3s according to circumstances. I would not bring my children to work early if I could help myself; but what am I to do?

At this time, due to the downturn in the American market, the Adams Stoke works, mainly serving the North American market, could only find enough work for a three-day working week.

To William Adams IV, the welfare of his workforce was paramount. His Grandson Percy W. L. Adams stated that

he was very fond of his workpeople, all of whom he knew personally, as well as most of their children; and it is said that he seldom made a mistake in their christian or surnames when addressing any of them. He used to take great delight in giving them little treats, and a very favourite game of his was to roll oranges down the Long Warehouse (a room of some 140 feet) for the youngsters to grab.

It is probable that Percy was referring to the long warehouse at the Greenfield Works, Adams' flagship factory, rather than the primitive Stoke works, which were mostly rented from other owners and were known to cause William some distress, his eldest daughter commenting in her diary that her father often came back from the Stoke works in anything but a peaceful frame of mind.

It would be appropriate to give William Adams IV the final word, through the testimony he gave during the Scriven enquiry:

I have been a manufacturer 20 years, or more. It is my usual practice to close my gates at six o'clock and not allow my people to work after that hour except in the oven which is unavoidable. I have adopted this practice from a conviction that it tends both to my own interest as well as theirs, as well to the employer as the employed. I know that I get more work done by the regular 12 hours than by allowing them to work overtime. It is a common thing in the Potteries for drunken and careless characters to work hard the middle and latter days of the week up to eight, nine, or ten o'clock, because they have neglected the first one, two, or three days and wasted their money at the beer-house in idleness and drunkenness. The consequences for children are evident, as they are obliged to work with them thus late, to the sacrifice of their health and strength and to the destruction of every principle of morality which they may have possessed.

ADAMS OF GREENFIELD William Adams IV (1798-1865)

203. Basford Hall, Wolstanton, the seat of Edward Adams (1802-1872). Photograph by Cecily Adams dated 1896

204. left: Edward Adams and family members taken at Basford Hall, dated 1857. From a daguerreotype (the first publicly available photographic process)

apprentice boys and girls in my works, they are not bound to me by stamped indentures, because the amount of duty is so high, when I take so great a number. I do not choose to use them; if it was reduced to 5s. I certainly should adopt them, and I believe everybody else would. There can be no doubt that this would improve the character of the lads, as they would thus feel under a moral obligation to remain with us. We should take a greater interest in them than we do now, and check in them any disposition to profligacy and vice.

[signed] Wm. Adams. Principal

As a direct result of the Scriven Report, Parliament passed legislation controlling hours and conditions of work for young people, but the overall effect was limited. It would take a further two decades before potteries would be officially classified as factories and

I believe that, under no circumstances, should I be compelled to continue my working hours more than 72 hours per week, provided I could get the people to come regularly. I have a great many

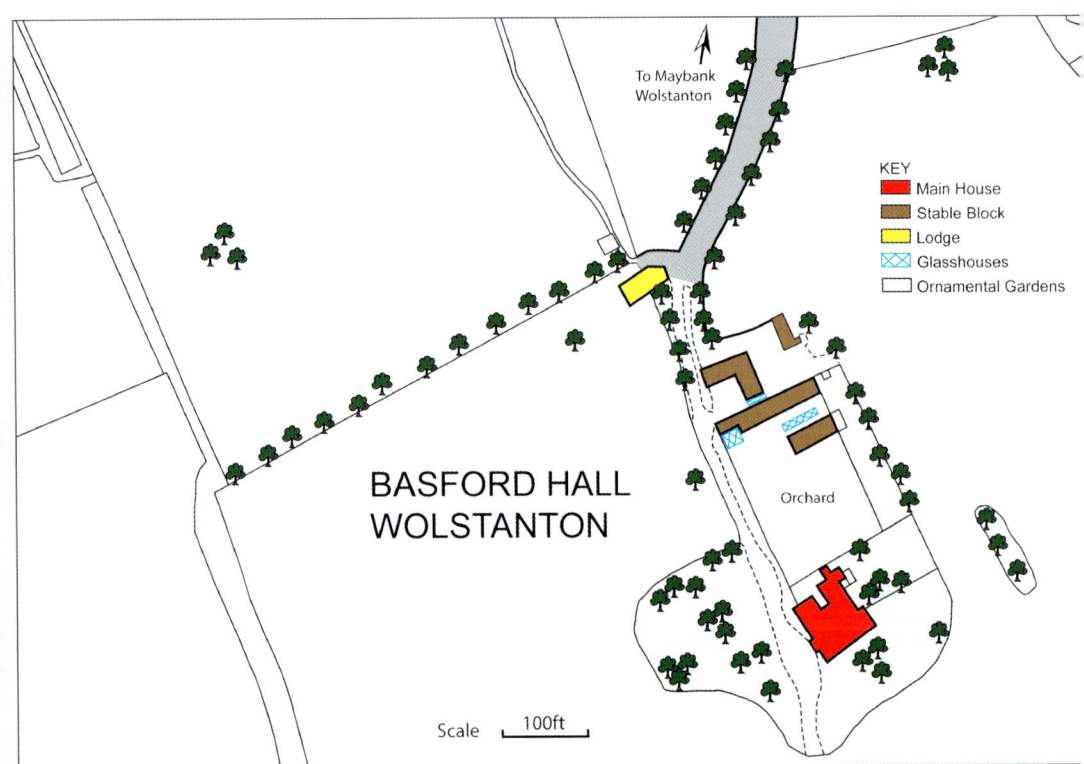

205. right: Layout plan of Basford Hall, Wolstanton, circa 1900

182   ADAMS Britain's Oldest Potting Dynasty

206. right: **Sarah Adams** (1828-1907), eldest daughter of William Adams IV

the rules of the Factory Acts rigorously applied. It would take until 1st August 1898 before legislation would be passed ensuring that no pottery manufacturer could employ anyone under the age of 14.

OMINOUS HEALTH WARNING

Strong trading relations were developed with America, the East Indies, West Indies, Java and South America as William sought to extend the company presence on the global stage, only taking flying visits to his home at Greenfield. Such a frenzied existence inevitably took a toll on his health, which broke down in 1847 when he possibly suffered a stroke that necessitated a drastic curtailment of his workload.

William had for nearly twenty years successfully negotiated the precarious business downturns resulting from the American Depression of 1837, which lasted for some six years and so scarred the Adams' trade that their Stoke factories reverted to a three-day week. The drastic effects of the American Civil War were looming on the horizon.

In 1853, taking decisive action, William dissolved the partnership, relinquishing entirely his interest in the Stoke works, in consideration of which Edward and Thomas gave him The Hadderidge works and some twenty cottages. William later bought out his brother Edward, becoming sole owner of the Greenfield works. Thomas was left to steer a faltering course at Stoke; his brother Lewis, often considered the most intelligent brother, had sadly died in 1850, and by 1861, on the eve of the American Civil War, poor Thomas had entered into bankruptcy.

Diary notes written in 1861/2 by William's eldest daughter Sarah reveal much of the latent tensions that existed within the Adams partnership. These were carefully recorded by Percy W. L. Adams in his *Notes on some North Staffordshire Families*, 1930. Sarah noted her father's repeated visits to the Stoke works:

after some sixty years of considerable prosperity we were doing badly. Great Uncle Lewis, a great asset to the firm, had died in 1850. His younger brother Thomas had spent most of his time at

Liverpool in connection with their shipping office there. Great Uncle Edward of Basford was easy going and I imagine did not trouble to go into details too much. William had severed his connection definitely with the Stoke Works since '53, still he naturally took a moral interest in them. Their Uncle Thomas used to ask them the names of shapes, and other questions which they should have been able to answer; - they seldom could. Workpeople made ware not ordered, rats from the neighbouring canal were getting into older parts of the warehouses, and doing damage to more expensive China. Thomas on visits was often very angry at the lack of supervision, and on enquiring why workpeople persisted in making certain wares without orders, he is known to have tipped up the boards which carried the ware on the answer being that they had no orders. On looking back one cannot help suspecting that Thomas should have abandoned the Liverpool office and come definitely to Staffordshire to help his brother Edward who was getting older.

Things got from bad to worse and it was at last decided to close the Stoke factories.

A WILD SPECULATOR!

Thomas Adams, the youngest of the dynamic Adams brothers, had spent several years managing his father's busy shipping office in Liverpool, handling not only the Adams wares but also acting as agent for other potting concerns. He was keen on travel and built up a good trade with Mexico, having travelled there on many occasions in pursuit of business, emulating his brother William's adventurous trading excursions. The world was at his fingertips, but sadly ominous signs appeared that threatened the status quo of what seemed to be a highly profitable and well-run business.

William, the eldest brother, became concerned by Thomas's increasingly worrying behaviour. Hot-headed by nature, Thomas speculated wildly in the railways and was increasingly drawn to racing and betting. This played heavily on William's mind, and ultimately affected his health.

Thomas seems to have 'gone off the rails' on the death of his elder brother Lewis, who was no doubt a steadying influence on the confrontational younger brother. Other influences were evidently in play that adversely affected a once reasonably stable character.

Lewis was a huge sporting enthusiast, often entering his horses in various race meetings. He held the post of Master of the North Staffordshire Harriers from 1836 to 1842, housing his hounds at kennels local to his seat at The Watlands, Wolstanton. On selling the pack in 1842, he joined the newly inaugurated North Staffordshire Hunt and was an active member until his death in 1850. Thomas, following his older brother, naturally gravitated to hunting and racing.

Given the close connections between the hunting fraternities in Staffordshire and adjoining Shropshire, it is not surprising to learn that Thomas Adams counted among his closest friends the celebrated John Mytton, one of England's most eccentric and colourful Regency squires.

JOHN 'MAD JACK' MYTTON OF HALSTON

John Mytton was born in 1796, the son of a wealthy Shropshire squire. His lineage stretched back some 500 years and he possessed an estate covering 132,000 acres in North Wales and Shropshire. He was left fatherless at the age of two and brought up by an indulgent mother who exerted little or no restraint on his early conduct. Incredibly, it is said that he owned his own pack of hounds at the tender age of 10 and regularly hunted in all weathers.

Unsurprisingly, Mytton grew up an unruly individual hardly able to conform to authority. He was expelled from the prestigious Westminster School, allegedly for fighting with a schoolmaster.

He was subsequently admitted to Harrow School only to be expelled on three separate occasions, eventually being taught by private tutors whom he mercilessly tormented with practical jokes.

207. *above:* **John Mytton** (1796-1834) *after William Webb, May 1818. Photogravure of the original miniature*

208. above: Halston House, the family seat of John Mytton, from A Tour of Wales *by Thomas Pennant (1726-1798)*

Having achieved virtually nothing academically, he was granted entry to Cambridge University, where he immediately arranged delivery of 2,000 bottles of port to sustain him during his studies. However, according to Alumni Cantabrigienses, it is doubtful that he even took up his place, seemingly preferring to embark on a short Grand Tour through Europe as a means of finishing off his education before returning to his beloved horses and hounds.

On 30th May 1816, aged 19, he joined the 7th Hussars and served as a cornet in the army of occupation in France. He found peacetime military life boring and whiled away the hours gambling and drinking heavily before finally resigning his commission some three years later.

No doubt he longed for the thrill of the chase, an outlook summed up by the horse racing phrase '*neck or nothing*' for a person who would risk all at gambling or hunting in search of excitement. It is fortunate that such an adrenalin junkie had not been involved in wartime exploits as he could well have led a suicidal cavalry charge on a par with the charge of the Light Brigade or worse!

On coming of age Mytton had inherited a vast estate of £10,000 a year and an accumulated sum of £60,000 in cash; a substantial amount of the latter was used to liquidate his mounting debts. Extravagant in the extreme, his new-found wealth just fuelled his insane indulgences. He is said to have borrowed £10,000 at a high rate of interest and immediately lent £9,000 to a friend who, according to his biographer,

has never been seen in Europe since!

Such flamboyant and excessive behaviour, when reported and chronicled in sporting journals, propelled Mytton to the realms of celebrity and conferred on him the well-deserved nickname of 'Mad Jack Mytton'.

209. John Mytton, Esquire, of Halston, Shropshire, by William Giller after William Webb, 1841

One of his friends, Charles James Apperley, writing under the pen name of 'Nimrod', chronicled his life and brought Mytton's exploits to public attention.

While Nimrod states that he had not in any way exaggerated Mytton's exploits, it must be remembered that the function of the 19th-century sporting journalist was to amuse and entertain as much as to record facts, making it difficult to separate truth from embellishments or even outright legend. If only a small proportion of these sensational exploits attributed to Mytton are true, we are still left with an overwhelming impression of the archetypal hard-drinking, hunting squire of his era, one who frittered away the best part of half a million pounds before his early demise at the age of 38.

In 1819, encouraged by friends, he stood for parliament as the Tory candidate for Shrewsbury, securing his seat by spending no less than £10,000 by offering freeholders £10 notes for their support in the ballot. After successfully winning the seat he was carried triumphantly through Shrewsbury. He is reported to have thrown himself through the window of the Lion Inn, where a reception was being held for him to deliver his speech of thanks. A somewhat unorthodox means of making an entrance!

In due course he took up his seat in the commons in June 1819, but according to the *History of Parliament* he

> *paid one visit to Westminster, but is said to have left after half-an-hour from boredom and restlessness (he never stayed anywhere for long), possibly because his deafness prevented him from hearing what was going on. He never the less appeared in the majority for the foreign enlistment bill on 10 June. He declined a contest in 1820, finding that a proper and punctual attendance to his parliamentary duties was incompatible with his present pursuits.*

So ended the political career of John Mytton, the last of his illustrious family members who had served their county as MPs since the time of Reginald Mutton, who was MP for Shrewsbury in the reign of Edward II.

Mytton was by all accounts a cruel practical joker, and many of his jokes seem to have backfired on him with often-disastrous consequences.

Foremost among his most outrageous exploits were:

'WHAT! NEVER UPSET A GIG?'

Nothing gave Mytton more of a thrill than driving his carriage. He often drove his gig at insane speeds, aiming for rabbit holes to see if he could overturn it, seemingly surviving such mindless actions without serious injury. It was stated that not only did he not mind accidents he positively liked them! On one occasion while driving his gig with a new companion, he enquired whether the nervous passenger had ever been upset in a gig, to which the trembling individual stated,

> *Thank God, I have never upset one.*

> *What! Replied Mytton, what a damn slow fellow you must have been all your life!*

and promptly drove the gig up a sloping bank, ejecting himself and passenger at high speed.

'STAND AND DELIVER'

On another occasion Mytton invited a local doctor and parson to dine with him at Halston Hall. After a convivial meal both guests departed unaware of the fate that awaited them. Mytton, disguised as a highwayman complete with blazing pistols, ambushed the departing guests on the road back to Oswestry, screaming out the instruction

> *Stand and deliver!*

Not content to simply terrify his genteel dinner guests to death, he is supposed to have chased the quivering unfortunates all the way back to Oswestry.

210-213. Illustrations from The Life of John Mytton, Esq., of Halston, Shropshire *by Nimrod, 1870*

"What! never upset in a gig?"

211

"Stand and Deliver"

"Fair Play's a Jewel"

"A new hunter - Tally ho! Tally ho!"

'FAIR PLAY'S A JEWEL'

This incident seems to have taken place at Warwick races, which Mytton was known to frequent. Family tradition has it that Thomas Adams, attending a card party after a day's racing with his friend Mytton, discovered that one player was cheating. So infuriated were the members that they grabbed the miscreant and attempted to throw him out of an upstairs window. It is recounted that but for Thomas's intervention the cheat would have undoubtedly been killed. It was an unexpected intervention from Thomas, who was known to have been hot-headed and easily angered.

Mytton, a profligate spendthrift, eventually lost all his money, but, astonishingly, kept his friends. Thomas Adams, by saving his friend from conviction for murder, would no doubt have strengthened their bonds of friendship.

'A NEW HUNTER'

Possibly the most outrageous of Mytton's pranks occurred at Halston Hall. Guests were gathered in Mytton's drawing room ahead of an evening meal when the host burst through the doorway dressed in full hunting gear, including spurs and whip, riding on a bear. The horrified guests scattered in all directions. To exercise some control, Mytton pricked the bear with the spurs, which immediately caused the agitated creature to turn round and bite his right leg.

Mytton had purchased the bear for thirty-five pounds from a travelling showman who was passing through Ellesmere; it had been in his ownership for seven years. Although partly domesticated, it was not to be trifled with by strangers.

John Mytton was a complex character, a person of celebrity,

> the 19th-century equivalent of a bad boy rock star, always in the public eye.

But, he was also extremely generous, kind, benevolent and charitable to the poor.

Scarcely a day passed when he seemingly did not want to put his life at risk, in what could be seen as series of failed suicide attempts while in a constant state of intoxication.

By the time he reached his late 30s he was a wreck, languishing in a dismal debtors' prison, bloated by drink, a tragic tale of reckless high living that led to inevitable poverty.

Mad Jack Mytton died on 29th March 1834, at the King's Bench Prison, Southwark, aged 38. England had lost one of its maddest eccentrics, but his legacy has lived on through the generations.

His body was taken for burial to the private chapel on his estate at Halston, and his funeral, one of the largest in the district, was reported by the Shrewsbury Chronicle:

FUNERAL OF THE LATE JOHN MYTTON ESQ

We last week announced the death of this gentleman. His body was conveyed from London, where he expired, to this town, with all solemnity. On passing through the town, many shops were closed; and crowds assembled to take a last look on his bier, and pay the homage of a sigh to the memory of John Mytton. We rejoice to say, that before his death the consolations of religion had been eagerly resorted to, and afforded him both comfort under affliction, and hope in the prospect of eternity.

A hearse with four horses (driven by an attached servant of the deceased), a mourning coach and four, and another carriage, formed the melancholy cavalcade through Shrewsbury. On the road to Oswestry, every mark of respect was paid; at the Queen's Head, the course was met by a detachment of the North Shropshire Cavalry (of which regiment the deceased was Major), who escorted them to the vault in the chapel of Halston, where the remains were deposited at three o'clock in the afternoon. The procession was exceedingly well arranged under the direction of Mr Dunn, of London, assisted by Messrs Hanmer and Gittins, of this town, and

entered the domain of Halston in the following order:

Four Trumpeters of the North Shropshire Cavalry
Capt. Croxton and Capt. Jones
Thirty-two Members of the Cavalry
A Standard of the Regiment covered with Crape
Forty-two Members of the Cavalry
Adjutant Shirley and Cornet Nicolls
Mr Dunn (undertaker) and Mr Gittins
Two Mutes
Carriage of the Revds W. Jones and J.D. Pigott
Two Mourning Coaches and Four, with the Pall-Bearers

Hon. T. Kenyon   A.W. Corbett Esq.
R.A. Slaney Esq., M.P.
J.R. Kynaston Esq.
J.C. Pelham Esq.
Rev. H.C. Cotton

The Hearse, drawn by Four Horses, with

THE BODY

In a Coffin covered with Black Velvet, with massive Handles,
Richly ornamented, the Plate inscribed
John Mytton, Esq, of HALSTON,
Born 30th of Sept. 1796,
Died 29th of March 1834
(The Hearse was driven by Mr Bowyer, the Deceased's Coachman,
who, with Mr McDougal, another Servant, attended him
in his last moments.)
Mourning Coach with two Mourners, the Rev. E.H. Owen
(Deceased's Uncle), and the Hon. And Rev. R. Noel Hill.
Mrs Mytton's Carriage
Lady Kynaston's Carriage, with Mr W.H. Griffiths and Mr Cooper
Carriage of A.W. Corbett, Esq.
Carriage of Rev. Sir Edward Kynaston, Bart.
Carriage of the Rev. E.H. Owen

214. left: Halston Chapel – an illustration from The Life of John Mytton, Esq., of Halston, Shropshire *by Nimrod, 1870*

> Carriage of R.A. Slaney, Esq., M.P.
> Carriage and Four of the Hon. Thomas Kenyon
> J.Beck, Esq. in his Carriage
> Dr. Cockerill and Lieut. Tudor, in Carriage
> Carriage of T.N. Parker, Esq.
> Carriage of W. Ormsby Gore, Esq., M.P
> Carriage of Viscountess Avonmore
> Several Cars, &c., with Friends
> Mr Broughhall, Agent.
>
> About One Hundred of the Tenantry, Tradesmen, and Friends on Horseback, closed the procession.

> *A mourning peal was rung at Oswestry, and the bells of Shrewsbury, Ellesmere, Whittington, Halston, &c. tolled during the day. The number of spectators was immense and the road along which the procession slowly moved was bedewed with the tears of thousands who wished to have a last glance.*

Among the large number of friends and acquaintances attending the funeral would undoubtedly have been Thomas Adams, who deeply mourned the passing of a faithful friend and companion.

WILLIAM ADAMS IV – MINING, POTTING AND OIL PROSPECTING

As a result of his ominous health scare in 1847, one would have thought that William might have sought a more tranquil existence, but such thoughts were far from his mind as he broadened his business portfolio to encompass a diverse range of mining activities.

In 1858 he acquired a portion of the nearby Newfield Hall estate, primarily for its valuable coal mines, and seven years later purchased the remainder of the estate. His son William Adams V added the Newfield pottery to their family holdings in 1872, having leased it for fifteen years previously. Valuable marls and clays were obtained from the Newfield brick and marl works which were still worked by the Adams family up until the middle of the 20th century.

The Newfield estate had been purchased from the prominent Child family who had owned it for nearly a century. Originally from Worcestershire, the Child family had migrated to Staffordshire where they built up a considerable landholding. By the time of their most illustrious son, Smith Child, Admiral of the Blue, their estate had been severely curtailed, but a fortuitous marriage made by Smith re-established the family's standing.

John Ward, in his book *The Borough of Stoke-Upon-Trent*, 1843, recounts a somewhat amusing tale of Smith Child Senior's visit north of the border. It also reveals the circumstances which led to his son joining the Navy:

> *Once, during a visit to Scotland, he was introduced to and entertained by the Duke of Hamilton, whom he accompanied on one of his hunting excursions, and being in that country during the expedition of the ill-fated Charles Stuart, in 1745, he was twice arrested, after the defeat of the rebel forces, on suspicion of being the Pretender, to whom he bore a strong resemblance. He travelled from Scotland in company with Lord Glenorchy, who advised him to bring his son up to the Navy, and introduced him to Lord Anson, the Circumnavigator, at that time one of the Lords of the Admiralty.*

And so, enjoying such patronage, the young Smith Child entered the navy in 1747 as midshipman, and by 1755 was commissioned as lieutenant, seeing action in the Seven Years War. During the peace of 1763, like many of his fellow officers, he applied himself to other tasks: returning home, he is known to have erected a large pottery works at Tunstall, producing a range of earthenware goods up until 1790, when William Adams I rented the works from him.

In 1765 Smith had inherited his uncle's seat, Newfield Hall at Tunstall–a large three-storeyed, five-bayed house–which, during another slack time in the navy, he rebuilt, taking up residence there in 1770.

Smith resumed his naval duties at the outbreak of the American War of Independence, being promoted to

215. below: **Greenfield Mill, Tunstall, dated 1860**

216. below: **Newfield Hall, Summerbank, Tunstall, photographed 1947** – sadly boarded up and awaiting demolition

captain by 1780. He took part in the important battle of Chesapeake Bay, serving with distinction. By 1799, he had been promoted to rear admiral and had moved up the ranks by 1810, becoming admiral of the blue, a junior position in the rank of full admiral.

Back in Staffordshire he was a highly regarded pottery manufacturer and a respected Justice of the Peace. He died at Newfield Hall on 21st January 1813 and was buried in St. Margaret's Church, Wolstanton. As his only son and heir John had died in 1811, the estate passed to his five-year-old grandson, who in later years became the Conservative MP for Staffordshire (North and later West) and noted philanthropist Sir Smith Child. An impressive clock tower situated in Tunstall marketplace commemorates Sir Smith Child, Bart. (1808-1896), the dedication plaque stating,

**IN HONOUR OF
Sir SMITH CHILD Bart.
A PHILANTHROPIST**
Who foremost in every good
Work, by generous gifts and wise
Counsel, sought to brighten the
Lives of the
WORKING CLASSES
And by noble Endowment of
Convalescent Homes offered a
Priceless boon to
THE SUFFERING POOR

217. below: **Clock tower in Tunstall Square erected in 1893 in commemoration of the Smith Child family**

218. below: *Poster issued to announce the celebrations in Tunstall to mark the end of the Crimean War*

219. right: Joseph Bull (1814-1872), *ironmaster of the Cliff Vale and Ravensdale Iron Works*

PEACE CELEBRATIONS OF 1856

The Treaty of Paris of 1856 heralded the end of the three-year-long Crimean War, fought between the Russian Empire and an alliance of Great Britain, France and the Ottoman Empire. The year-long siege of the Russian fortress at Sevastopol, the disastrous charge of the Light Brigade and the immense number of casualties, many of whom suffered in deplorable conditions, were temporarily forgotten, as the country erupted into wild celebration.

The public celebration of peace at Tunstall, on Thursday 29th May 1856, was vividly described in the Staffordshire Sentinel on Saturday 31 May 1856:

This busy and thriving portion of the Potteries had its rejoicing on Thursday, and we may safely assert that it lost none of its celebrity when compared with other parts of the district. The extensive arrangements, although commenced a very few days ago, were complete in every respect. On arriving there we walked under a number of garlands; and there were streamers and insignia from almost every shop window, as well as Union Jack banners from the windows of the poorest cottages. We noticed one device more than the rest in High street, at Mr Hind's, saddler, which was as follows:- 'God save Victoria our Queen, and may the balance of Europe continue in her hands: the arbitrator of peace and war. May she be the security of her allies, the terror of her enemies, the refuge of the oppressed, the delight of her subjects, and the blessed of God.'

The proceedings commenced with a PUBLIC BREAKFAST at the Sneyd Arms Hotel, at which upwards of one hundred ladies and gentlemen sat down, and a finer spread for the occasion by the hostess, Mrs Holland, it is scarcely possible to conceive. The Chief Bailiff (E. Wedgwood, Esq) who presided ... The room was beautifully decorated with festoons of evergreens, and banners bearing such devices as the following:

'May the treaty be firm and lasting;'
'Free Trade, Peace and Plenty;'
'May the Staffordshire Pots be broken all over the World;'
'Thanks to the Army and Navy;'

and a small brass band contributing to the harmony of the occasion.

(At 12 o'clock it was time for the procession to start) ...The six new bells of Tunstall Church were rung, for the first time, which greatly added to the novelties of the day... the procession was then formed and moved in the following order :-

**THE PROCESSION
FULL BRASS BAND**

The Scholars and Teachers of the Tunstall
Parish Church Sunday and National Schools,
with Flags and Banners,
St. John's Goldenhill
Tunstall Wesleyan Sunday and Day Schools
Goldenhill Welsh Sunday Schools
Tunstall Primitive Methodist Sunday Schools
Pitt's Hill Primitive Methodist Sunday Schools
Goldenhill Primitive Methodist Sunday
Schools
Tunstall Methodist New Connexion Sunday
Schools
Tunstall Independent Sunday Schools
Full Brass Band
The Clergy, Chief Bailiff, and Ministers of
other Denominations, Churchwardens and the
Inhabitants,
The Lodges of the United Free Gardeners
Drum and Fife Band
The Temperance Society and the Independent
Order of Rechabites
Full Brass Band

ADAMS OF GREENFIELD William Adams IV (1798-1865)

220.above: Bradwell Lodge, Wolstanton–originally built by Joseph Bull, ironmaster between 1859-60. (Unfortunately for Joseph his time of residence was short as he was declared bankrupt in March 1861)

221. below: **A wind direction indicator installed on the stairwell of Bradwell Lodge– used by Joseph Bull to monitor the wind prior to firing up his blast furnaces**

222. below: **Close up of the dial of the wind direction indicator**

223. above: **Weather vane on the roofline, connected directly to wind direction indicator**

224. above: **Mary Bull (1834-1895), the youngest daughter of William Adams IV and the wife of William Simms Bull**

225. above: **William Simms Bull (1837-1919). A prominent alderman of Cheltenham and one-time mayor of the town. In the late 19th century he owned a North Wales slate quarry**

MR. BULL'S WORKMEN, IN SIX DIVISIONS OF ABOUT ONE HUNDRED EACH
First Division: Two Leaders of Procession on horseback – The Ravendale Flag – Tunstall Brass Band, brought up by a captain on horseback.

The Workmen and Operatives of the several Manufactories, Iron-works, Collieries and other Trades in the District with Flags and Banners The Fire Brigade and Engine.

The procession was supposed to be a mile and a half in length; the Sunday school scholars numbered upwards of 3,000; the Gardners of different lodges were very numerous and we must not omit to mention that there were upwards of 500 workmen of Mr. Bull's in the procession, headed by a large flag, on which was inscribed 'Long life to Joseph Bull, Esq., and success to the Ravensdale Ironworks.' Mr Monham, the manager, and eleven other officials, rode on horseback. The procession, on the whole, was very imposing, white rosettes and medals being worn, with an extraordinary display of flags and banners; the streets were thronged with spectators, and the shop windows, more particularly in the High-street, had the appearance of large picture frames filled with living family portraits. On the return to Market-place they formed a dense crowd, numbering upwards of 7,000 persons.

226.right: **William Adams IV** (1798-1865) and wife Jane (1804-1864) photographed in later life

(After reading the proclamation of peace and singing the National Anthem)

... the vast concourse of human beings separated; the scholars retiring to their respective school rooms, where they were regaled with tea and buns; and the following manufacturers also entertained their workpeople with cold collation, or tea:- Mr. Bull, Ravensdale Works; Messrs. Podmore, Walker, and Co., Messrs Woolliscroft and Galley, Mr. Meir, Mr W. Emberton, Mr Adams, and Messrs. M & J. Butterfield. There was also a gratuitous tea party of the widows and infirm, held at the Town Hall, served up by Mrs Holland when upwards of three hundred sat down. After tea, each of them was presented with sixpence, by a kind friend whose name was not divulged, and each sixpence was of the reign of George the Fourth. There was also an excellent dinner served to the police and fire brigade at the Sneyd's Arms.

At nine o'clock at night, the general illumination commenced, which was really beautiful, and the fireworks at Belle Vue Gardens were both extensive and admirable. The rejoicings were exceedingly well sustained throughout the day.

Among the top contributors to the Tunstall Peace Celebration Fund we find J.L. Ricardo, MP, Smith Child, MP, Joseph Bull, E. Challinor and William Adams IV.

Joseph Bull was a prominent iron master, owning two local iron works: the Ravensdale Works, Wolstanton, and Cliff Vale Works in Stoke-on-Trent. William Adams IV's youngest daughter, Mary, would later marry Joseph Bull's eldest son, William Simms Bull, at Christ Church, Tunstall, on 4th January 1865.

OIL PROSPECTING

Visitors to the Greenfield works in 1862 would no doubt be puzzled by the strange constructions that were beginning to appear on land adjacent to the pottery. It would soon become clear that the mysterious structures were oil retorts, built for the purpose of making crude oil from cannel coal (a form of bituminous coal).

Informed by his network of American connections, William Adams IV would have been alerted to the financial rewards that could be achieved through such a refinery, as in his days oil was obtained from whales and was prohibitively expensive. His innovative idea was to produce crude oil from coal and shale and convert it into paraffin, the success of which later resulted in the formation of the North Staffordshire Oil Company Limited, complete with a state-of-the art refinery at Bradwell Wood.

The company yielded considerable profits until 1869 when America discovered its own petroleum oil wells and flooded the British market with a much cheaper product. The fledgling company was run down and the Bradwell Wood works sold.

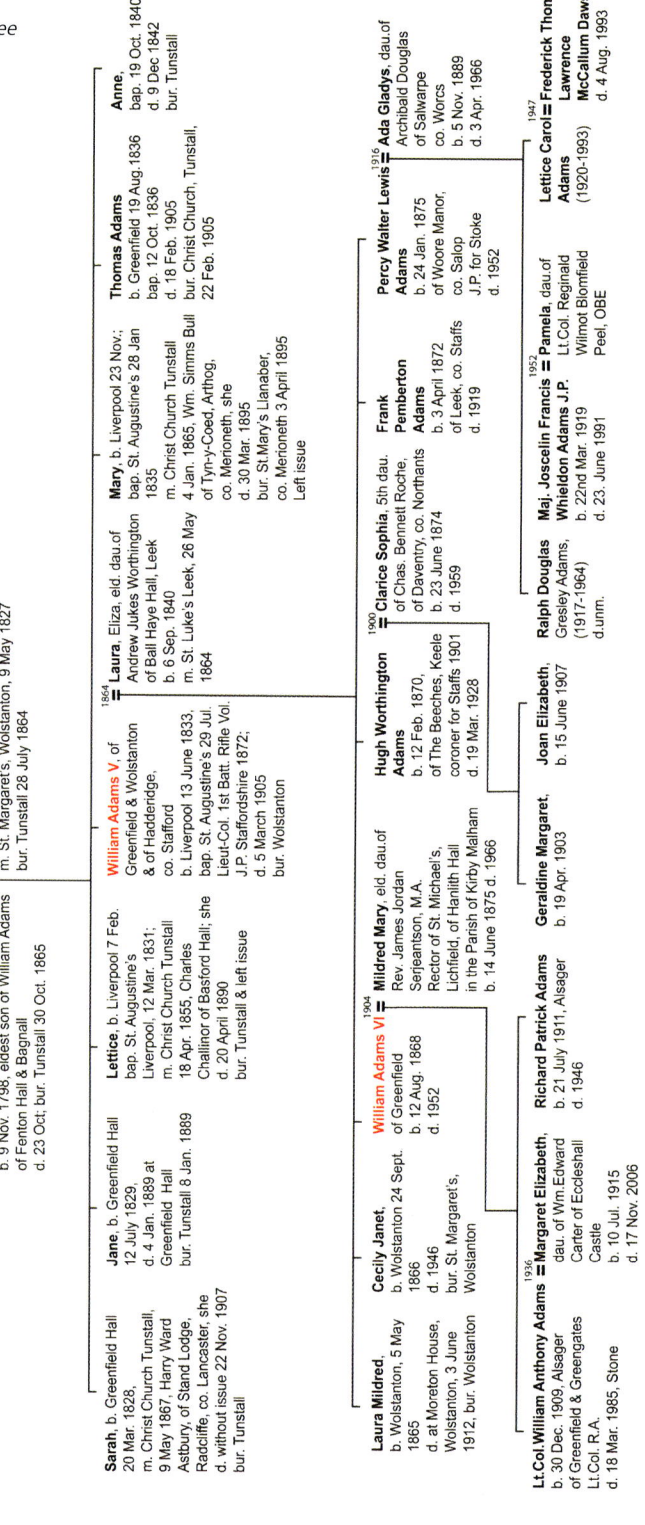

227. Adams of Greenfield family tree

William Adams IV, the thoughtful man of quiet tastes, had certainly proved his worth in business, both as a seasoned entrepreneur and high-powered salesman with the common touch.

On one hand a strict churchman of the old school who avidly attended Burslem Church (occupying the Breeze family pew, inherited by his wife), and on the other grounded in the traditions of his day, the Fairs and Wakes that so infatuated the inhabitants of Burslem must have equally held a fascination for William, who throughout his life showed a great interest in boxing. Fighting was in his blood–an interest perhaps kindled from early recollection of professional pugilists nimbly dispatching their drunken challengers with skill and dexterity. He revelled in prize fighting and was often called upon to referee matches, which he undertook with great enthusiasm. A poignant reminder of his dedication to the sport is embodied in his stopwatch, which, until recent times, was preserved within the family.

William Adams IV died in 1865 aged 66 while staying at his favourite holiday location–Rhyl on the North Wales coast. Waiting in the wings to take on the mantle of master potter of Greenfield was his eldest son William Adams V–one who would prove to be a worthy successor to his ambitious, well-liked father.

228. left. **William Adams IV** (1798-1865)

230. right: 1st Staffordshire Administrative Battalion Officers shoulder-belt plate

9

1833-1952
DAWN OF THE TWENTIETH CENTURY
William Adams V of Greenfield & Wolstanton

William Adams V was born on 13th June 1833 at the family residence in Everton, Liverpool; an area considered a fashionable address at the time. To date, the children born to William Adams IV and his wife had been girls and great celebrations would have been held to commemorate the birth of an heir and future master potter to continue the family's potting traditions.

William received his early education at a small school only a mile away from the family seat at Greenfield Hall, where, according to family tradition, he learnt very little but rubbed shoulders with many local children, one of whom was the son of a local pork butcher whose father, it is said, supplied the school with meat in lieu of school fees.

After a period spent at Newcastle Grammar School, William was admitted to study at Rugby School. One of his first letters home, dated August 1849, left no doubt in his parents' minds as to how delighted their son was to be installed in this great public school:

Rugby,
August 1849

I am glad to say that I like the school better than I thought. We have pretty good studies and I have with me a very nice fellow. They do not see our letters and we may write as often as we like. I am as happy as a king.

I am, your affectionate son,
W. Adams

Rugby school was part of the select group of institutions that sought to satisfy the demand for a 'gentleman's education'. The Clarendon Report, established in 1861 to investigate the state of leading schools in England, aptly expressed in its concluding paragraphs the underlying philosophies so widely admired:

These schools have been the chief nurseries of our statesmen; in them, and in schools modelled after them, men of all the various classes that make up English society, destined for every

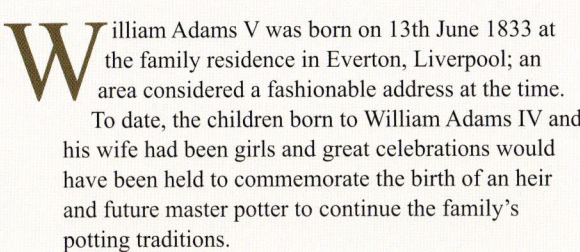

229. left: The Adams Clock Tower, Tunstall Park, Staffordshire, erected in 1907 to the memory of William Adams V of Greenfield by the employees of William Adams & Co.

231. above: **The Close, Rugby School,** circa 1890

profession and career, have been brought up on a footing of social equality, and have contracted the most enduring friendships, and some of the ruling habits of their lives; and they have had perhaps the largest share in moulding the character of an English Gentleman.

Other letters written by William during these formative years reveal his wide range of friends, foremost among whom was the first Lord Goschen, English banker and statesman, who later held the post of First Lord of the Admiralty under Lord Salisbury and subsequently Chancellor of the Exchequer in the same administration, where he was remembered for managing to reduce the national debt and introduce the first UK road tax.

William Adams V left Rugby in 1851 and joined the family business–a no doubt most welcome addition to the management team, especially considering his father's failing health and the disappointing lack of commitment from his uncle Thomas.

Tuesday 13th June 1854 was a joyous occasion at Greenfields, with great celebrations held to commemorate the coming-of-age of William Adams V. The Staffordshire Sentinel and Commercial & General Advertiser reported the joyous festivities on Saturday, 17th June:

FETE AT GREENFIELDS. – On Tuesday, the 13 inst. Mr William Adams, jun., son of W. Adams, Esq., of Tunstall, attained his majority, and a fete was held in celebration of the occasion. The factory and adjoining houses were decorated with flags, bearing different mottoes; and in front of the mansion a red flag floated conspicuously. The amusements commenced early in the morning by the firing of cannon, which was repeated at intervals during the day; and in the evening a very pretty display of fireworks was made. A commodious tent had been erected on the grounds; and about four o'clock in the afternoon upwards of 300 persons – workpeople, tenants, and visitors – sat down under it, to a plentiful and excellent repast. The Tunstall Brass Band was present, and played a number of enlivening compositions. After ample justice had been done to the varied and well-dressed viands, the tables were cleared, and the usual toasts were drunk in

232. right: *Donkin's House, Rugby (now Bradley House) where William Adams's son Percy boarded under housemaster A.E. Donkin*

bumpers of nut-brown ale, especially tapped for the occasion. A highly gratifying address was then presented to the hero of the fete, who acknowledged it in a very appropriate speech, which he concluded amid vehement cheering. After these ceremonies had been performed, the company abandoned themselves to enjoyment. Mr. Adams jun., led off the dance with a young lady, and was followed by a considerable proportion of the ladies and gentlemen present. A large number of the young workpeople engaged in juvenile sports, which they practised in the best of humour, and with evident gratification. The festivities continued until after nine o'clock at night, when amid a brilliant discharge of fireworks, the company broke up. Altogether, the proceedings betokened the existence of the best feelings between the family and their dependants; and it must have been greatly gratifying to Mr. Adams to see the large number of relatives and friends who gathered round him on the occasion. Amongst the visitors present, we noticed –in addition to the different members of the family – the Rev. Hurston Foreshaw, Mr. and Mrs. Bateson, of Liverpool, J. Llewellyn, Esq., Mr Day, Mr. John Baker, manager of the manufactory, and other. The festivities, we are informed continued on the following day.

FORMATION OF THE RIFLE VOLUNTEERS

Following France's defeat of the Austrians in northern Italy in 1859, a fear of invasion gripped the country. On 12th May 1859 the Secretary of State for War, Jonathan Peel, issued a letter to the county Lord Lieutenants authorising them to form volunteer rifle corps and artillery formations in the coastal towns.

Alfred Tennyson captured the mood of the country in his poem 'Riflemen Form' that was printed in The Times on the 9th May 1859:

233. right: *Captain W.E. Twigg of the Burslem Corps of Rifle Volunteers (photographed April 1867)*

Dawn of the Twentieth Century

Riflemen Form!

There is a sound of thunder afar,
Storm in the South that darkens the day!
Storm of battle and thunder of war!
Well if it do not roll our way.
Storm, Storm, Riflemen form!
Ready, be ready against the storm!
Riflemen, Riflemen, Riflemen form!

Be not deaf to the sound that warns,
Be not gull'd by a despot's plea!
Are figs of thistles? Or grapes of thorns?
How can a despot feel with the Free?
Form, Form, Riflemen Form!
Ready, be ready to meet the storm!
Riflemen, Riflemen, Riflemen form!

Let your reforms for the moment go!
Look to your butts, and take good aims!
Better a rotten borough or so
Than a rotten fleet and a city in flames!
Storm, Storm, Riflemen form!
Ready, be ready against the storm!
Riflemen, Riflemen, Riflemen form!

Form, be ready to do or die!
Form in Freedom's name and the Queen's
True we have got – such a faithful ally
That only the Devil can tell what he means.
Form, Form, Riflemen Form!
Ready, be ready to meet the storm!
Riflemen, Riflemen, Riflemen form!

By 1862, 134,096 rifle volunteers had joined the rallying call. In the Potteries, the 2nd Staffordshire RVC (Rifle Volunteer Corps) was raised in Longton, near Stoke-on-Trent, on 30th September 1859. This was quickly followed by others in the area, and by May 1860 there were sufficient numbers to form the 1st Staffordshire Administrative Battalion under the command of Lieutenant-Colonel Coote Manningham Buller, an officer who had previously served with the Rifle Brigade during the Crimean War.

234. left: Major William Adams (1833-1905) of the Staffordshire Rifle Volunteer Corps–by John Nash-Peake

235. below: Quarter-Master Sergeant W. Dodd, who served in the Staffordshire Rifle Volunteers

All volunteers were exempt from the Militia Ballot with the proviso that they had to perform drill eight days in every four months. Initially volunteers were expected to provide their own uniform, arms and equipment although some items were paid for by public subscription as the need arose, and although by 1861 government arms were issued countrywide to all the 40 Volunteer Corps. By 1862, a Royal Commission recommended that each Rifle Volunteer attend nine drills a year and a minimal grant was given as an encouragement to practice their marksmanship.

236. *Staffordshire Rifle Volunteers camp, Langley, North Staffordshire,* circa 1860

237. left: Lt. Col. William Adams of the 1st Administrative Battalion, Staffordshire Rifle – a post he held from 1867 until 1872

William Adams V was one of the first to enthusiastically offer himself as a volunteer for the newly formed RVC's in 1859 and was appointed as the first Captain of the 9th Company based at Tunstall on 4th January 1860. On the 7th March that year, William, in the company of other fellow officers, was presented to Queen Victoria at St. James's Palace.

On 28th November 1863, William was promoted to major and in a later meeting was presented with a sword by members of the 9th Company as a mark of esteem for his leadership. Making the presentation at Tunstall Covered Market, Mr Smith Child (later Sir Smith Child) declared,

> *Receive this sword, Sir. May you long wear it with honour; may it never be drawn in anger except in self-defence or to smite an invader of your country; and in that hallowed cause, Sir, may it never be sheathed while an enemy's foot desecrates her soil; and after you have honourably borne it, may your children regard it as a valued heirloom as evidence that your services were appreciated by your valued townsmen; as of evidence that you did your duty in your day and generation, that you made yourself useful among your fellow men, and that to the best of your ability you endeavoured to promote, to maintain and to preserve the honour and happiness of your native town.*

True to form, the sword became a treasured heirloom passed down with pride through the Adams family to the present day. In 1863, an oil painting of William Adams V, in the uniform of the Rifle Volunteers, was painted by a friend of his, John Nash-Peake, and commissioned on William's promotion to major.

By 1867, William Adams' leadership skills must have been recognised as he was appointed Lieutenant-Colonel of the 1st Battalion of the Staffordshire Rifle Volunteers, a post he was to hold until 6th April 1872, when he resigned his commission.

On 26th May 1864, William Adams V had married Laura Eliza, eldest daughter of Andrew Jukes Worthington of Ball Haye Hall, Leek, and by all accounts a very festive atmosphere pervaded the town. Two of the bridegroom's friends were in attendance: Captain John Nash-Peake (tile manufacturer and artist) and Lieutenant J. Bull (brother-in-law).

After the death of his father in 1865, William and Eliza took up residence at Greenfield Hall and William and his brother Thomas took over the Greenfield works.

While William was the senior partner of the Greenfield Pottery, he owned a quarter share in common with his brother Thomas. The remaining half was owned by their uncle Edward Adams who remained a non-executive partner until his death in 1872, when his share was bought out. Confusingly, Thomas chose also to be a non-executive partner but to recognise his business capital the firm was renamed W & T Adams.

238. below: **Wolstanton Church from a watercolour, circa 1800**

With William at the helm, the reported weekly output of the Greenfield works in 1865 was enormous–in the region of 73,000 dozen plates and a thriving export trade centred on South America, Africa and the East Indies–but surprisingly little of the output found its way to the home market.

WOLSTANTON CHURCHWARDEN

William Adams V, in common with his illustrious ancestors, was an avid supporter of the Church, serving upwards of 20 years as churchwarden of the ancient parish church of Wolstanton.

The first Wolstanton church had its origins at least 200 years prior to the founding of Hulton Abbey in the year 1223. Ancient track-ways of probable monastic origins criss-crossed the area connecting Wolstanton to Hulton Abbey, where, since medieval times, generations of potters–Adams' foremost among their number–plied their wares until they relocated to larger potteries centred at Burslem.

From its Saxon origins, Wolstanton Church remained intact until 1623 when significant alterations were made to the ancient fabric.

South Elevation

ST. MARGARET'S CHURCH WOLSTANTON

Sneyd Effigy

ADAMS MONUMENTS

VESTRY

Sneyd Effigy

Plan from an 1858 sketch of pew ownership

CHANCEL

FONT

Scale 10ft

Memorial Stained Glass
William Adams V of Moreton House
Charles Challinor of Basford Hall

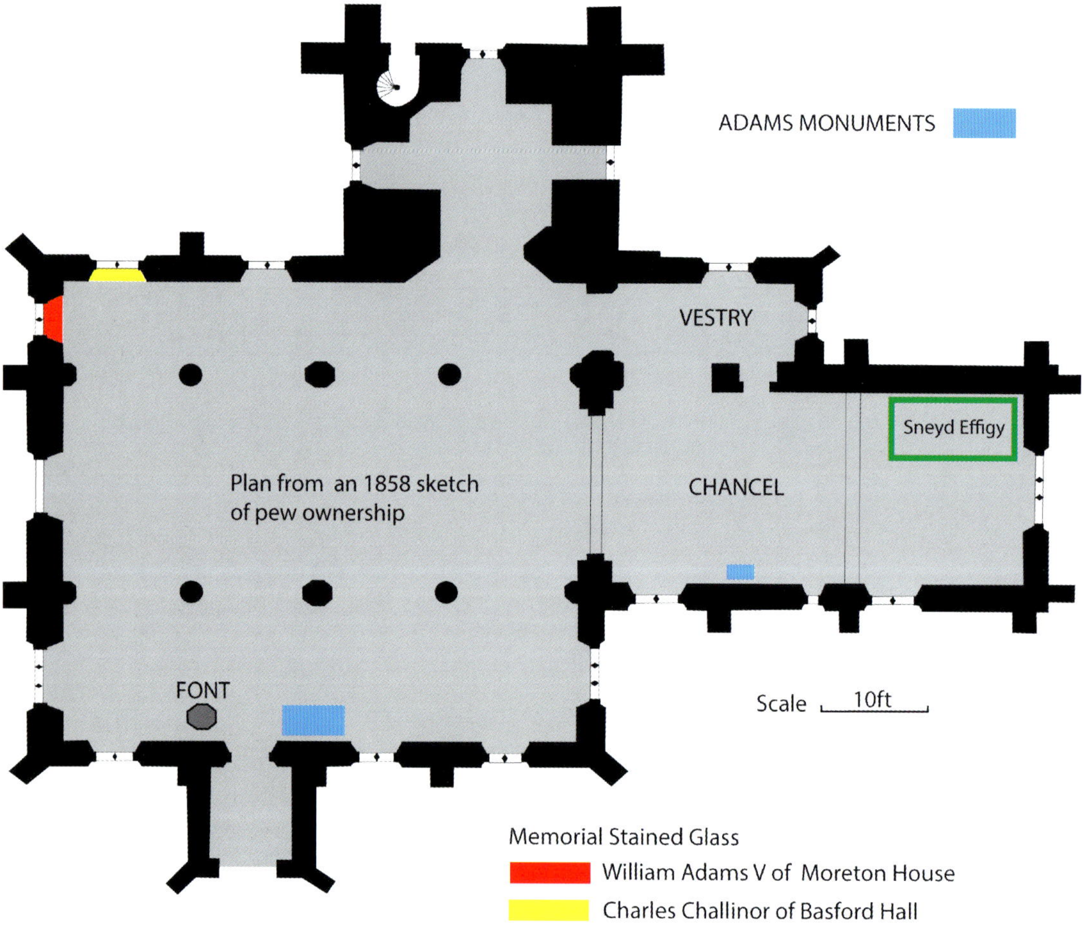

239. Plan of St. Margaret's Church, Wolstanton

240. right: The gravestone of Sarah Smith who died in 1763–with its provocative inscription which alleges she was poisoned

Wolstanton Church today is a most graceful structure. From its elevated site it serves as an elegant landmark, its slender tower concealing what is thought to be foundations dating back to the 13th century. Its historic churchyard was once famous for its earthenware memorials, crafted with care by generations of peasant potters. These are now only housed in distant museums.

One 18th-century tombstone had carved on it for eternity the initials of the perpetrator of a deadly crime:

Here lieth the body of Sarah Smith daughter of Samuel and Martha Smith of Bradwell Park who departed this life Nov: 27, 1763, in the 21st year of her age –

It was G-SB-W,
that brought me to my end
Dear Parents mourn not for me.
For God will stand my friend.
With half a Pint of Poyson
He came to visit me.
Write this on my grave
That all that read it may see.

Buried within the churchyard are Admiral Smith Child of Newfield Hall and many members of the Greenfield Adams.

Ward, in *The History of the Borough of Stoke-upon-Trent*, published in 1843, provides a description of the church twenty years before its partial rebuild in 1859:

The nave appears to belong to an early period, as well as proportions of the side aisles, and the red sandstone of which they are constructed is much decayed by the corroding hand of time. These parts of the sacred edifice may have been of Saxon formation, but the upper parts of the body of the church and the battlements are probably of the date of 1623, when the present roof appears to have been constructed according to a superscription on the wall plate of the South aisle as follows: -

Sir Thomas Colloclough, Knight 1623, John Brett, Esquire, Ralph Bourne, John Macclesfield,

John Woode, Churchwardens, Anno Domini 1623. The Steeple, which is a tower seventy-eight feet high, surmounted by a spire rising sixty-five feet higher, stands on the North side and not as usual on the West side.

By 1858, the church had become so dilapidated that it was considered unsafe and was comprehensively restored under the direction of Messrs. Ward and Son, architects of Hanley, with the admirable brief of restoring the principal features as faithfully as they previously existed. The interior makeover was equally as extensive: stonework was re-dressed, the church re-pewed, the aisles paved with Minton encaustic tiles and some stained-glass windows installed. The impressive 16th-century alabaster altar tomb, erected in memory of Sir William Sneyd and his wife Dame Anne, was restored and re-instated complete with likenesses of their fifteen children carved in panels on the front and sides.

Within the church are numerous shields of the coats of arms of notable local families, foremost among which are the Sneyds of Keele and Bradwell, Moretons of Moreton House, Adams of Greenfield and Bennetts of Dimsdale.

Dawn of the Twentieth Century

241. *St. Margaret's Church Wolstanton, viewed from the east (Photograph by Attic Tapestry)*

242. below: **Stained-glass window in memory of William Adams V and his wife Laura, by Kempe**

By 1871, William Adams V and his young family were installed at The Oaks, Wolstanton – a substantial house with four female servants in the desirable Porthill area. William's unmarried brother Thomas remained at the family seat of Greenfield Hall until he died in 1905. In 1908, realising the mining potential of the site, William's son William Adams VI demolished Greenfield to make way for further coal mining.

In 1872, aged 39, William Adams V was appointed Chief Bailiff of Tunstall and also began to serve as Justice of the Peace for the County of Staffordshire the same year. His public service record is exemplary, with a string of further appointments added, among which were: Commissioner of Taxes, one of the first County Council members, Member of Wolstanton and Burslem Board of Guardians, Churchwarden and School Governor.

The lofty steeple, standing so proudly against the skyline, has been struck numerous times by lightening. In 1843 Ward commented that

it had been so injured by the electric fluid as to be obliged to be twice partly taken down and repaired

In the Cecily Adams family photographic collection is an interesting photograph which she took in October 1908. It is an image that clearly shows workmen repairing Wolstanton Church steeple, possibly after another lightning strike.

243. right: **Steeplejacks working on the tower of Wolstanton Church, 1908**

Dawn of the Twentieth Century

244. left: **William Adams VI, circa 1892**

In 1875, disaster struck the Greenfield Works when a fire broke out, destroying many business records and all-important pattern books from the days of his father's Stoke works. To enable the works to function, the offices were relocated to their Newfield Pottery which was only a mile to the north of the stricken Greenfield site.

COMING-OF-AGE CELEBRATIONS

In line with family tradition, Monday 12th August 1889 was a day of huge celebration in Tunstall as the whole workforce turned out to celebrate William Adams VI attaining his majority. The Staffordshire Sentinel of Wednesday 14th August captured the mood of the event:

On Monday evening last, about 450 workpeople of the firm of Messrs. W. and T. Adams manufacturers, at the request of Mr. W. Adams, J.P., of Porthill, sat down to an excellent repast in the Court-room of the Town Hall, to celebrate the coming of age of his eldest son, Mr. W. Adams, jun. the following ladies and gentlemen were amongst those present :- Mr. and Mrs. W. Adams,

and Mr. H. Adams, Mr. Llewellyn, Mr. Lodge, and Dr. Massingham. During the tea Messrs. Morfey Bros. band played a number of suitable selections. After the repast, the company moved into the large hall, where a concert was held, followed by a presentation and a dance. The presentation to Mr. Adams was made by Mr. Baker, and consisted of a gold watch and chain and ring, the watch bearing the inscription: - Presented to William Adams, jun., Esq., on his attaining his majority by the employees of Messrs. W. and T. Adams, August 12th 1889. The ring had the crest of the family, a boar's head, chased upon it. The presentation was accompanied by a lengthy and suitable speech. Mr Adams, jun., made a suitable response, and remarked that he was glad of that opportunity of thanking them for their uniform kindness and courtesy towards him during the time he had been with them learning the business of a potter. He appreciated the gifts as tokens of their good feeling towards him, and assured them that he should study their interests as well as his own. Mr. Baker next proposed the health of Mr. Adams, the toast being honoured musically – Dancing was then commenced, and after an interval, Mr. Adams, Sen., rose and said what a great pleasure it gave him to see so many of his workforce there; and hoped that they would all be present at their next gathering. He remarked upon the position of his son, and hoped he would look to the interests of the workpeople. (Applause.) The proceedings were brought to a close by the National Anthem.

A LOOMING FINANCIAL CRISIS ON THE HORIZON

Throughout the 1860s Greenfield's eight bottle ovens were constantly in use to meet the endless demand for Adams wares, but by the mid-1870s the Potteries' prosperity was in decline, blamed partly on the international competition that forced potteries to cut their prices.

These were indeed challenging times for the Adams works, as a catalogue of misfortunes unfolded, events that were to seriously threaten the very existence of the ancient firm.

245. above: **Greenfield Colliery,** circa 1900

Historically, generations of Adams potteries had taken full advantage of the availability of cheap coal sourced from their own coalmines. The fact that six times as much coal as clay is used in the potting process indicates how financially desirable it was to have their own mines, but this cheap energy source was abruptly ended when the Greenfield's pits became intractably water-logged, forcing the company to source this expensive commodity from other suppliers, much to the detriment of its profitability.

The disastrous Greenfield's fire of 1875 heralded the deteriorating trading conditions that lasted for the next two decades, when the world suffered a severe economic recession, woefully referred to as the *Long Depression*. Staffordshire's potting industry was hit hard; even the massive Minton potting concern made

> *continuous losses from 1887 until the end of the century and in early 1890s acute financial crisis made failure a very real possibility.*

(*Business Structure, Business Culture and the Industrial District: The Potteries, c.1850-1900*. Andrew Derek Popp, 1997)

With profits and capital squeezed by low prices and crippling tariffs, some manufacturers looked at cheapening the goods, speeding up production or controversially cutting wages.

By 1892, W. & T. Adams were in a dire financial situation: the pottery gates were shut for a period of two weeks while the management grappled with the crisis that had unfolded. The Newfield works was put up for sale in an attempt to avert collapse.

Crucially, William Adams VI had joined the company as partner in 1889 when his father was 67 years of age, and he must have played a key role in successfully securing outside capital to enable the company to weather the storm.

246. Watercolour of Greenfield Pottery in the 1890s, by Charles M. Evans (2021), 20 x 26 inches

Dawn of the Twentieth Century

247. above: **Greenfield Works, October 1898–with packing crates clearly visible in the foreground**

It was at this pivotal stage of the company's history that William Adams I's historic Greengates Pottery came up for sale, the Meir family wishing to retire from the business which had been in their family since purchasing it from Benjamin Adams in 1822.

It was a unique business opportunity that the Greenfield Adams could in no way resist: the factories lay adjacent to each other and would naturally allow the company to expand, and to add a further enticement, the Greenfield board no doubt knew that lurking within the dusty Greengates storeroom lay all the tools and moulds used by William Adams I in the making of his famous jasper ware, kept in cupboards that had not been used since the reign of George III.

A twenty-one-year mortgage was secured and the historic Greengates works was once more under the control of an Adams master potter.

The two factories together employed a workforce of some 700, with Greenfield Pottery concentrating on low-value mass production ware while Greengates concentrated on higher value products. It would take a few more years until the arrival of the younger son of William Adams V, Percy Adams, before jaspers would once more roll off the production line at Greengates, marking what was to be the second period of jasper production at Greengates–a period that would eventually span some four decades.

GREENGATES JASPER PRODUCTION PERIODS

1st **Period**–Wm. Adams I (1779-1805)
2nd **Period**–Wm. Adams & Co.–Wm. Adams & sons (1900-1936)
3rd **Period**–Wm. Adams & Co. –Trials on reintroducing Jaspers 1960s

In 1896, with the departure of Thomas Adams and the appointment of William's youngest son Percy, the business was re-designated Adams & Co.

248. *Extract from the jasper-ware catalogue produced by Percy W.L. Adams between 1900 and 1939*

249. *Jasper workers at Greengates Pottery 1907–Percy W.L. Adams seated front right*

250. *The Duchess of Teck visiting Leek, March 1895*

251. *left: Reverend Augustus Theodore Wirgman DD (brother-in-law to Eliza Adams), Senior Chaplain of the Cape Colonial Forces and Hon. Chaplain to the King in 1905*
252. *above: Duchess of Sutherland's coach during the Duchess of Teck's visit to Leek, March 1895*

253. *below:* *William Adams V and his wife at Moreton House, September 1902*

By the time of the visit of Her Royal Highness Princess Mary, Duchess of Teck, to Leek Silk Mills in 1895, the company was once more on a firm financial footing. William Adams V and family would have shared in the joyous occasion which was made even more memorable as the Duchess visited William's brother-in-law's premises, one of the larger Silk Mills of the town, namely A.J. Worthington & Co. of Portland Mills, Leek.

William's talented daughter Cecily captured unique photographic images of the arrival of the Duchess at the beginning of her tour of the Mill, ably conducted by her Uncle, Reverend Augustus Theodore Wirgman, Rural Dean of Port Elizabeth, South Africa 1884-96 (author of *Storm and Sunshine in South Africa*, 1922) and later Hon. Chaplain to the King in 1905.

WOLSTANTON SCHOLAR'S TREAT

Facilitating an annual treat for the scholars of various church and Sunday schools in the parish seems to have been a regular event organised by William Adams V. Photographs exist in the family archive of the 1901 occasion, held on the outskirts of Wolstanton. *The Staffordshire Sentinel* of 11th August 1880 conveys the excitement of the participants at that time:

> *The annual treat to the Sunday and day scholars' attending the various Church schools in this parish, was held on Monday. The scholars, to the number of about 800, were entertained to tea at the Central Schools, after which they marked in procession, proceeded by their banners, to the Oaks, the residence of Mr. William Adams, where a field had been kindly placed at their disposal. The children heartily entered into the different sports provided, and thoroughly enjoyed themselves, until the gathering twilight proclaimed the close of the day which had been looked forward to with eagerness, and will be remembered with pleasure. As the little ones left, three hearty cheers were given for Mr. and Mrs Adams; cheers, which also expressed the thankfulness of the children to those kind teachers and friends, who by their untiring exertions so largely contributed to the day's enjoyment. Much regret was expressed at the unavoidable absence of the vicar, and by none more so than by the children whose spiritual and temporal welfare he had always so much at heart.*

SAVED BY THE BELL!

Friday 3rd July 1903 might well have been a catastrophic day in the history of Greenfield Pottery had not the Tunstall Fire Brigade responded so swiftly to the call to action!

It seems that a smouldering fire was detected in the factory's packing house and a messenger despatched to Tunstall for the Fire Brigade. It appears that the firemen were summoned to action by means of an electric call bell installed in the house of each of the firemen, which enabled a swift deployment of the fire fighters to the scene, fighting the blaze in under twenty minutes. Three water jets supplied from a nearby pond enabled the flames to be subdued, saving extremely valuable stock from almost certain destruction.

THE OAKS, PORTHILL, WOLSTANTON

254. above: Watercolour of The Oaks, Wolstanton–the home of William Adams V from 1864-1892–by F.P. Langley, portrait and animal painter of Wolstanton (6.5 x 4.5 inches)

255. below: **Photograph of the Adams family at The Oaks dated 1892, possibly just before they relocated to Moreton House, Wolstanton**

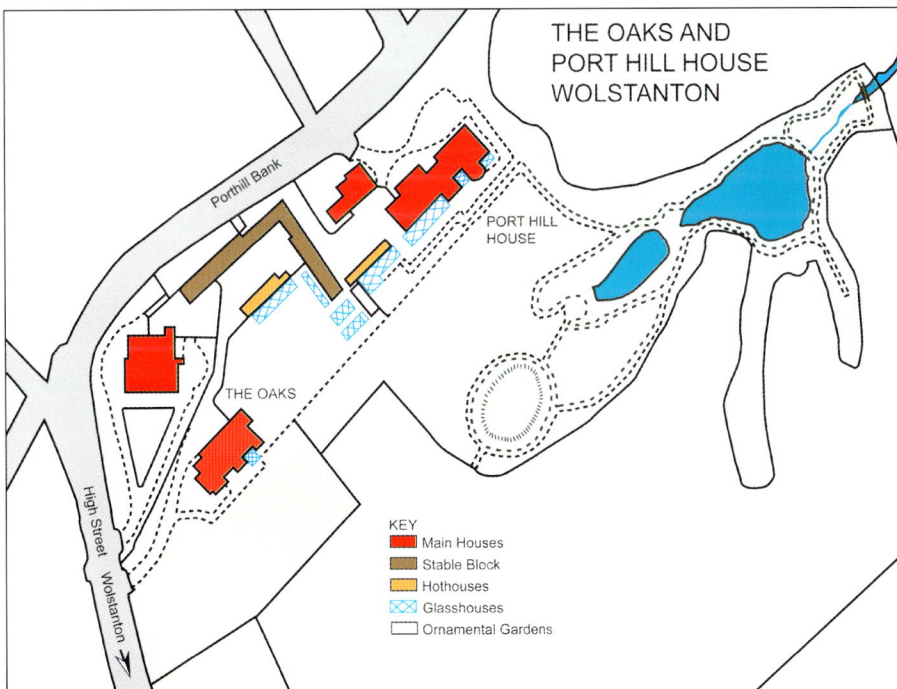

256. above: **Layout plan of The Oaks and Porthill House, Wolstanton, circa 1900**

Dawn of the Twentieth Century   231

257. Wolstanton Sunday School Annual Treat, 1901 (provided by William Adams V)

232

258. right: *William Adams VI of Greenfield and Greengates and wife, Mildred Mary, daughter of Reverend James Jordan Serjeantson M.A., photograph dated 1904*

The Staffordshire Sentinel of 3rd July 1903 commented,

There can be little doubt that but for the promptitude of Captain Pemberton and his twelve assistants, very great damage would have resulted, and the Brigade are to be heartily complimented upon their smartness in turning out.

The whole episode conjures up a graphic image of horse-drawn fire equipment tearing through the cobbled streets and hand-pumped hoses furiously fighting the raging flames, all adding to our sense of disbelief that they turned out so swiftly.

On a happier note, Friday 23rd December 1904 was a joyous day for the employees of William Adams and Co. as the entire workforce of some 600 in number were invited for tea and entertainment in Tunstall Town Hall to commemorate the recent marriage of William Adams VI and Miss Mildred Mary Serjeantson, and to be thanked for their generous wedding gifts of a grand piano, sideboard, silver bowl and illuminated address.

The Staffordshire Sentinel of Tuesday 27th December 1904 reported:

The large assembly hall of the Town Hall was thronged with workpeople and the magistrates' room had to be requisitioned, and this was also filled. A knife and fork tea of the most generous order was served, this being excellently catered for by Mr. Frewer, of the Sneyd Arms Hotel, Tunstall, afterwards a few toasts were proposed, including that of Mr. and Mrs. William Adams, jun., of Oaklands and this was drunk with great heartiness and enthusiasm, and then a further presentation was made by the combined workpeople of the two manufactories and brickworks, this time to Mrs. Adams junior, of a beautiful gold bracelet.

At the head table there were among others the host and hostess (Mr. and Mrs. William Adams jun.) Miss Adams, Miss Cecily Adams, Mr. and Mrs. Hugh W. Adams, Mr. Percy Adams, the Rev. D.H. Briggs, (Vicar of Christ Church), the Rev. W. H. Heale (Vicar of Wolstanton), Miss Heale ...

Mr. Aaron Heath, manager of Greengates Works, then proposed 'The health of Mr. and Mrs. Wm. Adams jun.'

He said there were not many firms in the Potteries that had worked so well as that of Wm. Adams and Co. had done during the last eight or nine years, and this was in no small measure due to the way in which Mr. Wm. Adams jun. had looked after the business... the toast was received with much cheering and singing of He's a jolly good fellow.

Dawn of the Twentieth Century

259. below: Illuminated address given by the workforce of Greenfield and Greengates Works to Mr & Mrs William Adams VI on their wedding – Friday 23rd December 1904

After the gift of the bracelet was given, William Adams junior arose to respond and said

there was only one regret he had that night, that his father was unable to be present. They knew as well as he did that there was no place his father liked to be at better than the works ...

Commenting on his coming-of-age presentation of 15 years before when he stood before them he said,

There is only one difference between now and 15 years ago, and this was that instead of seeing before him 350 workpeople he now saw that night over 600. (Applause) How had that occurred? It was through the good feeling and co-operation of all concerned, and the interest everyone took in the work that they were producing that they had made such strides. He took that opportunity to impress upon them the lesson that everyone, from the paper cutter to the glost fireman, in these days of competition must do his best if they were to make progress.

An enjoyable social time was experienced by all, with a tinge of sadness due to the fact that Mr. William Adams senior was unable to be present on account of suffering ill health.

On the morning of Sunday 5th March 1905 William Adams suffered a heart attack and died at his home, Moreton House in Wolstanton, aged 72, just 100 years after the death of his eminent predecessor William Adams I of Greengates. He was buried in Wolstanton churchyard on Ash Wednesday, 8th March, and a tablet was erected in his memory on the south aisle of the church.

In 1907, the Adams workforce and the company erected a clock tower in Victoria Park, Tunstall, to William Adams V's memory and that of his predecessor William Adams of Greengates. A bronze portrait medallion of William Adams V was installed on the north side of the tower facing his beloved Greenfield, and over the door on the south side his coat of arms was incorporated into the wall.

260. below: **William Adams V of Greenfield** (1833-1905)

Dawn of the Twentieth Century   235

261. left: The Adams Clock Tower, Tunstall Park

An Aberdeen granite slab has the following inscription:

> Erected in the year 1907,
> By the workpeople & firm of William Adams & Co., of Greenfield,
> Greengates, & Newfield, to the memory of
> WILLIAM ADAMS, OF GREENFIELD, ESQUIRE
> Born June 13th, 1833 Died March 5th, 1905
> A well-known manufacturer of this Town
> On the organisation of the Volunteer movement of 1859, he was one of the first to offer himself, & in 1867 was made Lieut-Colonel of the 1st Vol. Batt., N.S. Regiment. In 1872 he was appointed on the Commission of the Peace for the County; & in the same year he
> Became Chief Bailiff of this Town.
> He was descended from a long line of Master Potters who helped
> Considerably to achieve the world wide repute which English Pottery
> Had attained. One of the factories he controlled was founded by his
> Predecessor,
> WILLIAM ADAMS
> THE FAMOUS STAFFORDSHIRE POTTER
> Baptized June 15th, 1746. Died January 10th, 1805
> Who built the first important Potteries
> in this Town.

Other inscriptions on each side of the tower read:

> North–William Adams held lands in Tunstall 1307
> South–William Adams worked a pottery near here 1590
> East– John Adams, Chief Constable of Tunstall Manor Court 1616
> West–Richard Adams owned coalmines within the sight of this Tower 1487

262. Left: Bronze portrait medallion in memory of William Adams V (1833-1905) of Greenfield, on the north side of the Adams Clock Tower, Tunstall Park

263. right: **Postcard showing the main entrance gates to Victoria Park (Tunstall Park) circa 1913**

Standing on the top of a landscaped mound, the stone tower was erected in 1907, with its clock added a year later following the official opening of the park at a cost of £98 including its installation.

It had been intended that the official opening of Victoria Park would commemorate the Diamond Jubilee of Queen Victoria in 1897 but unforeseeable delays made this impractical. The official opening of the park had to be delayed until 1908, by which time its impressive gates, donated by the Nash-Peake family, had been installed.

The opening ceremony was performed by Mrs Peake, widow of John Nash-Peake, a fervent promoter of the Victoria Park scheme. The Peakes were connected to the Adams family by marriage, as Eleanor Peake was sister-in-law to Mary Adams (William Adams V's sister).

The Staffordshire Advertiser of June 20th 1908 declared that Nash-Peake's gates were

> *the finest work in wrought iron in the district – always excepting the magnificent Trentham Hall gate. Their design is a happy combination of the historic with the modern, and are altogether a highly-decorative and craftsman-like work. The gates are in three sections, and are hung upon four pleasingly moulded and enriched piers. Above the central and principal gate is the coat of arms of the town, and below this the inscription :- In memory of Thomas Peake by his children, whilst the gates on either side bear the words Floreat Tunstall. The cost of the gates is estimated at £450; they are the work of Mr. W. Durose, of Tunstall, and the stonework has been executed by Mr. W. Bonner also of Tunstall. The only matter for regret is that Mr. John Nash Peake did not live to see their erection and the completion of the work on which he had set his heart.*

Following the opening ceremony a garden party and fete–including maypole dances, gymnastic displays and musical entertainment from the Silverdale Prize Band – were held for the benefit of Tunstall Hospital.

As the daughter of a prominent Tunstall iron master, Mrs Eleanor Peake would no doubt have admired the

264. above: **Eleanor Peake (seated) and her sister Elizabeth Blaikie, née Bull**

Dawn of the Twentieth Century

265. Tunstall Park Gates in 2021 after extensive restoration

Dawn of the Twentieth Century

266. Moreton House, Wolstanton (2021)

267 right: Layout plan of Moreton House, Wolstanton, circa 1900

268. below: **Laura Eliza, wife of William Adams V and her daughter Mildred, outside Moreton House, September 1898**

269. right: **William Adams VI at the wheel of his new car outside Moreton House, with Mildred and Percy Adams to the rear**

Dawn of the Twentieth Century

271 right: Laura Eliza, eldest daughter of Andrew Jukes Worthington of Ball Haye Hall, Leek, and the wife of William Adams V

wonderful craftsmanship involved in making the gates, which today, after their recent magnificent renovations, must look very much like the gates she viewed on that summer's day in 1908.

In 1905, William Adams VI became joint proprietor with his youngest brother Percy W.L. Adams, and had taken over as the senior partner of the Greenfield and Greengates Potteries and Newfield Brick Works, eagerly taking on the mantle of master potter of this long and illustrious lineage.

A DYNAMIC BUSINESSMAN

William Adams VI had joined the family business as a director in 1889, and by the death of his father in 1905 had already had sixteen years of managerial experience that stood him in good stead as he enthusiastically launched into the formidable challenges that were on the horizon.

He had played a pivotal role in the acquisition of the Greengates factory – a shrewd business purchase that enabled the Adams board to capitalise on Greengates' buoyant home market, which was – a perfect antidote to the Adams' ever-declining overseas trade, not to mention the historical re-entry of an Adams into the potentially profitable jasper market.

Laura Eliza Adams, William Adams V's wife, died on the afternoon of Monday 27th April 1914 and was buried beside her husband near the northwest corner of Wolstanton church tower. The Vicar of Wolstanton, Reverend C. J. Winn, writing in the *Parish Magazine* described Laura Eliza Adams as

> *a beautiful example of solid English piety at its best. Such people are rare in any age; we have therefore great reason to thank God that this parish has been so long possessed of her. She has gained the love of many & the respect of all ...*

By the onset of the First World War the Adams potteries were once more on a firm financial footing with a wide range of successful lines and seemingly ready to weather the turbulent times ahead.

Fortunately, their ovens were kept going through the dark days of war with no trade restrictions on their manufactured goods as they continued with a healthy export trade, supplementing this by orders for the government to provide institutional and hotel ware for use of the Military, Hospitals and Civil Service.

By the end of hostilities in 1918, the directors of Adams Potteries could look back with a considerable sense of relief: they had paid off the mortgage on Greengates and the prospect of peace heralded a hoped-for post-war boom.

The early 1920s witnessed a period of refurbishment and general improvement especially focussed on the Greenfield works, where a new office block was added on the north front.

A range of successful products flowed from the Adams Potteries, foremost among which were their wide-ranging Titian ware available in a vast range of free-hand painted patterns, which struck a note with consumers who sought their vibrant ceramics as an antidote to the gloom of post-war Britain.

270. left: William Adams VI of Greenfield and Greengates Works – painting by Edward Halliday R.B.A. of London

272. Drawing of Greenfield Pottery (left) and Greengates on the horizon, circa 1900

The stark reality of international competition was dawning on the Adams directors as close copies of Adams ware began to appear in Eastern markets, and, as their international trade floundered, the company also witnessed a slump in their home market, all of which adversely affected their profitability.

Steering the Adams companies through such troubling times must have taken its toll on William Adams VI, who in 1922 embarked on a tour of the West Indies primarily for the benefit of his health, but, like the seasoned entrepreneur that he was, he kept an eye open for potential trade opportunities.

The Staffordshire Sentinel of Monday 13th February 1922 reported on the complimentary dinner held by Adams' employees to welcome their managing director home:

> There was a very happy gathering at the Sneyd Hotel, Tunstall, on Friday evening when staffs of Messrs. William Adams and Sons at Greenfield and Greengates Potteries and the Newfield Brick and Marl Works gave a complimentary dinner to Mr. William Adams, as a welcome home on his return from a trip to the British West Indies … [addressing the gathering William said]:
>
> He was very pleased to get back again for he was fearfully home-sick (Laughter.) Proceeding, Mr Adams said he had been at the factory for 33 years, and they had been the happiest times of his life. He was only sorry that his health had been so bad during the last few years; it had rather taken the spirit out of him at times. But there was plenty of life left in him yet, and he felt in the best of spirits that night. He did not deserve all the praise which had been meted out to him, but all the same, it was a great pleasure to know that his efforts had been appreciated. He had wanted to leave the factory in a better state than when they took it over. They had an unlucky period during the colliery slump in North Staffordshire, when the mines were flooded, but he did not think there was any firm stronger under foot than they were at the present time, and it was not entirely due to his endeavours, but to the cooperation of the managers and the workpeople. The great thing

273. right: **Percy Walter Lewis Adams (1875-1952)**
J.P. F.S.A., of Greenfield and Greengates Potteries

was to pull together, and for everybody to take a pride in their production; although they were going through a very serious depression at present – he was afraid there would not be a very great change this year – they must hope for the best, and he was certain the firm would do their best to get through it with as little unemployment as possible. Mr. Adams concluded by giving a resumé of his trip to the West Indies, which was exceedingly interesting.

True to his word, William proved that there was plenty of life left in him, as he went on to manage the Adams diverse holdings for a further thirty years, dying in post aged 84 years in 1952.

On 28th January 1925, William Adams and Sons became a public limited company with William Adams VI and Percy Walter Lewis Adams as directors. In future they would trade under the name of William Adams & Sons (Potters) Ltd with a workforce of over 600, one of the largest firms in the potteries.

Further improvements were carried out at Greenfields in 1926 and then the focus switched to Greengates, where offices were refurbished and a new showroom was built to display the company's ever increasing range of wares. Sales were buoyant and the balance sheet healthy, when in 1929, disaster struck and the world was shaken to its core by the Wall Street Crash in the autumn of that year.

Adams' crucially important American market was devastatingly hit and remained deflated for a further three years. In a targeted attempt to increase penetration of the home market, Adams launched their Calyx Ware in 1930 – a green glazed fine earthenware range that was hoped would revive their flagging sales. The depression of the 1930s had seen a reduced demand for more expensive products and thus heralded the death knell for sales of jaspers, which had ceased at Greengates by 1936. Adams' strategy was to introduce a new catalogue of reduced cost wares, fielding as wide a possible range to grasp at any opportunity for trade.

274. below: Greengates Pottery circa 1930

275. below: **William Anthony Adams photographed in the Site Manager's office at Greengates,** circa 1930

It was at this critical phase in the company's search for new markets that William's eldest son, William Anthony (Tony) Adams, joined the family business in 1930 as a junior director with particular responsibility for sales. In line with his role, he undertook a number of European fact-finding visits notably to Denmark, Norway and Holland and an extended sales tour of Australia and New Zealand during 1934-5.

Although suffering the aftermath of the Great Depression–the most severe depression ever experienced by the industrialized Western world–the morale of the Adams workforce seems to have been remarkably high, no doubt reflecting the effective management in place at the time.

The noted author of *The Good Companion,* J.B. Priestley, visited the Adams works in 1933 and, as part of his social study *English Journey,* described the potteries as

276. *Percy W.L. Adams (left) and William Adams VI, at their Greenfield office,* circa 1930

277. below: J.B. Priestley (1894-1984). Novelist, playwright, scriptwriter, social commentator and broadcaster

a modern industry rooted in a traditional craft, where all the employees show a pride in the exercise of their skills, which removes them from the ordinary ranks of modern workmen. They are left to themselves to get on with the job, are trusted and respected. The happy result can be read on their faces.

In 1938 William Adams and Sons were honoured when H.R.H Queen Mary placed an order for their wares. Further royal purchases were forthcoming in 1939 when during her tour of the Pottery Section of the British Industries Fair at Olympia, Her Majesty Queen Mary visited the showroom of William Adams & Sons where she purchased richly enamelled dinnerware and specimens of 'Calyx and Cries of London' ware. A cheque dated 10th April 1933 from Queen Mary, preserved in the family archives, show that Her Royal Highness had purchased 'Cries of London' ware some five years previously.

In 1939, on the brink of war, William Adams VI was 72 years of age, his brother Percy 65. William Anthony Adams was sales director and aged 31, while Percy's son, Joscelin, had recently been admitted as junior director on his 21st birthday.

Skilled pottery workers were not liable to be called up to join the forces; likewise, directors essential for the running of the firms could be retained. On admirable patriotic grounds, the senior partners concluded they could continue at the helm, releasing their sons to join the war effort for what it was mistakenly thought would be a relatively short conflict.

WARTIME SERVICE
Major Joscelin Francis Whieldon Adams

On leaving Uppingham School in 1937, Joscelin Adams joined the Territorial Army, and on 28th May that year he was commissioned as Second Lieutenant, serving in the 46th (North Midland) Division of the Royal Engineers, attached to the 214th Field Company, stationed at Tunstall.

It is interesting to note that the North Midland Divisional Engineers Territorial unit was created in 1908 by a conversion of a volunteer infantry battalion from Staffordshire whose origin lay in the 1st Staffordshire Rifle Volunteers, the corps which Joscelin's grandfather, William Adams V, had served in with distinction, achieving the rank of Lt. Col. some six decades previously.

278. left: Cap badge of the Royal Engineers, with motto, 'Everywhere' and 'Where Right and Glory Lead'

The 214th (North Midland) Army Field Company fought in France as part of the British Expeditionary Force. The allied forces could not withstand the devastating speed and violence of the German advances and were forced to withdraw to Dunkirk to avoid complete annihilation. The 214th Field Company were actively involved in demolitions that covered the allied withdrawal, but on 27th May it was ordered to abandon all its equipment and march to Dunkirk, later taking cover in ditches near the town, which was being mercilessly bombed. Later that evening the Company moved to the beaches, and were miraculously transferred to boats and to safety in England the following evening.

After the Dunkirk evacuation the 214th Field Company reassembled in England, subsequently fighting with the 78th Division (Battle Axe) in North Africa in 1942, followed by Sicily and Italy, building bridges, often under continuous mortar fire, and clearing mine fields in addition to infantry duties.

This *sapper* (combat engineer) company took part in three heavily fortified river crossings in Sicily and took part in the Battle of Cassino.

> *The 214th Field Company's finest achievement was probably their quick action on 3rd October 1943. 78th Division were leading the Army advance up to the east coast of Italy when the Germans counter-attacked suddenly. The River Biferno, in spate, was in rear of 78th Division and it was essential to bridge this quickly to reinforce the Division to meet the crisis. For this 214th Field Company built a 100ft Class 30 high level Bailey bridge over the two damaged piers. Four Squadron bricklayers laid 5,000 bricks in 9 hours to repair the piers and the bridge was completed after 30 hours of continuous work in the rain and under fire.*

Through such commendable action the 214th Field Company had

> *probably, the most distinguished record of all the Staffordshire Companies in the Second World War. In all, members of the Company won some 12 Military Crosses and 20 Military Medals.*

(*The History of the 125th (Staffs) Corps Engr. Regt. (TA)*, Stafford, June 1963)

Major-General Campbell, late Engineer-in-Chief, described the 214th Field Company as

the finest Field Company in the British Army.

In a letter to Percy Adams, dated 2nd June 1944, the commanding officer of the 214th Field Company expressed his disappointment that Joscelin was being posted home to take up training duties:

> *It was a great surprise to me that he was to be posted home, and we feel his absence very much. Jos after so many years with the 214th had become an institution, and without him things seem very different.*

279. above: Lieutenant Joscelin F.W. Adams of the Royal Engineers, circa 1944

280. left: **Lt. Col. William Anthony Adams of the Royal Artillery**

After the war Major Joscelin Adams continued in the T.A., serving in the newly constituted 125th (Staffordshire) Army Engineer Regiment, and went on to command a squadron later designated 214th Field Squadron, stationed in Tunstall.

LT. COL. WILLIAM ANTHONY ADAMS

William Anthony Adams was commissioned to the Royal Artillery in April 1940. In December 1943 he was posted to India.

At the outbreak of the Second World War, the Indian Army numbered some 205,000 men and as the war progressed that rose to 2.5 million, the largest all-volunteer force in history.

Specialist training officers from Britain were deployed to assist with the training of this vitally important element of the British Empire's forces, and William Anthony Adams was part of that contingent.

The British Indian Army fought with distinction against the Axis forces in North Africa but the bulk of their forces were committed to fighting the Japanese Army in Malaya and Burma, as part of the largest British Empire army ever established. These campaigns were to cost the lives of over 87,000 Indian service men. Their undisputed valour was recognised through the awarding of some 4,000 decorations, including 18 Victoria/George Crosses, a record aptly voiced by Winston Churchill who paid tribute to *the unsurpassed bravery of the Indian soldiers and officers.*

In a letter written to his Aunt Cecily Adams on 14th December 1944, William Anthony stated,

I was started off in a Depot not very far from Bombay and then spent a few months with a Regiment in the Central Provinces; now I am commanding a Training Regiment about 90 miles north of Delhi. I like my job and have a lot of work to do, all Indian troops which I have come to like very much; I am really extremely well accommodated in a comfortable bungalow and have an excellent bearer who comes with me on all my travels ... Originally I had hopes of getting to a more exciting job than this but someone seems to think that I am a specialist in training, so I am landed here for a while.

It was a more settled outlook than the frustration voiced in a letter to his uncle Percy on 15th June 1944:

We are rather bored with life out here and wish we were in Europe now – we feel we are rather forgotten out here in India.

Presumably, William Anthony Adams remained in India until the Allied victory over Japan was achieved, celebrated as VJ day, 15th August 1945, some three months after VE Day (victory in Europe) – 8th May 1945.

WARTIME TRADE

During the early years of the war exports continued unabated and Adams continued to exhibit at International Exhibitions–the 1940 International Exhibition in New York being a case in point. The German invasion of France and the Low countries put an end to trade with Eastern Europe, a situation that would continue for the duration of the war. Atlantic trade continued despite the terrific losses as a result of German submarine attacks that were by 1943 destroying one in four of all the Atlantic shipping.

281. left: Badge of the Royal Regiment of Artillery

market–measures introduced to preserve much-needed fuel supplies after the war and which were only lifted in 1952.

On 27th December 1952, William Adams VI died at his home in Oulton Cross, Stone, in his 85th year, and very sadly his younger brother Percy W. L. Adams had died only three weeks previously. Both brothers left a substantial fortune in potteries, quarries, property and land that by implication attracted substantial death duty charges.

By 1946, both William Anthony Adams and Joscelin Adams had returned home from war. Joscelin re-joined the firm while William Anthony Adams took several months sick leave before later taking up his post in the family business.

Birthday Presentation

Saturday 9th July 1949 became a memorable day for William Adams VI as a delegation of long-serving Adams employees gathered at his home to present an oil portrait of himself to mark his 80th birthday. The entire workforce of Greenfield and Greengates Potteries had contributed to the subscription, but as William had been in poor health for some time it was decided to present the portrait at his home at Oulton Cross, Stone.

A select group of some 33 long-serving operatives had gathered for the presentation, none of whom had less than 40 years' service with the Adams firm. Sadly, the longest serving employee, Fred Greatbach, with 58 years service, was unable to attend. The presentation was made by Mr. Arthur Grocott (head packer at the Greenfield factory) who had 56 years service, and Mr. T. Barrow (head biscuit placer at Greengates) who had spent 55 years with the firm.

While exports remained strong the Staffordshire potters were very much stifled by government restrictions on selling decorated wares to the home

282. above: Christening party, at Lea Head Manor, of Richard Christopher Adams, son of William Anthony Adams, 28th March 1948

Dawn of the Twentieth Century

283. *A presentation to William Adams VI, Chairman of the Directors of William Adams & Sons (Potters) Ltd, of his portrait from the employees of Greenfield and Greengates Potteries, August 1949*

William Adams VI was held in high regard by his employees, to whom he was known by his christian name. In addition to managing the potteries, William had taken over the family firm of George Davenport Adams, silk manufacturers of Leek. He had built up a considerable amount of property and owned some 260 houses in the Greenfield area, which were occupied by his employees.

In his younger days he had played rugby football for Stoke, becoming captain of the team for four years. He was a keen cricket supporter, actively supporting his son William Anthony Adams, who was captain of the Staffordshire team from 1936-39.

In the funeral address at Christ Church, Stone, the vicar Reverend Harold Glew said that

the name of Adams had enriched the industrial development of North Staffordshire and had made pottery a thing of world renown. It had been interwoven with both tradition and adventure for a period of almost seven centuries, and had been prominent in the wide expansion of the ceramic industry of the late 18th and 19th century. Mr. Adams, he said, was no mean representative of that name. He inherited the tradition and enriched it by his personal worth and high character. There was a bigness about him that called out for admiration and emulation.

He was, like so many of his ancestors, an avid supporter of the Church throughout his life and served as churchwarden in total for no fewer than three parishes.

284. left: Bellringers of Wolstanton Church, November 1904 (William Adams VI seated front left)

P.W.L. ADAMS - A GENEALOGIST AND HISTORIAN OF NOTE

The Adams family are indeed fortunate to count among their midst such an accomplished genealogist and historian as Percy Walter Lewis Adams, the youngest son of William Adams V of Greenfield.

Following family tradition, Percy was educated at Rugby School and subsequently entered the family potting business, becoming a director at the age of 21 in 1896. While his older brother William concentrated on the sales, Percy gravitated towards the design side of the business.

It was an exciting time for the artistically motivated Percy; the Adams company had recently taken over the historic Greengates works which, one hundred years earlier, had been the domain of the hugely talented William Adams I, and Percy would have the privilege of re-introducing jasper production to the old works, employing many of the old tools, moulds and designs which had lain dormant since the time of George III, perfectly preserved in purposely built cupboards.

It may well have been while searching through the rich Greenfield and Greengates archival materials that Percy first developed his interest in genealogy. Indeed, preserved in the Adams family archives are notes of his, including one his early forays into family history in the form of a written pedigree, constructed, as he noted, from old deeds, documents and family recollections. This document is dated July 25th 1897, a year after he joined the firm. It is evident at this early phase in his life that Percy was already fascinated by all things genealogical as he speculates on the differing Adams' branches and hypothesises that the Adams family,

> *perhaps with the Wedgwoods are the oldest Potters ...*

At the end of the handwritten account, Percy noted that:

> *there is nothing more I know to put down as I am very tired of writing, I stop.*

Fortunately for the family and the wider Stoke community, he did not stop; in fact he went on to pursue genealogical research and local history for the rest of his life, chronicling a definitive account of the distinguished *Adams Family of North Staffordshire* in 1914 and producing a range of other historical publications, widening his already extensive areas of research to encompass local antiquities in addition to the demands of running a thriving potting company with a workforce in excess of seven hundred.

285. above: Percy W. L. Adams (1897)

In 1902, in his late 20s, Percy assisted William Turner in the production of his book *William Adams: An Old English Potter*, which was subsequently published in 1904. Turner acknowledged that Percy offered to supply information and assist in forming a catalogue, but in reality it is likely that the book was almost an Adams in-house publication with wide-ranging factory support evident. Turner's book was in some way an incentive for Percy to gather a collection of Adams ware from many sources with the aim of providing illustrations for the book, a collection that would ultimately be donated to Tunstall Museum between 1903 and 1908, by which time no less than thirty pieces of Adams I jaspers had been gifted.

The Staffordshire Advertiser of Saturday January 29th 1910 reported the important additions to the Museum collection that had been curated by Percy Adams and T. Batty, as by 1910 both were honorary curators for Tunstall Museum:

Messrs. Wm. Adams and Co., the successors to the historic family of potters have contributed an exceedingly valuable collection of Adams ware, probably the most representative that has ever been brought together. The collection, which occupies some four cases, represents various periods and different classes of ware, from the primitive slip decorated ware of the 17th century to the refined classic products in jasper of the 18th and 19th century. The earliest piece is a slip-decorated cradle as were frequently produced by the early Staffordshire potters. This piece, which has been in the Adams family for two hundred years, is attributed to Adam de Holden, and is believed to have been made at the Abbey Works in about 1690. Next in chronological order come several pieces of salt glaze, including a small teapot of what is known as the Astbury period – belonging to the early part of the 17th century. This is of special local interest, having been used

286. left: Percy W. L. Adams (aged 60), photographed in 1934 for the Staffordshire Advertiser's *series on County Notabilities*

287. below: A section of the Tunstall Museum, circa 1911, showing mostly Adams wares

by the ancestors of the Adams family at a breakfast on the occasion of Prince Charles Edwards's visit to Bagnall in 1745 ... other salt glaze pieces include a jug of the early 'scratched blue' variety and a fine soup tureen of the later period ... finely modelled Parian ... But the most important section is the large and representative collection of 18th century Adams jasper, mostly blue with white reliefs. There is a considerable variety of design and decoration, though, of course, the classic feeling pervades all these products, and the execution invariably shows a refinement, which gives them a high place amongst that signally beautiful ceramic of the 18th century jasper.

This valuable collection was transferred to Hanley in 1911, becoming part of The Potteries Museum collection when the six Staffordshire Potteries towns were amalgamated into the Federation of Stoke-on-Trent. It is interesting to note that Percy stated that the collection had cost him in the region of £250 but that they were now worth considerably more. The majority of the pieces had been purchased through Christie's salerooms and acquired from famous collectors and had not been passed down though the family. Even the great Josiah Wedgwood was known to have been sorry that he had not kept all representative samples of his work–clearly Adams too must have been negligent in this respect.

From 1911 to 1931 Percy was Hon. Secretary and Treasurer of the Staffordshire Parish Register Society and worked diligently to transcribe and print many records which otherwise might have been lost.

Among his well-received books were *A Short History of Wolstanton* and *Notes on North Staffordshire Families* and his magnum opus *The Adams Family of North Staffordshire*; in addition he contributed to other Staffordshire history publications.

In 1933 he received the Garner Medal from the North Staffordshire Field Club for his considerable

288. New Trubshaw Cross – erected on the ancient base at the junction of the three roads, Burslem, Tunstall and Porthill – presented to the city by Percy W.L. Adams, November 1949

contributions to the genealogical knowledge of Staffordshire, foremost among which was his work in transcribing and publishing the important Manor Rolls of Tunstall.

His association with the William Salt Archaeological Society spanned some fifty years, during which time he was appointed member of the council and a Trustee of the William Salt Library in Stafford. In recognition of his valuable historical work he was accepted as a Fellow of the Societies of Antiquaries of London.

His interest in local antiquities resulted in the repairing and restoration of a number of artefacts of considerable local historical importance, all of which were personally funded by Percy Adams:

1. 1932–the repair and restoration of the Saxon font in Stoke Parish church, which was re-dedicated by the Dean of Lichfield in March 1932, and the restoration of the ancient stone altar.

2. 1935–the re-erection of a fragment of a Pre-Norman Cross in Stoke churchyard which had been unearthed by the sexton in 1876 in the course of digging out a grave.

3. 1935–the repair and repainting of the church gates at St. John's Church, Burslem, and the planting of twenty poplar trees.

4. 1949–the erection of a new stone cross at Trubshaw Cross, installed on the old stone base where an ancient stone cross was situated. While laying out the roadside planting the City Parks Authorities had discovered an ancient stone plinth; this was re-erected at the centre of the traffic roundabout at Trubshaw Cross and has

289. above left: Fragment of a Pre-Norman Cross re-erected near its original position in the 25th year of the reign of George V (1935) by Percy W.L. Adams

290. above middle: The old Saxon font, prior to being relocated in Stoke parish Church

291. above right: Old Saxon font now installed at the north-east end of the nave of the parish church of Stoke-upon-Trent– restored by Percy W.L. Adams F.S.A. in 1931

Dawn of the Twentieth Century

292. below: *Poster announcing the Coronation festivities at Wolstanton on Thursday 22nd June 1911 (Councillor Percy Adams was to light the bonfire at 9pm)*

Wolstanton United Urban District Council.

CORONATION FESTIVITIES,

THURSDAY, June 22nd, 1911.

PROGRAMME OF EVENTS.

DIVINE SERVICE at St. Margaret's and St. Andrew's Churches at 11 a.m. And **UNITED SERVICE** at Wesleyan Chapel at 11 a.m.

THE PROCESSION which will include Cyclists (who are competing in the Parade), Friendly Societies, Police, Fire Brigade, P.E.T. Ambulance Corps, Boy Scouts, and Members of the Council, will assemble in the Ellison Street Council School Yard, from **1 30** to **1 45**, and will leave the Schools at **2** o'clock prompt, headed by the Silverdale Town Prize Band, taking the following Route—Orchard Street, Lily Street, High Street, St. Andrew's Church, Watland's View, Dimsdale Parade, Silverdale Road, into High Street, and on to May Bank, returning to the Marsh to join the Children's Assembly.

THE CHILDREN will assemble at the various Sunday Schools in accordance with their own Local Arrangements, and proceed to the Marsh for **2 45**, where they will be marshalled in the following order (so as to form a square around the Flag). St. Margaret's, St. Andrew's, Wesleyan New Connexion, Primitive, Congregational, and May Bank. The marshalling of the Children will be in charge of **Scout Master Slack**.

O'CLOCK
3 0—The Flag will be unfurled by Mrs. Henry Walklate. The Children will salute the flag, during which they will sing (accompanied by the Band) the National Anthem, and a selection of Coronation Music. The singing will be led by Messrs. Holdcroft, Wyborn and Taylor.

3 30—Entertainment by the Morris Dancers.

4 0—Children proceed to their various Schools for Tea.

O'CLOCK
4 0 to 5 0—INVITATION TEA to the Aged People will be served in the Ellison Street Council School.

5 0 to 6 0—Selections by the Silverdale Prize Band, and Performances by the Morris Dancers.

6 30—Distribution of Prizes by Mrs. C. J. WINN, to the successful competitors in the Cycle Parade.

7 0—MAYPOLE DANCE by St. Margaret's School Children, under Miss FROST.

Greasy Pole Climbing Competition, &c.

THE BONFIRE on the May Bank side of the Marsh will be lighted at **9 0** by Councillor P. W. Adams.

RESIDENTS (particularly those in the Route of Procession) are kindly requested to decorate their premises.

This Programme is subject to slight alterations or partial abandonment, should the weather turn out unfavourable.

By Order, and on behalf on the Committee,

HY. WALKLATE, Chairman.
WM. SIMON, General Secretary.

June 17th, 1911.

293. below: *Bonfire to mark the Coronation of George V, Wolstanton 1911*

since become a familiar landmark in the locality. The locality was named after a certain Thomas Trobbeschawe who was a juror at the great court of Tunstall held Tuesday 4 May 1378 in the first year of the reign of Richard II.

5. Additionally, a number of plaques and monuments in memory of the Adams family, erected in several Staffordshire churches, the oldest tablet installed in St. John's, Burslem, in 1917.

As part of the three days of celebration to mark the Coronation of King George V in June 1911, Wolstanton joined in with the national festivities; a poster chronicling the day's events announced a bonfire to be lit on the May Bank side of Wolstanton Marsh, to be lighted at 9 o'clock by Councillor P.W.L. Adams.

294. below: **Exhibition of modern pottery ware in the King's Hall, Stoke-on-Trent, 22nd and 23rd April 1913**

ROYAL TOUR OF THE POTTERIES IN 1913

On 22nd April 1913, King George V and Queen Mary visited Stoke as part of their tour of Staffordshire. The royal couple had intimated that they were keen to inspect articles of earthenware and china manufactured in the area.

The Mayor of Stoke had organised a committee representative of the pottery industry to arrange an appropriate display; the venue chosen was King's Hall Stoke. Percy Adams was nominated as honorary secretary to the committee and he must have worked tirelessly to ensure the event was a success. Manufacturers were invited to send examples of their wares, and, if possible, to be displayed in their own showcases.

In a letter dated 26th March 1913, Percy informed participants that

we are pleased to state that in conjunction with the display of the modern products alluded to, a large and fine Collection of 18th Century Pottery, selected from the Museum in the County Borough, for the purpose of illustrating the development of the Art of Potting, will be on view. Their Majesties are particularly interested in both modern and antique Pottery ...

It is highly probable that Percy's 18th-century Adams ware, deposited in the museum in 1908, formed a significant part of the museum's display.

295. below: Woore Manor, Shropshire–home of Percy W.L. Adams and family, photograph 1942

The *Staffordshire Advertiser* of Saturday, 19th April 1913 outlined the organisation of exhibits:

1. **Slip Decorated Pottery** (2 cases)
2. **Elers, Twyford and Astbury ware** (1 case)
3. **Salt-glazed ware** (4 cases)
4. **Whieldon Period ware** (4 cases)
5. **Jasper** (5 cases, Wedgwood, Adams, Turner, Neale & Co.)
6. **Stoneware** (1 case)
7. **Black Basalt** (2 cases)
8. **Cream-coloured Earthenware** (1 case-Wedgwood Queen's ware)

GIFTS TO THE KING AND QUEEN

Many gifts were presented to the Royal couple and William Adams & Co. headed the list:

For His Majesty the King – One earthenware bowl decorated from engravings (delicately coloured) of pictures from the works of Charles Dickens.

For Her Majesty the Queen – One pair of vases, 11 inches high on square plinths, in sage green jasper, cameo decoration in white relief of four Grecian female figures, emblematical of the seasons, each figure divided by Corinthian columns, bordered with interlacing circles; acanthus leafage in shape and form to a pair of Adams vases in the British Museum, made by William Adams, the well-known Staffordshire potter (1746-1805).

(*Melton Mowbray Times*, Friday 2nd May 1913)

The Royal presents were removed for display in Harrod's London. J.F. Blacker in *London Opinion*, 17th May 1913, commented,

I do hope some of you went to Harrods's to view the pottery exhibits removed from the King's Hall, Stoke which included the gifts to the King and Queen. I spent much time there, and I came to the conclusion that the potters had honoured themselves in presenting our illustrious

296. above: **Mrs Percy Adams in the morning room at Woore Manor, Shropshire**

Sovereigns with such a beautiful collection of fine porcelain and pottery. The Queen and Princess Mary visited the well-known Knightsbridge stores to see the splendid exhibition which in their recent tour, could only receive only scant attention from their Majesties. You will be glad to know that the Queen expressed herself as highly pleased and satisfied. Congratulations to the potters! Make no mistake; English wares are the best the world can produce.

On 26th April 1916, Percy married Ada Gladys, daughter of Archibald Douglas of Kingsland, Newcastle, Staffordshire, and High Park, Salwarpe, Worcestershire, a prominent Newcastle solicitor. An article in *The Lady* of May 27th described the occasion under the headline of *A Fashionable Marriage* and noted that it was held at St. George's, Newcastle, and officiated by The Reverend F.W. Greasley Douglas of Maidstone. The brother to the bride was assisted by Reverend C.J. Winn, Vicar of Wolstanton, and Mr. F.P. Adams attended his brother as best man. After a reception at the family home of Kingsland, Mr. and Mrs Adams drove to Stafford en route for London and a honeymoon in Torquay.

The newlyweds took up residence at Woore Manor, a large house standing in an elevated position in the middle of the village of Woore, shaded by fine tall trees. Percy had purchased it in 1911, some time after an earlier engagement to the daughter of Col. Charles James Briggs, J.P., D.L., of Hylton Castle, County Durham.

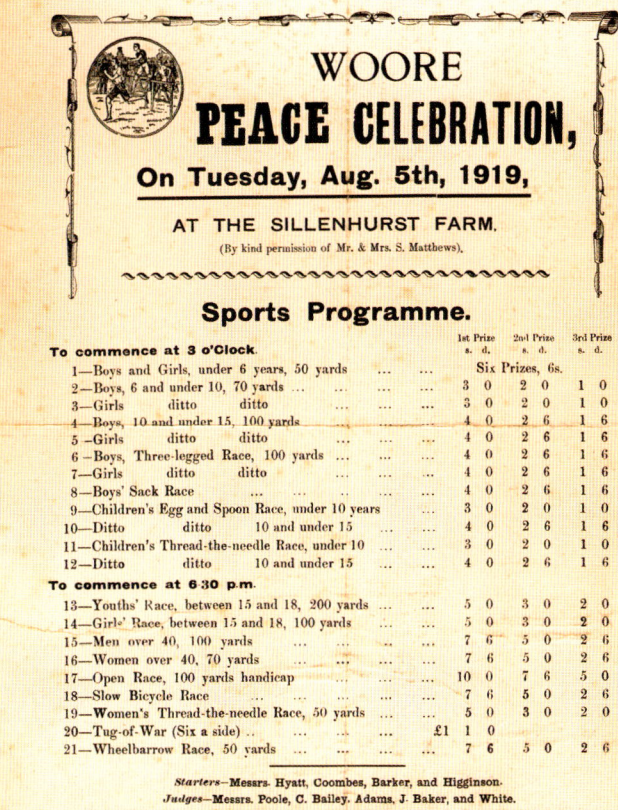

297. right: **Poster announcing the Peace Celebrations in the village of Woore, Tuesday 5th August 1919**

Percy was to spend the rest of his life at Woore Manor, a much-loved family home complete with Adams ceramic fireplaces bedecked with jasper figures, and, we are told, two different styles of water closets, each of course made by Wm. Adams & Co.

WOORE PEACE CELEBRATIONS 1919

Although the guns fell silent on 11th November 1918, the First World War did not officially end until the signing of the Treaty of Versailles in June 1919 when peace could be officially celebrated.

A month later, on 19th July, a massive victory parade was held in London with some 15,000 British Empire servicemen taking part, led by Allied commanders including Field Marshal Sir Douglas Haig and Marshall Ferdinand Foch. The architect Sir Edwin Lutyens had designed the Cenotaph as a focus for troops to salute the honoured dead as they marched along Whitehall, but the dignified memorial was yet to be built. On the victory parade a temporary structure of wood and plaster had been erected, the permanent stone memorial being finally erected in 1920.

Away from the capital many communities planned their own celebrations with Percy Adams and his family joining in with planned celebrations at Woore on 5th August 1919.

The local newspaper reported that the village was thronged with joyous spectators who lined the streets, awaiting the procession, which was headed by

the Madeley Silver Band, the finest ever witnessed in the township.

The local Lodge of Foresters was well represented by its members, with their regalia and banner. The humorous get-ups and antics of the 'Woore Surprise Band' caused continuous merriment. There was much competition for the prizes offered for the turn-outs, and the ingenuity and taste displayed were most commendable. The decorated waggon of the first prize winner in that section had tableaux vivants denoting parts of the Empire, surmounted by a beautiful representation of Peace. Most of the other conveyances had decorations that were admirably conceived and executed. There were many original ideas embodied in the humorous costumes, and all the prize-winners proved to be members of the redoubtable Surprise Band. The fancy costumes and trimmed hoops and wands of the School children were beautifully done and the Judges had a hard task in making their selections.

The Procession after its journey round Ireland's Cross and Gravenhunger, was drawn up in Woore Square, and presented a most interesting sight. Led by the Madeley Band, nearly 2,000 people, including many visitors joined in singing heartily three verses of the hymn, God our help in ages past, and also two verses of the National Anthem.

Through the generosity of Percy Adams, Esq.,

Dawn of the Twentieth Century

298. left: Advertising leaflet for Adams Calyx ware with The 'Chinese Bird pattern'

J.P., Manor House Woore, each child residing in the Shropshire part of Woore Parish was presented with a beaker in remembrance of England's Victory and the signing of the peace.

It is likely that Percy's commemorative beakers were made in Greengates works, which in 1919 concentrated on dinner and tea ware, jaspers and commemorative ware, while Greenfields produced mostly hotel and hospital ware.

An afternoon and evening of sporting events followed, held at a local farm, which, according to the poster of events, provided generous prize money for the winners.

Throughout the early decades of the 20th century, Percy, in his role as artistic director, was heavily influenced by early Adams ware, forever delving into old factory records for long forgotten patterns that could be revived–the 1910 revival of the chinoiserie pattern, the 'Chinese Bird', being a classic example of a pattern first employed by William Adams I in the late 18th century.

He also took inspiration from Charles Dickens and from illustrations in William Gilpin's 18th-century travel novels, as represented in the Adams' popular 'Doctor Syntax' wares. The late 1920s saw the introduction of their most acclaimed series, that of 'The Cries of London'. Based on the prints by Francis Wheatley, they portrayed a range of 18th-century London street vendors hawking their wares.

JOSIAH WEDGWOOD BICENTENARY CELEBRATIONS

From the week commencing 19th May 1930, Stoke-on-Trent took on a carnival feel, its smoke-grimed walls temporarily hidden by brightly coloured flags and buntings. The transformation was complete when individuals appeared in the city streets dressed in 18th-century apparel and it signalled the commencement of a week's celebration of two hundred years since the birth of Josiah Wedgwood.

Organisers promised a week of culture and entertainment with magnificent displays of modern and historical pottery complemented by historical pageants that would bring North Staffordshire's history alive for the masses.

On Sunday 18th May, an Inaugural Service was held at Stoke Parish Church of St. Peter ad Vincula with the Bishop of Winchester, the Right Reverend Theodore Woods, D.D., giving the sermon. Prior to arriving at the church the procession had halted at the grave of Josiah Wedgwood where the Lord Mayor laid a laurel wreath.

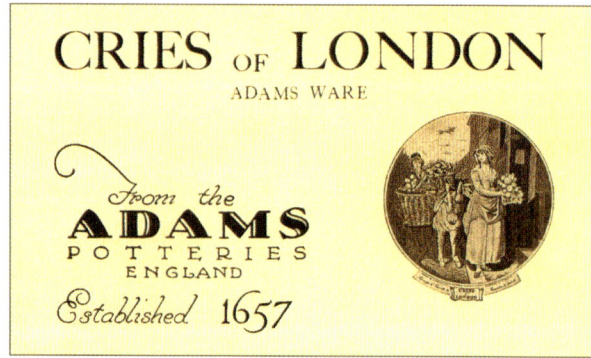

299. above: Adams 'Cries of London' series advert– introduced in the 1920s

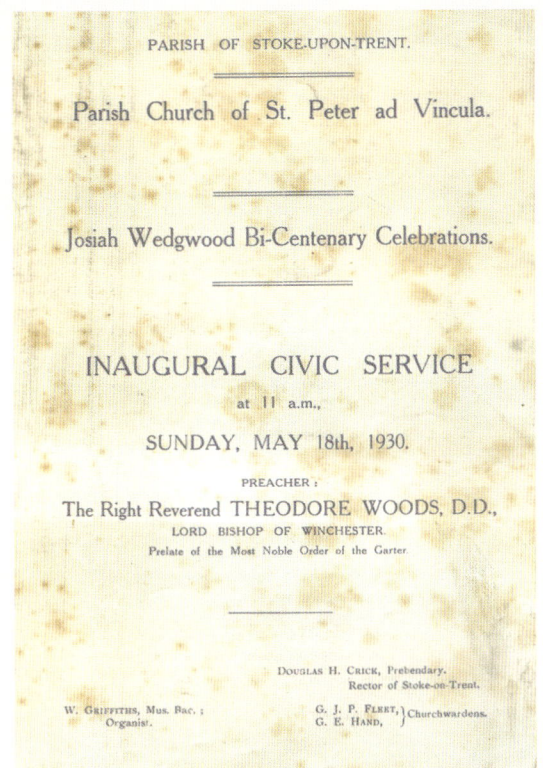

300. above: Cover of the Inaugural Civic Service at the Parish Church of St. Peter ad Vincula in 1930–part of the Josiah Wedgwood Bicentenary Celebrations

301. above: H.R.H. the Princess Royal and Countess of Harewood, (1926)

On Monday H.R.H. Princess Mary, Countess of Harewood, officially inaugurated the proceedings, arriving at Stoke Town Hall at 10.30 a.m. to a civic reception and the official opening of the Modern Pottery Exhibition in the King's Hall Stoke and later the Historical Exhibition at Hanley. After luncheon, Her Royal Highness proceeded to Hanley Park to witness the first of the planned Pageants of the History of the Potteries.

The spectators were further entertained in the evening to a Military Tattoo to close the first day's schedule of events. Each of the successive days followed the same organisation, although different distinguished guests opened each day's busy schedule:

Tuesday:	Transport Day
Wednesday:	Ceramic Day
Thursday:	Industrial Day
Friday:	Overseas Day

HISTORICAL POTTERY EXHIBITION

The historical exhibition had been housed in Hanley Museum and was comprised of both ceramic art and, interestingly, portraits aimed at illustrating the rise of the potter's craft from the late 17th century to the days of Wedgwood and his contemporaries. Listed among the portraits was Sir Joshua Reynold's studies of Josiah Wedgwood and his wife and the famous group painting of the Wedgwoods by the much-acclaimed George Stubbs. Among other portraits of early Staffordshire potters were paintings of Josiah Spode, William Adams and Thomas Minton.

Notable among the ceramic exhibits were prized examples of Wedgwood ware kindly lent by Her Majesty the Queen from her Windsor Castle Collection, including two cameo portraits of George III and Queen Charlotte.

302. above: **Josiah Wedgwood Bicentenary Celebrations**

Leading Staffordshire pottery firms were asked to provide examples of their most characteristic modern ware for the Stoke Exhibition and a number pledged to allow exhibition guests to visit their factories as part of the week's celebration, foremost among which were J. Wedgwood and Sons, Ltd., Etruria, William Adams and Sons, Ltd., Tunstall and Mintons Ltd., Stoke-on-Trent.

The Historical Pageant displays at Hanley Park were perhaps the most memorable attraction for many of the visitors, a significant number being children who had been given an afternoon's holiday each day of the celebrations. A covered auditorium had been erected in the park that seated 3,000 spectators. The sloping ground provided a spectacular view of the unfolding episodes that for the duration of the events consisted of a prologue and eight separate historical happenings in the history of North Staffordshire from the time of the Early Britons down to the present age. The episodes were designed to show the gradual growth of the Staffordshire pottery industry building to a climax with 'The Life of Wedgwood' represented in episode Six.

Episode Four took the audience back to the time of Hulton Abbey and the sad surrender of the abbey to the officers of Henry VIII. The entire scene, planned and acted mostly by teachers, education staff and senior pupils, was vividly described in the *Staffordshire Sentinel* of Thursday 8th May 1930:

It depicts the arrival of the Receiver General of Henry VIII outside the Abbey, cursing the slowness of the monks for keeping him waiting till the very cold eats into the marrow of our bones – a touch that the weather made it easy to be realistic about. The monks arrive in slow

303. above: Josiah Wedgwood Bicentenary Celebrations–the Ceramic Queen and her attendants. All represent famous potteries: Spode, Copeland, Minton, Wedgwood, Doulton, Adams, Booth and Meakin

procession, chanting and thereafter the scene is a contrast between the deep emotion of the monks at the loss of the Abbey and the matter-of-fact salesmanship and irreverence of the Receiver. It is a clever psychological study.

The Abbot was played by the vicar of Norton, the Rev. J. G. Hamlet, perhaps as a concession for lending valuable chalices and pattens, altar cloths and sanctuary chairs as props!

Episode Six involved 'The Life of Josiah Wedgwood' and was enthusiastically presented by employees of the Wedgwood firm, with over £200 subscribed by the company for dresses alone! A very polished performance was given by the cast, after, it is said, the endless practices in Etruria Park. All 900 employees of J. Wedgwood Ltd. were presented with a booklet entitled *The Story of Josiah Wedgwood* and a copy of the Wedgwood commemorative plate made in honour of the celebrations.

In addition to the historical narratives, each pageant was provided with musical accompaniment, both choral and orchestral, with carefully arranged displays of dancing, each episode lasting some two hours.

Altogether more than 5,000 individuals had participated in the pageants over the weeklong celebrations and over 50,000 had attended the performances; an equal number is thought to have attended the exhibitions.

THE ARRIVAL OF A LITERARY GIANT

Without art the crudeness of reality would make the world unbearable.

304. left: **George Bernard Shaw** (1856-1950). *Anglo-Irish playwright and political activist*

'You cannot know how I feel when I face such a magnificent company as I face today.' He said, 'I will have to write a play for you. It is such a splendid thing to think that I could have all this magnificent company and I should not have to think of the salaries list.' (Laughter)

In February 1933, The Princess Royal purchased some of 'The Cries of London' plaques, paying with a cheque which has been carefully preserved in the family archives. Additional royal purchases ensued in 1939 when H.R.H. Queen Mary bought a number of items from this popular series that was to continue to sell well for nearly sixty years.

As artistic director of William Adams and Sons, Percy was in a unique position, able to call on talented individuals to assist with his ventures. While compiling his epic tome on the Adams family of North Staffordshire, he is known to have dispatched artists working for the pottery far and wide to distant relations, with the aim of having family portraits of long-gone ancestors copied in order to enhance his publication and 'of course' to grace the walls of Woore Manor.

In his mission to produce imagery of his illustrious potting ancestors, Percy employed the services of Arnold Machin, a former Wedgwood designer and the creator, in 1966, of arguably the most reproduced work of art in history–the iconic portrait bust of the Queen which has appeared on more than 320 billion Royal Mail stamps since 1968.

Arnold Machin was a native of Stoke-on-Trent, born the year of the launch of the *Titanic*, and was a prolific and talented sculptor who rose to be a Master of Sculpture at the Royal Academy.

Percy is known to have commissioned at least one sculpture of an Adams family worthy from Arnold Machin A.R.A., in the form a magnificent bronze of William Adams of Bagnall (1736-1802) and possibly a similarly crafted bronze of Ralph Adams (1687-1766).

The organisers could well look back on a successful event that did much to bring Stoke and its staple industry to the notice of the country and beyond, but there was one last surprise visitor with a passion for art who anonymously attended an exhibition, that is, until he was recognised.

The *Belfast News Letter* of Friday 23rd May 1930 leads with the story:

Among the visitors to the Wedgwood Bi-centenary celebrations at Stoke-on-Trent yesterday was Mr. George Bernard Shaw, who motored over from Buxton.

He was first detected waiting patiently in the queue outside the exhibition of modern pottery. On being recognised, he was taken into the exhibition, and afterwards visited the exhibition of historic pottery, and went to the pageant in Hanley Park. Towards the close of the last episode in the pageant, Mr. Shaw addressed the thousands of performers from his box.

305. *Left:* Bronze bust of William Adams of Bagnall (1736-1802), by Arnold Machin

hard-working population, he unequivocally states that the Potteries were not worthy of the Potters, who overwhelmingly worked hard and took great pride in their labours.

It is not surprising that Priestley took time to visit the potteries and view at first hand the workforce at their toil, and it is revealing that he visited William Adams and Sons factories in the course of his research.

Possibly Percy or William had arranged for Priestley to be shown around the works by a young foreman who, he noted, referred to all the workpeople as either ladies or gentlemen. Even the young girls of sixteen, all sticky with printing ink, and the youths plastered in clay, were equally described in such a respectful manner.

ENGLISH JOURNEY

As previously mentioned, the renowned English novelist and playwright J.B. Priestley visited the city of Stoke-on-Trent as part of the research for what would become one of his most influential books, *English Journey*. The book professed to be a

rambling but truthful account of what one man saw and heard and felt and thought during his journey through England during the autumn of the year 1933.

Travelling by motor coach, Priestley shared his insights through some of his most memorable writing, on subjects from the last echoes of old rural England to the hideous deprivation of the industrial cities.

His perception of Stoke-on-Trent was still of six discreet little towns with everything seemingly on a small scale: there were no towering factories or huge warehouses and even the potbanks were, in his eyes, of a diminutive scale. The houses were described as stretching out in a ribbon development for miles upon miles, nearly all being primitive workmen's cottages.

In a scathing social commentary, he expressed outrage that good craftsmen, whose families had been working for generations, perhaps, for Wedgwood, Adams or Spode, should be condemned to live in such miserable circumstances. Expressing his admiration for the

306. *above: Cover of* English Journey *by J.B. Priestley*

Dawn of the Twentieth Century

307. above: **Civic Ceremony to open the first pair of semi-detached houses built on the old Greenfield site on Furlong Road (Percy W.L. Adams far right)**

Priestley described the pottery as a modern industry rooted in a traditional craft, a view possibly gleaned while watching a potter throwing a large meat dish on the wheel–an extremely challenging task which he performed with ease, as, probably, had his father and grandfather before him.

Priestley noted that the personal pride in their work set these pottery workers apart from the ranks of modern workmen, stating that they perceived that they were not merely doing a menial job, they were craftsmen doing a job that they were highly proficient at; they did not dawdle as was often the stance of workers who 'clocked in'; they were trusted and well respected by the management and the happy result of this mutual respect could be read in their faces.

It was a glowing accolade for the Adams management which was borne out by images in an Adams promotional booklet commissioned in the 1930s illustrating production both at Greenfield and Greengates works.

Post WW2 the family business was still overwhelmingly under control of the senior partners, William Adams VI and his brother Percy, respectively aged 76 and 70 in 1945, with neither showing any sign of standing down in favour of the younger Adams directors, namely Tony Adams and Joscelin, who had returned to the works after their wartime service.

In October 1945, the *Staffordshire Sentinel* reported a Civic Ceremony was held to formally open the first pair of semi-detached houses on the Furlong Road, Tunstall, where 330 houses were due to be constructed on land formerly part of the Greenfield works; 250 were scheduled to be sold and the remainder let. The cost of the houses to be sold was set at £850 freehold including all legal charges.

The news report concluded that Aneurin Bevan's talk of racketeers profiteering from such developments was not always the case. One firm in question had, between the two wars, raised their business to such efficiencies that they were able to build a thousand houses on the profit basis of £5 a house!

Among the dignitaries who formally opened the first pair of semi-detached houses were the Lord Mayor of Stoke-on-Trent, the Town Clerk, the Architects, Chairman of the Housing Committee and Mr Percy Adams (former owner of the site).

Although the Greenfield works continued to operate, its days would be numbered. By 1955, requiring extensive modernisation and suffering from subsidence due to coal mining by Adams in the 19th century, the historic pottery was abandoned and put up for sale.

A few years prior, on July 10th 1947, Lettice Carol Adams, Percy's only daughter, married Mr Frederick Lawrence MacCallum Dawson, BSc., son of Mr Frederick Lawrence McCallum Dawson, barrister-at-law of Redlands, Long Stanton, Cambridgeshire and of Pyapon, Burma. The fashionable wedding took place at St. Leonard's Church, Woore, and was conducted by the Rt. Reverend R.L. Hodson, the Lord Bishop of Shrewsbury. A reception for some 200 guests was held at Woore Manor after which the bride and groom left for a honeymoon on Exmoor. Among the many presents received was a handsome oak clock from the officials and office staff of Messrs. William Adams and Sons.

The wedding of Percy's son, Major Joscelin Francis Whieldon Adams R.E., T.D., took place in 1952 in less austere times. He married Miss Pamela Joan Peel, only daughter of Lieut. Colonel Wilmot R.B. Peel, O.B.E., and Mrs Peel of 50, Pont Street, London. The ceremony took place at Holy Trinity Church, Brompton, London, followed by a reception at the Hyde Park Hotel, after which the couple left to spend the honeymoon in Paris.

As was the established custom, the staff and employees of William Adams and Sons made a collection and presented the young couple with a television set.

A MAN OF ACTION REMEMBERED

Tragically, Percy Adams died aged 77 while visiting friends at Atherton, Cheshire, on the 6th December 1952, only three weeks before the demise of his older brother William Adams VI.

308. below: **St. Leonard's Parish Church, Woore**

309. left: Hugh Worthington Adams (1870-1928), the 2nd son of William Adams V

He had been a staunch church worker all his working life–for 30 years a member of the Woore Parochial Church Council and churchwarden of Woore and Wolstanton–and he had formed close associations with St. John's Parish Church, Burslem, and Stoke Parish Church.

His association with William Adams and Sons as a director had spanned more than half a century and in addition he had been a director of the Hope Silk Mills of Messrs. George Davenport Adams and Co. Ltd., Leek.

In the funeral address Preb. Linsley, former Vicar of Tunstall, said,

The generation in which Mr Adams lived was one of great changes, and any man who could adjust himself to the changes was a man of noble being and character. Mr Adams had been steeped in the nobility and fibre of a former generation, yet had adapted himself to modern conditions. He described Mr Adams as a student of rightful tradition, a man of research and lover of all that was good and true. He was a man of action who applied himself to good works with a sense of duty, courtesy and justice, tempered with charity. Mr Percy Adams rendered great service to both his Church and his contemporaries; he had a spirit of service to his fellow men, and was a quiet, self-effacing Christian.

His family later presented St. Leonard's Church Woore with entrance gates in memory of Percy, but his greatest legacy survives in the plethora of books he produced on North Staffordshire life and family histories, and his immensely valuable artistic contribution to Adams Ceramics in the 20th century.

HUGH WORTHINGTON ADAMS

Hugh, the second son of William Adams V, in line with family traditions, was educated at Rugby School, an institution in which he maintained a close interest throughout his life, being an authority on its early history–an interest he no doubt passed down to his youngest brother Percy.

Diverging from the family potting business, he followed a career in law, articled to Mr A. P. Llewellyn, a successful Tunstall solicitor, and was admitted a solicitor in 1893. By 1896 he was appointed Deputy Coroner and in 1901 Coroner for North-West Staffordshire, which at the time included the whole of the present city of Stoke-on-Trent. It was a post he was to hold for twenty-seven years.

During his long tenure, he conducted many important inquiries, including a number of colliery accidents, including the devastating Minnie Pit disaster of 12th January 1918, the worst ever recorded in the North Staffordshire Coalfield, when 155 men and boys died in an explosion due to firedamp (coal mine gases – predominantly methane). Although the official investigation failed to establish the cause of the ignition of the flammable gases, it did conclude that the explosion would not have been so extensive had the coal dust in the mine been systematically removed.

His glittering legal career came to an all-too-early end when he died on 19th March 1928. *the Staffordshire Advertiser* of March 24th 1928 summed up the loss to North Staffordshire:

Mr Hugh W. Adams was laid to his last resting place on Thursday, but it is hard to realise that we shall see him no more. For he was one of the biggest figures in the life of North Staffordshire. He was big in every sense of the term; tall and commanding of figure, large hearted, full of the zest for life, spacious in his capacity of friendship, conviviality and sympathy, possessed of a boundless sense of humour, and a doughty hater of shams, swanks, prigs (intellectual or moral) bores, and all smug and conceited persons were anathema to him. He brushed them out of his path like insects. He had a keen eye for the beauties of nature, and he detested cruelty either to children or animals, any guilty person whom he prosecuted for cruelty could rely only on just treatment, relentless and without trimmings. Hugh was easily the biggest figure amongst local advocates, and he was a great Coroner; indeed, in the opinion of the many journalists who have come to North Staffordshire from all corners of

310. left: Frank Pemberton Adams (1872-1919), 3rd son of William Adams V and sole proprietor of George Davenport Adams & Co. Silk Mills, Leek

the kingdom the best 'crowner' (as he always called his office) in the country.

For the last few months of his life Hugh had, on the orders of his doctor, journeyed to an Italian resort hoping it would aid his recovery, but it was sadly to no avail.

He was laid to rest in Stone Cemetery; an alabaster tablet with his family crest and with arms impaling that of his wife's was placed on the east wall of the chancel in Christ Church, Tunstall, bearing the following inscription:

Sacred to the memory of Hugh Worthington Adams of Stone in this County, Esquire, born 12th February 1870, died March 19th, 1928, Solicitor of this City, and for 27 years H.M. Coroner for North-West Staffordshire. (Second son of William Adams of Greenfields, near Tunstall, and Wolstanton. Lt. Col. 1st Batt. Rifles Vol., J.P., Staffordshire, a Warden of this Church, 1859-60)

After 28 years of marriage, he left a widow, Clarice Sophia, and two daughters: Geraldine Margaret born 1903, and Joan Elizabeth born 1907.

THE SILK MILLS OF DAVENPORT ADAMS & CO.

Frank Pemberton Adams, the third son of William Adams V, like his older brother Hugh, had chosen to follow a different career to his potting brothers William and Percy, joining his uncle's business running one of the largest silk mills in Leek.

Frank was educated at Repton School, later joining his uncle, Mr Ernest Andrew Worthington, at Messrs. A. J. Worthington and Co., Portland Mills. Some years later, with a sound knowledge of the trade, he set up in business on his own account under the name of Messrs. George Davenport, Adams and Company.

The pressure of running a large business must have taken its toll on Frank, whose health had been failing for many years, and came to its tragic end when he died aged only 48 on 5th November 1919 at his home, Roche Mount, Leek.

In his will, dated 26th March 1918, he left an estate valued at £39,476 and, after various bequests– including £500 to his manager Mr Fred Coates, who no doubt had been his mainstay in the challenging latter years–the residue of his large estate was shared equally among his three brothers and sister Cecily. The three brothers subsequently became directors of George Davenport, Adams and Company.

A GLIMPSE OF VICTORIAN STAFFORDSHIRE

Cecily Janet Adams was the second daughter of William Adams V and through her passion for photography she has gifted us a unique window into the privileged existence of the Victorian and Edwardian élite of Staffordshire.

311. right: Cecily Janet Adams (1866-1946), youngest daughter of William Adams V

312. A selection of portraits by Cecily Janet Adams (1894-1900)

A SELECTION OF PORTRAITS BY CECILY ADAMS

1896

William Simms Bull Junior. Cecily's cousin. He had a very successful career in musical theatre, becoming manager of the D'Oyly Carte Opera Company

1894

Old Slater, the gardener at William Adams V's home, The Oaks, Wolstanton. Cecily photographed many of the family's servants over a period of 20 years

1900

left. *A member of the 2nd Gloucester Regiment photographed in the yard of Moreton House*

1900

above. *A member of the 1st. South Staffs Regiment photographed in Wedgwood Street, Wolstanton*

left. *Robert Jeffcock of Harpenden, died in the Great War*

1896

Dawn of the Twentieth Century

Haymaking at Moreton House Farm 1902

313. CECILY'S IMAGES OF RURAL LIFE

Challinor's shooting party September 1890

Moreton House Servants 1898

314. SERVANTS AT WOLSTANTON

Moreton House servants 1905

315. left: *Cecily Janet Adams* (1866-1946)

From the early 1850s, women in the upper and middle classes had been attracted to photography, although the sheer cost of photographic materials and equipment meant that it was the pursuit of the most affluent in society. In this respect, Cecily Adams, the younger daughter of William Adams V, was well placed to pursue her hobby.

Her early attempts at photography, dating from the 1880s when she was still a young adult, focus on her immediate family and are seen as domestic photography, narrating family life and capturing many images of her parents, siblings and close relatives – an admirable example of the typical treasured Victorian family album.

The classic Victorian album was designed to resemble the traditional family Bible, often with heavily embossed leather bindings and sturdy metal clasps. The Adams album, preserved in the family archives, became a treasured repository of family photographs, or, as one Victorian commentator predicted,

> *the family album will supersede the first leaf of the Family Bible and become an illustrated book of genealogy.* (Anon. 1861)

As her expertise developed, she broadened her focus to encompass images of her friends and social groupings, providing us with a unique insight into the privileged world of leisure experienced by Staffordshire's élite in the late Victorian and early Edwardian period, with endless rounds of shooting parties, tennis, cricket and hockey matches.

The early 1890s saw her focus shift to portrait photography. Her striking images demonstrate an awareness of the importance of lighting in capturing an effective portrait, and the need to put sitters at their ease in order to capture a natural expression. Her self-portraits taken at this time exude a striking air of confidence with a remarkable attention to detail and general composition, skills that had been honed through years of practice and through entering a great many photographic competitions in the *Amateur Photographer*. Through such entries she was able to elicit valuable professional feedback that she systematically entered into her photographic albums.

Carrying her unwieldy tripod and mounted plate camera she sought to capture the world around her, from the industrial landscape to local antiquities and many important buildings that have long since vanished from the county. She captured friends and family on holidays on the North Wales coast and further afield in Whitby and the Lake District.

Her rich and varied portfolio, entrusted to the care of descendants, remained relatively undiscovered for well over a century, and now yields a rare insight into her privileged life.

Curiously, her photographic work seems to have come to an abrupt end in 1913, with no further examples of her work having been preserved in albums. Aged 47 years, Cecily switched her attention to charity work and in 1914 she took on the post of president of the Potteries Division of the Soldiers, Sailors and Airmen Association–a position she held until 1938–and also generously supported many local good causes.

She maintained a great interest in Staffordshire County Cricket and the local Porthill Park Cricket Club that was based near to her home, The Little Croft, in Wolstanton.

Cecily died on 28th of June 1946 aged 80 and was buried beside her sister Mildred and her parents in Wolstanton churchyard, the parish church she had been such an avid supporter of throughout her life. An armorial tablet to her memory was erected on the south wall of the chancel of St. Margaret's Church, Wolstanton.

THE BAGNALL, FENTON HALL & GREENFIELD LINE OF ADAMS MASTER POTTERS

WILLIAM ADAMS III
1772-1829

WILLIAM ADAMS IV
1798-1865

EDWARD ADAMS
1803-1872

LEWIS ADAMS
1805-1850

WILLIAM ADAMS V
1833-1905

WILLIAM ADAMS VI
1868-1952

PERCY W.L. ADAMS
1875-1952

WILLIAM ANTHONY ADAMS
1909-1985

JOSCELIN F.W. ADAMS
1919-1991

317. right: The Adams backstamp—used from 1966 when William Adams & Sons (Potters) Limited became a subsidiary of Wedgwood Limited

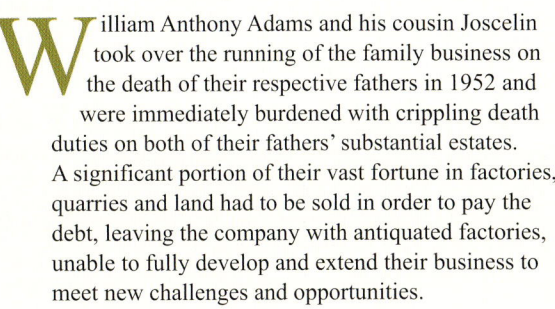

10
1909-1966
THE LAST OF THE ADAMS MASTER POTTERS

William Anthony Adams and his cousin Joscelin took over the running of the family business on the death of their respective fathers in 1952 and were immediately burdened with crippling death duties on both of their fathers' substantial estates. A significant portion of their vast fortune in factories, quarries and land had to be sold in order to pay the debt, leaving the company with antiquated factories, unable to fully develop and extend their business to meet new challenges and opportunities.

The lifting of the government's restriction on the selling of decorated ware in 1952 resulted in a much-welcomed improvement in home sales that necessitated an increase in production. This was achieved by the replacement of two of Greengates' old inefficient bottle kilns with tunnel kilns in 1955. A year later the remaining bottle ovens would be redundant, forced to shut down as a result of the Clean Air Act of 1956.

The level of trade seems to have been sufficient to support both factories, but the management, realising that Greenfield needed modernising, instigated a structural survey which revealed extensive subsidence due to the coal workings carried out by the family over the previous century. The land would not support any building work or, for that matter, an updated kiln. The fate of the historic pottery was sealed: its work was transferred to Greengates and the Greenfield site was abandoned in 1955. It was later put up for sale, eventually selling after many years in 1959.

The latter years of the 1950s looked more encouraging for the Adams family, with only the Greengates Works to manage and a workforce of some four hundred. At this time 60 per cent of the factory's output went overseas and the home market appeared promising as Britain came out of the bleak years of post-war austerity.

318. right: Greenfields Pottery, circa 1960

319. Aerial photograph– Greengates Works in the foreground, the Greenfield Works in the distance

The Last of the Adams Master Potters 289

320. below: **Plan of the Adams' Works at Greengates, Greenfield and Newfield,** Tunstall, circa 1900

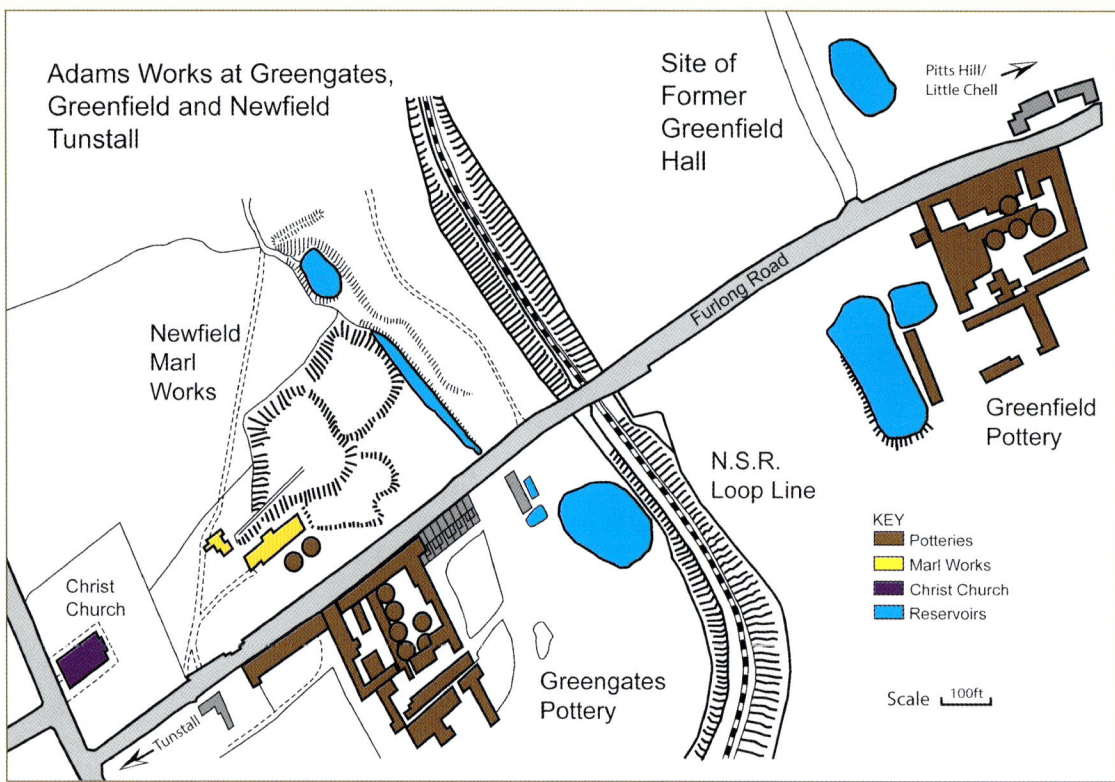

With William Anthony Adams at the helm as managing director, Joscelin sought to develop new innovative products. Working with the British Ceramic Manufacturer's Association, he developed 'Micratex', a ceramic body that was as strong as porcelain but less prone to chipping than Adams ironstone ware. Micratex was primarily aimed at the hotel and catering market, where its greater strength and anti-chipping properties were seen as a highly desirable feature.

But the cards were stacked against them: they had an ageing pottery facility that desperately required modernising, and much of their output was still painted in the costly freehand method (as opposed to that of many competitors who used the considerably cheaper lithography techniques).

In 1963, aware that the end was in sight, Joscelin left the family firm and took up a position as a director at Murray Curvex Printing Limited of Gloucester, leaving William Anthony Adams to continue at Greengates. Realising that its future was limited, he reluctantly sold the historic works to Josiah Wedgwood Ltd. in 1966 and retired to Stone in Staffordshire.

A poignant newspaper cutting preserved in the family archives dated 1966 captures the sad demise of the historic firm:

The end – after 517 years

The famed Adams pottery firm – the oldest family business in Britain – is finally to surrender its independence. After 517 years.

321. below: Joscelin Francis Whieldon Adams (1919-1991) of Greenfield and Greengates

As news was released that the whole of the Adams share capital has been bought by the Josiah Wedgwood concern, 56-year-old managing director Anthony Adams – the 17th generation – admitted: 'This is a sad day. I cannot pretend it is not.'

Mr Adams is the last of the family still in the firm. He has two sons, 17-year-old William – over the centuries tradition had decreed that every eldest Adams must be named William – and Michael, 11. Both are still at school.

Mr Adams said: 'The takeover happened very quickly. Negotiations began only two months ago. The merger takes effect on January 1st'

Mr Adams added: 'We are very proud of our history here. But nowadays the dice is loaded against the feudal type factories which family businesses are apt to be.

Yesterday Mr Arthur Bryan, managing director of Wedgwoods, promised: 'The Adams name and identity will be retained.'

Said Mr Adams: 'I shall be staying on for a while. But I hope the family tradition we have been so proud of will always remain.'

Ironically, the merger brings history full circle. For the original Josiah Wedgwood was once a tenant of an Adams factory. When the then William Adams came of age he took it over – and Josiah left to found his own firm in 1759.

POIGNANT MEMORIES OF THE END OF AN ERA

In later retirement Joscelin Adams reflected on his personal impressions of the three decades he spent working in the family business, recording these important recollections of the final years of William Adams and Company.

It is wholly appropriate to permit the last of this historic line, the seventeenth and sadly the final generation, to portray the works as witnessed by him, and where possible to quote directly from Joscelin's own accounts:

I began work at Greenfield after leaving school in 1936. Greenfield had been reduced somewhat in size to a five bottle oven factory having been a seven bottle oven. We had just had the depression in the early thirties.

An estate map of the Adams works, showing Greenfield, Greengates and Newfield (image 320) encapsulates the extent of the family's potting concerns, still intact in Joscelin's time.

He recalled that

> Greenfield was a very well laid out factory … the design was very good on the whole and work flowed from department to department. A five oven factory such as Greenfield would normally consist of two biscuit ovens and two glost ovens; with these in full production you could expect to do two biscuit ovens per week, and four or possibly five glost ovens per week. In addition there were three enamel kilns which were used before World War I, although most of the decorating was done at Greengates.

Raw materials came into a railway siding between Greenfield and Greengates in waggons, with William Adams written on the sides, as opposed to in the 19th century when canal transport had been relied upon to transport the raw materials.

From the sidings, it was a short haul to take the clay to the claybank at Greenfield where it would stay for some time to be weathered. Transporting the clay to the factory would no doubt have been by horse and cart.

Joscelin noted:

> We did actually have five carters and five carthorses. They used to take tremendous pride in their horses. The leather and brass work would be beautifully polished. I remember one shire called 'Prince', it was one of the most beautiful animals I think one could ever see and so docile and quiet.

From the claybanks the clay would be taken to the blungers where it was stirred up with water and ground calcined (burnt) flint and other materials were added. The resulting mixture entered a filter press where the water was extruded.

Image 322 outlines the pottery production at Greenfield and contemporary images for both Greengates and Greenfield factories have been furnished with a commentary by Joscelin.

Although predominantly based at Greenfield, Joscelin did occasionally venture to the adjoining works. One such foray was noted by him:

> As soon as I left school I went to work at Greenfield where I didn't really know much about what was going on at Greengates. If I had a bit of spare time I would go up there and have a look around. In fact I found a couple of jasper vases in the clay state and surreptitiously took them back to Greenfield where I had them fired. We have them here now at Coombe House. They are quite interesting in being the last pieces of jasper ever made by us and one is not quite complete although that is not very easily noticed.

Preserved in the family collection are two of the most likely vases that Joscelin so carefully rescued:

1. A scroll-handled vase and cover.

2. A light blue dip, jasper bowl with pedestal and drum stand decorated in applied white relief, which together with its missing lid would have been an Adams second period jasper product c.1900-1936 described as a potpourri lidded pedestal urn.

Either or indeed both jasper vases are symbolically highly important, as they could well be the last jasper ever to be produced in the historic Greengates.

Joscelin's intentions were to describe the Greengates works in the late forties and early fifties, but sadly his vivid recordings stop abruptly as his health took a turn for the worse.

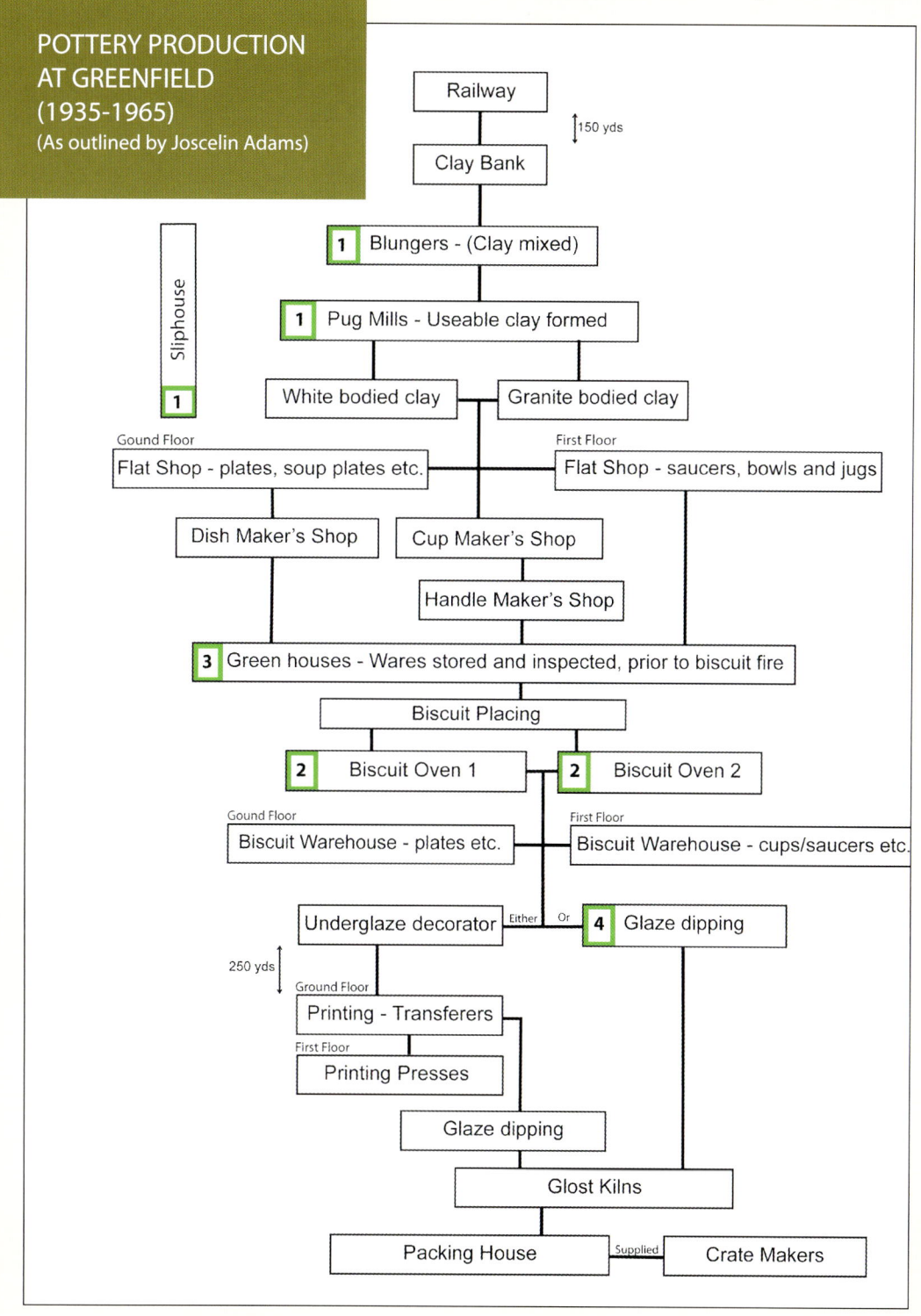

322. below: A flow chart of the pottery production at Greenfields between 1936 and 1965 as outlined by Joscelin F.W. Adams

GREENFIELD FACTORY

SLIPHOUSE

From the claybank, clay would be taken to blungers where the clay was stirred up with water ready to be mixed with the ground materials. The filter press extruded the water and clay was taken out in slabs

DIPPING

From the biscuit warehouse the ware went either to the underglaze decorator or into the dipping house where it was dipped with glaze and then went on to the biscuit ovens

323. Joscelin F.W. Adams' recollections of the Greenfield Works

INTERIOR OF BISCUIT OVEN

It took exactly a week to place, fire and draw a biscuit oven. We produced ware from two biscuit ovens every week. I cannot remember exactly how much but my guess is that somewhere between 50,000 dozen ware were made at Greenfield each week

(Commentary by Joscelin Adams)

BISCUIT PLACING

The glost kilns like the biscuit were old intermitted bottle ovens and the ware would be placed in saggers. The saggers were made on our own premises ... from our own brick and marl works

GENERAL OFFICE

The main office for both factories was at Greenfield so that there was a general office and a private office which was the main office where all the accounting etc was done

The Last of the Adams Master Potters

GREENGATES FACTORY

GRINDING MILL AT GREENGATES

There was no grinding mill at Greenfield after the turn of the century. It had an old beam engine and the beam broke but by that time we obtained the Greengates factory and used the Greengates mill

MODELLING AND MOULD MAKING - GREENGATES

Head of Modelling - Ezra Ball, and his son worked with him and later his grandson. He was still working part time at aged 86 and was given the B.E.M. for long service

UNDERGLAZE PAINTING

FREEHAND PAINTING - GREENGATES

There were one hundred and twenty paintresses working at Greengates with many starting their employment straight from school

PRINTING SHOP GREENGATES

Greenfield was still being rebuilt in the mid-twenties and it wasn't until that was finished they started to rebuild Greengates. The outputs of both factories would be about the same, except many more facilities for decorating at Greengates

(Commentary by Joscelin Adams)

The printing shop was at least two hundred and fifty feet from the biscuit warehouse and all the ware had to be carried in the open air by hand

325. below: **William Adams and Sons letter heading,** circa 1950s

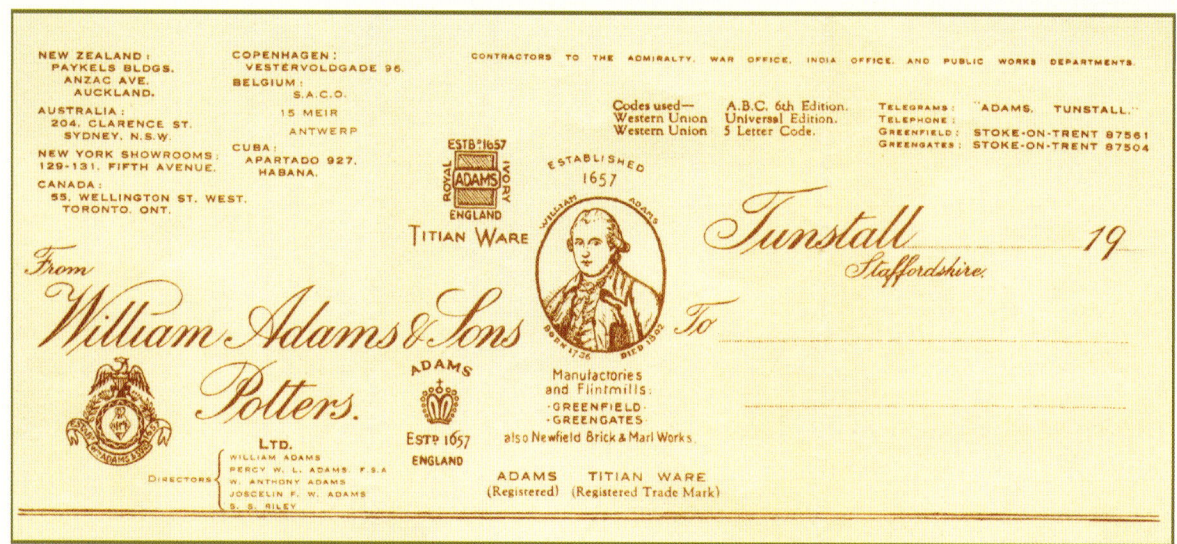

GREENGATES POTTERY UNDER WEDGWOOD

On merger, William Adams & Sons Ltd. was incorporated into the Wedgwood Fine Earthenware Division and received an injection of capital. Production in the first year increased by 92 per cent and the workforce increased from 340 to 410–a welcome trend that was maintained into the 1970s.

In 1984 the Wedgwood Group merged with the Waterford Glass Company and sadly William Adams (Potters) Ltd did not survive the subsequent reorganisation.
By 1992 all commercial activities had ceased at the

326. right: Possibly the last jasper ware to be produced at the historic Greengates Pottery, described as a:

Light blue dip jasper vase with white upward curving handles ending in scrolls. The vase rests on a square plinth. White relief decoration includes four female figures each within an arcaded columned segment, acanthus leaves, interlocking circles, and lotus leaves.
Circa 1900, 11 inches high

Adams Ceramics, 1999

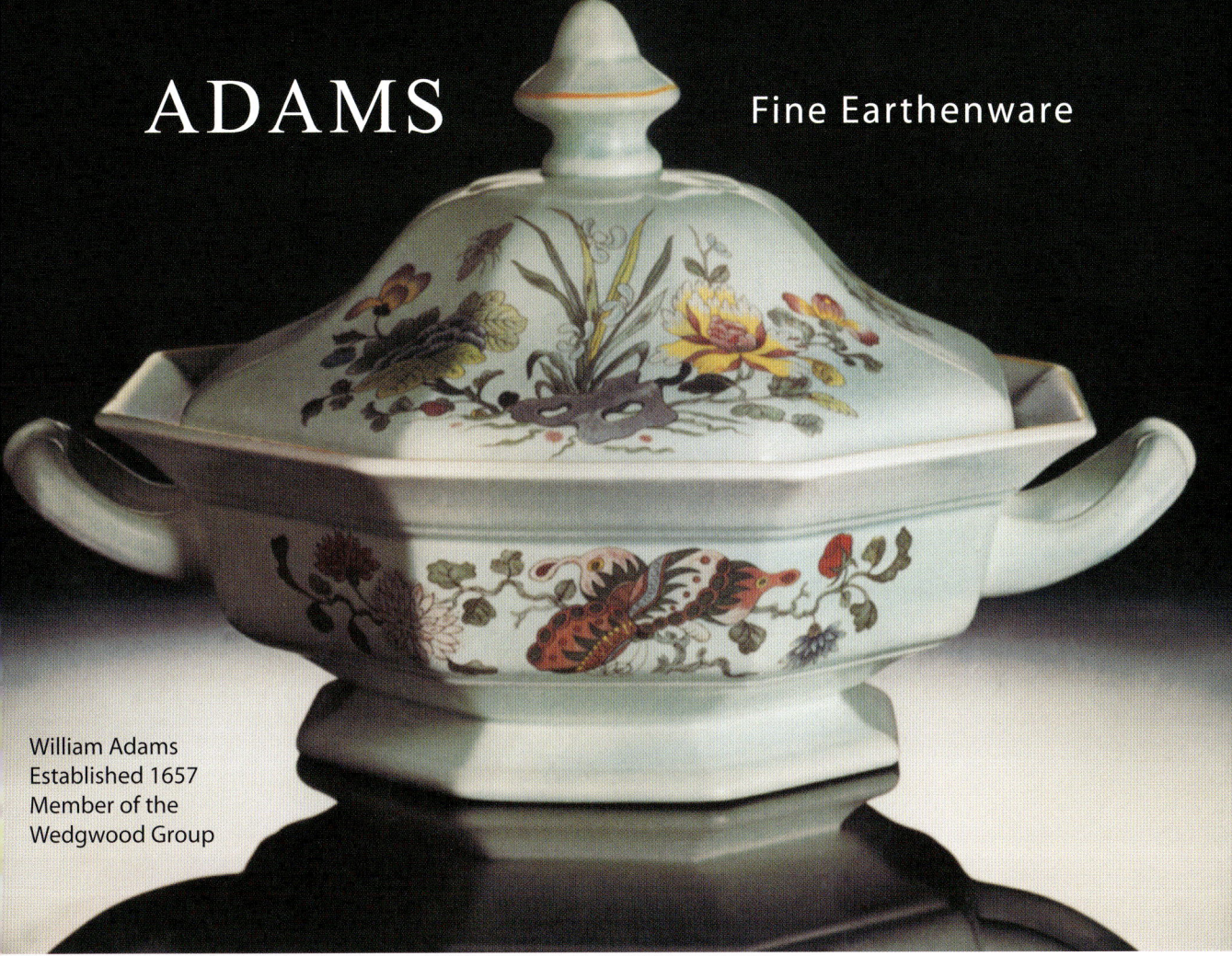

327. above: Cover of a Wedgwood Group leaflet for the earthenware series, Ming Jade–recognising the fact that many Adams' designs were influenced by the Orient

Greengates factory and it was put up for sale, only to be badly damaged by fire and threatened with demolition.

Protestors quickly mobilised in an attempt to save this important part of Stoke-on-Trent's potting heritage. In a final flourish Joscelin's widow Pamela Adams enthusiastically added her weight to the rescue attempt, commenting in an article in the *The Staffordshire Sentinel* of 15th September 1995 that

> preserving the frontage of the historic Greengates factory would be a worthwhile contribution to our dwindling industrial heritage.

But to no avail. The historic pottery was deemed unsafe and, despite many protestations, was demolished in 1995.

With it disappeared the last visible remains of Adams' two-hundred-year-old link to Tunstall's important potting history.

PHOTOGRAPHIC CREDITS

Every effort has been made to secure the permission of the copyright holders of images used and credits listed as requested. Any deficiencies brought to our attention will be corrected in subsequent editions.

For the many individuals and institutions who allowed images to be used free of charge, the author would like to offer sincere thanks for their generosity and support.

All numbers are reference to images in the book

Adams Family Archive 9, 21, 22, 24, 32, 41, 49, 57, 63, 83, 102, 103, 108, 109, 110, 114, 115, 116, 117, 118, 120, 124, 125, 129, 130, 131, 133, 134, 138, 139, 140, 141, 142, 144, 145, 147, 148, 149, 150, 152, 153, 156, 157, 159, 160, 164, 167, 168, 173, 175, 177, 178, 179, 181, 182, 188, 189, 190, 193, 194, 195, 196, 202, 206, 215, 216, 218, 219, 224, 225, 231, 232, 233, 234, 237, 238, 244, 248, 253, 254, 262, 264, 270, 271, 272, 274, 275, 276, 279, 280, 282, 283, 284, 285, 286, 287, 288, 290, 292, 294, 295, 296, 297, 298, 299, 300, 302, 303, 305, 307, 309, 310, 316, 317, 318, 319, 321, 323, 324, 325, 326, 327

Alamy 14, 26, 71, 236

Author's Collection 4, 5, 7, 25, 35, 48, 50, 51, 52, 53, 62, 85, 89, 111, 112, 123, 126, 135, 136, 137, 146, 154, 158, 180, 192, 199, 201, 203, 204, 210, 211, 212, 213, 214, 226, 228, 230, 235, 243, 245, 246, 247, 249, 250, 251, 252, 255, 257, 258, 259, 260, 263, 268, 269, 273, 293, 311, 312, 313, 314, 315

British Library 3

British Museum 99, 132

Jonathan Gray 163, 166, 169

The Metropolitan Museum of Art 27

The Nelson-Atkins Museum of Art 54

The Potteries Museum and Art Gallery 1, 43, 67, 90, 101, 113

V & A Museum 29, 56

Wedgwood Museum 33

P. N. Williams (photographs) 6, 12, 13, 37, 38, 39, 58, 61, 65, 73, 77, 78, 79, 84, 104, 151, 162, 217, 220, 221, 222, 223, 229, 239, 240, 242, 261, 265, 266, 289, 291, 308

Wikipedia 2, 11, 15, 19, 23, 28, 30, 31, 34, 36, 42, 44, 46, 47, 55, 59, 68, 69, 74, 75, 76, 80, 81, 82, 93, 95, 96, 97, 98, 100, 105, 106, 107, 121, 122, 174, 183, 184, 185, 187, 198, 207, 208, 209, 241, 277, 278, 281, 301, 304, 306

BIBLIOGRAPHY *By Chapters*

The following publications were extensively utilised during the writing of this book and are clearly identified as sources that relate to a number of different chapters:

P. W. L. Adams, *A History of the Adams Family of North Staffordshire and of their connection with the development of the Potteries* (London, 1914): Supplement 1, 1925; Supplement II, 1940; Supplement III, 1949

P. W. L. Adams, *Notes on some North Staffordshire Families, including those of Adams, Astbury, Breeze, Challinor, Heath, Warburton &c.* (Tunstall, 1930)

Robert Nicholls, *Ten Generations of a Potting Family: Founded Upon 'William Adams: An Old English Potter'* (Stoke-upon-Trent, 1949)

Derek Peel, *A Pride of Potters* (London, 1957)

William Turner, *William Adams: An Old English Potter* (London, 1923)

John Ward, *The Borough of Stoke-upon-Trent* (London, 1843)

Chapter 1 – Early Adams Ancestors (1299-1534)

P. W. L. Adams, Burslem Parish Registers (Staffordshire Parish Registers Society, 1913)

W. Boyd, 'The Muster for Staffordshire AD 1539' (Hundreds of Cuttlestone and Pyrehill). Copied from the original in the Public Record Office, pp. 233-324. Published in 1902 by the Staffordshire Record Society, *New Series Volume 5*

William Burton, *Josiah Wedgwood and His Pottery* (London, 1922)

Raphael Holinshed, *Holinshed's Chronicles of England, Scotland, and Ireland*, ed. Vernon F. Snow (New York, 1965)

Eliza Meteyard, *The Life of Josiah Wedgwood From His Private Correspondence and Family Papers* (London 1865)

Harold Owen,	*The Staffordshire Potter* (London, 1901)
Robert Plot,	*The Natural History of Staffordshire* (1686)
Z. Razi, ed.,	*Medieval Society and the Manor Court* (1996)
G. W. Rhead and F. A. Rhead,	*Staffordshire Pots & Potters* (New York, 1907)
J. Ritson,	*The Jurisdiction of the Court Leet* 1809 (Google Books)
Simeon Shaw,	*History of the Staffordshire Potteries, and the rise and progress of the manufacture of pottery and porcelain, with notices of eminent potters* (London, 1900)
Samuel Smiles,	*Josiah Wedgwood his Personal History* (London, 1894)
John Thomas,	*The Rise of the Staffordshire Potteries* (Bath, 1971)
J. C. Wedgwood,	*Staffordshire Pottery and its History* (London, 1913)
Wikipedia,	'Court Leet' (www.wikipedia.org)
Wikipedia,	'Frankpledge' (www.wikipedia.org)
Wikipedia,	'Manorial Court' (www.wikipedia.org)

Chapter 2 – Hulton Abbey and the Dissolution (1223-1536)

P. W. L. Adams,	*Wolstanton* (Tunstall, 1908)
Steve Birks,	'Notes on the history of Stoke-on-Trent: Abbey Hulton' (www.thepotteries.org)
B. J. Bridgwood and Ingval Maxwell,	'The Potteries and Surrounding Areas Part 1: Understanding the Region'- (A COTAC Regional Study, 2019)
British History Online	'Houses of Cistercian monks: The Abbey of Hulton'(www.british-history.ac.uk)

William Burton,	*Josiah Wedgwood and His Pottery* (London, 1922)
L. Butler,	*The Cistercians in England and Wales* (1982)
P. H. Ditchfield, ed.,	*Memorials of Old Staffordshire* (London, 1909)
Vincent Eley,	*A Monk at the Potter's Wheel* (Leicester, 1955)
M. W. Greenslade,	'A History of Burslem': Being an extract from *The Victoria History Of The County Of Stafford, Volume III* (Reprinted, Staffordshire County Library, 1983)
Arthur Hayden,	*Chats on Old Earthenware* (New York, 1909)
F. A. Hibbert,	*Dissolution of the Monasteries* (London, 1910)
F. A. Hibbert,	*Monasticism in Staffordshire* (Stafford, 1909)
C. Lynam,	'Recent Excavations on the Site of Hulton Abbey, Near Stoke-upon-Trent, Co. Stafford', *Journal of the British Archaeological Association* (1885)
A. R. Mountford,	'Hulton Abbey, Stoke-on-Trent, Staffs – Excavations and Restoration 1959-1966', *SOTMAS Report 2*, 15-20
G. W. Rhead and F. A. Rhead,	*Staffordshire Pots & Potters* (New York, 1907)
Simeon Shaw,	*History of the Staffordshire Potteries* (Hanley, 1829)
Stebbing Shaw,	*History and Antiquities of Staffordshire* (Stafford, 1801)
John L. Tomkinson,	'A History of Hulton Abbey' (*Staffordshire Archaeological Studies No. 10*, 1997)
E. J. D. Warrilow,	*A Sociological History of the City of Stoke-on-Trent* (Hanley, 1960)
G. W. O. Woodward, Wikipedia,	*The Dissolution of the Monasteries* (1985) 'Cistercians' (www.wikipedia.org)
Wikipedia,	'Dissolution of the Monasteries' (www.wikipedia.org)

Chapter 3 – Butterpots, Tygs and Quagmires (17th and 18th century)

T. Allbut,	*View of the Staffordshire Potteries. Burslem* (1800)
B. J. Bemrose,	*Newcastle under Lyme: its contribution to the growth of the North Staffordshire pottery industry 1650-1800* (unpublished MA thesis, University of Keele, 1972)
C. F. Binns,	*The Story of the Potter* (London, 1898)
Anthony Burton,	*Josiah Wedgwood: A Biography* (New York, 1976)
William Burton,	*Josiah Wedgwood and His Pottery* (London, 1922)
William Chaffers,	*Marks and Monograms on European and Oriental Pottery and Porcelain* (London, 1891)
G. Cooper,	*Farmers and Potters: A History of Pre-Industrial Stoke-on-Trent* (Leek, 2002)
P. H. Ditchfield, ed.,	*Memorials of Old Staffordshire* (London, 1909)
E. A. Downman,	*English Pottery and Porcelain* (New York, 1904)
R. G. Haggar, R. Mountford and J. Thomas,	*The Staffordshire Pottery Industry* (Stafford, 1981)
Arthur Hayden,	*Chats on Old Earthenware* (New York, 1909)
B. Hodgkiss,	*Mother Burslem: A Burslem History* (Leek, 2001)
Llewellynn Jewitt,	*The Ceramic Art of Great Britain: From Pre-Historic Times Down to the Present Day* (London, 1878)
Alison Kelly,	*The Story of Wedgwood* (New York, 1962)
A. Meigh,	*The Potters of the Staffordshire Potteries* (Privately Published, 1937)
R. Plot,	*The Natural History of Staffordshire* (Oxford, 1686)
F. Redfern,	*History of the Town of Uttoxeter* (1865)

G. W. Rhead,	*The Earthenware Collector* (New York, 1920)
Simeon Shaw,	*History of the Staffordshire Potteries* (Hanley, 1829)
L. N. Solon,	*The Art of the Old English Potter* (New York, 1906)
J. Thomas,	*The Rise of the Staffordshire Potteries* (Somerset 1971)
L. Weatherill,	*The Pottery Trade and North Staffordshire 1660-1760* (Manchester, 1971)
J. C. Wedgewood,	*Staffordshire Pottery and its History* (1913)

Chapter 4 – The Mysterious Dutchmen of Bradwell (1688-1700)

P. W. L. Adams,	'The Rise and Progress of the Art of Pottery in North Staffordshire' in *Memorials of Old Staffordshire*, ed. P. H. Ditchfield (London, 1909)
P. W. L. Adams,	*Wolstanton* (Tunstall, 1908)
Cyril Andrade,	*Old English Pottery: Astbury Figures* (London, 1924)
Diane Baker,	*Potworks: The Industrial Architecture of The Staffordshire Potteries* (London, 1991)
William Chaffers,	*Marks and Monograms on European and Oriental Pottery and Porcelain* (London, 1891)
A. H. Church,	*English Earthenware* (London, 1884)
A. H. Church,	*Josiah Wedgwood: Master-Potter* (London, 1903)
Brian Dolan,	*Wedgwood – The First Tycoon* (London, 2004)
Major Cyril Earle,	*The Earle Collection of Early Staffordshire Pottery* (London, 1915)
G. W. Elliott,	'Staffordshire Red and Black Stonewares' – A paper read by G.W. Elliott at the Victoria and Albert Museum on 18 October 1975

Gordon Elliott,	'The Elers in Staffordshire', in *Aspects of Ceramic History: A Series of Papers Focussing on the Ceramic Artifact as Evidence of Cultural and Technical Developments* (2006)
Frank Falkner,	*The Wood Family of Burslem* (London, 1912)
Ann Finer and George Savage, eds,	*The Selected Letters of Josiah Wedgwood* (London, 1965)
W. B. Honey,	'Elers Ware', a paper read at 9, Queen Anne Street W. on December 13th 1932, E.C.C. trans., Vol.1, No 2 (1934)
Llewellynn Jewitt,	*The Ceramic Art of Great Britain: From Pre-Historic Times Down to the Present Day* (London, 1878)
Llewellynn Jewitt,	*The Wedgwoods: Being a Life of Josiah Wedgwood* (London, 1865)
Alison Kelly,	*The Story of Wedgwood* (New York, 1962)
Stephen Leslie, ed.,	'Elers, John Philip', *Dictionary of National Biography* (Oxford, 1889)
Eliza Meteyard,	*The Life of Josiah Wedgwood From His Private Correspondence and Family Papers* (London 1865)
Robert Plot,	*The Natural History of Staffordshire* (1686)
B. Rackham,	*Early Staffordshire Pottery* (1960)
G. W. Rhead and F.A. Rhead,	*Staffordshire Pots & Potters* (New York, 1907)
W. Scarratt,	*Old Times in the Potteries* (Stoke-on-Trent, 1906)
Simeon Shaw,	*History of the Staffordshire Potteries* (Hanley, 1829)
L. N. Solon,	*The Art of the Old English Potter* (New York, 1906)
Wikipedia,	'Elers brothers' (www.wikipedia.org)

Chapter 5 – Adams of Longcroft, Brick House and Cobridge Hall (1536-1869)

William Chaffers, *Marks and Monograms on European and Oriental Pottery and Porcelain* (London, 1891)

Robert Chambers, *Select Writings of Robert Chambers: History of the rebellion of 1745-6* (Edinburgh, 1840)

David Daiches, *The Last Stuart: The Life and Times of Bonnie Prince Charlie* (New York, 1973)

Robert K. Dent and Joseph Hill, *Historic Staffordshire* (Birmingham, 1896)

Brian Dolan, *Wedgwood – The First Tycoon* (London, 2004)

Alex. Charles Ewald, *The Life and Times of Prince Charles Stuart* (London, 1883)

Rev. Robert Forbes, *Jacobite Memoirs* (Edinburgh, 1834)

Arthur Hayden, *Chats on Old Earthenware* (New York, 1909)

Christopher Hibbert, *The Grand Tour* (London, 1987)

B. Hodgkiss, *Mother Burslem: A Burslem History* (Leek, 2001)

John Home, *The History of the Rebellion in the Year of 1745* (London, 1802)

Llewellynn Jewitt, *The Wedgwoods: Being a Life of Josiah Wedgwood* (London, 1865)

Charles Louis Klose, *Memoirs of Prince Charles Stuart* (London, 1846)

Moray McLaren, *Bonnie Prince Charlie* (New York, 1972)

Eliza Meteyard, *The Life of Josiah Wedgwood From His Private Correspondence and Family Papers* (London 1865)

Charles Sanford Terry, *The Rising of 1745* (London, 1900)

J.C. Wedgewood, *Staffordshire Pottery and its History* (1913)

Wikipedia,	'Watt steam engine' (www.wikipedia.org)

Chapter 6 – Adams of Greengates (1746-1821)

P. W. L. Adams,	*John Henry Clive 1781-1853 of North Staffordshire and his Descendants* (Newcastle, 1947)
P. W. L. Adams,	*Wolstanton* (Tunstall, 1908)
J. Akin,	*The Country around Manchester* (1795)
Diane Baker,	*Potworks: The Industrial Architecture of The Staffordshire Potteries* (London, 1991)
Belfast Monthly Magazine	'Account of James Brindley, a Self-Instructed Genius, and Introducer of the Mode of Still Water Navigation' Vol. 13, No. 72 (July 31, 1814)
William Burton,	*Josiah Wedgwood and His Pottery* (London, 1922)
William Chaffers,	*Marks and Monograms on European and Oriental Pottery and Porcelain* (London, 1891)
A. H. Church,	*English Earthenware* (London, 1884)
Marjorie Deaton,	'Adams of Greengates' in *Apollo,* Vol. LVII, No. 338 (April 1953)
Brian Dolan,	*Wedgwood – The First Tycoon* (London, 2004)
Ann Finer and George Savage, eds.,	*The Selected Letters of Josiah Wedgwood* (London, 1965)
Arthur Hayden,	*Chats on Old Earthenware* (New York, 1909)
Meteyard, Eliza,	*The Life and Works of Wedgwood.* 2 vols, (London, 1865)
N. Hudson Moore,	*Wedgwood and his Imitators* (New York, 1909)
G.W. Rhead,	*The Earthenware Collector* (New York, 1920)

Samuel Smiles,	*James Brindley and the Early Engineers* (London, 1864)
Samuel Smiles,	*Josiah Wedgwood* (London 1894)
W. Turner,	'Adams Ware', *The Queen,* 10th September 1904
W. Turner,	'Eighteenth Century Adams Ware', *The Connoisseur – An Illustrated Magazine for collectors*, Vol. IX (May-August 1904)
Josiah C. Wedgwood,	*Staffordshire Pottery and its History* (London, 1913)
Richard H. Weir,	*Six of the Best … A Potteries Companion* (Leicester, 1988)
Wikipedia,	'James Brindley' (www.wikipedia.org)
Wikipedia,	'Turnhurst' (www.wikipedia.org)

Chapter 7 – Adams of Bagnall and Fenton Hall (1660-1829)

William Adams & Co.,	'Bi-centenary booklet of Richard Adams Master Potter of Stoke-on-Trent' (1739-1811)
British History online,	'Fenton' (www.british-history.ac.uk)
Brian Dolan,	*Josiah Wedgwood: Entrepreneur to the Enlightenment* (London, 2004)
Brian Dolan,	*Wedgwood – The First Tycoon* (London, 2004)
Dr. David Furniss,	'Adams Notes', No.7 Summer 1990
Jonathan Grey,	'William Adams III (1772-1829) and family', *English Ceramic Circle Transactions*, Vol.30 (2019)
Pat Halfpenny,	'Thomas Whieldon: his Life and Work', *English Ceramic Circle Transactions*, Vol.16, No.2 (1997)
Arthur Hayden,	*Chats on Old Earthenware* (New York, 1909)

A. T. Morley Hewitt,	'Early Whieldon of the Fenton Low Works', *English Ceramic Circle Transactions,* Vol.3, No.3 (1954)
B. Hodgkiss,	*Mother Burslem: A Burslem History* (Leek, 2001)
Llewellynn Jewitt,	*The Ceramic Art of Great Britain: From Pre-Historic Times Down to the Present Day* (London, 1878)
Llewellynn Jewitt,	*The Wedgwoods: Being a Life of Josiah Wedgwood* (London, 1865)
N. Hudson Moore,	*Wedgwood and His Imitators* (New York, 1909)
Arnold Mountford,	'Thomas Whieldon's Manufactory at Fenton Vivian', *English Ceramic Circle Transactions,* Vol.8, Pt.2 (1972)
G. W. Rhead,	*The Earthenware Collector* (New York, 1920)
David Sekers,	*The Potteries* (1981)
Staffordshire Sentinel,	'Bicentenary of Richards Adams – Eighteenth Century Potter', Wednesday 26 April 1939
Cathryn Walton and Lindsey Porter,	*Lost Houses of North Staffordshire* (Ashbourne, 2010)
L. Weatherill,	*The Pottery Trade and North Staffordshire 1660-1760* (1971)
J.C. Wedgewood,	*Staffordshire Pottery and its History* (1913)
Wikipedia,	'Thomas Whieldon' (www.wikipedia.org

Chapter 8 – Adams of Greenfield (1798-1865)

Neil Ewins,	'Supplying the Present Wants of Our Yankee Cousins … Staffordshire Ceramics and the American Market' *Journal of Ceramic History,* Vol. 15 (1997)
D. A Furniss, R. J. Wagner and J. Wagner,	*Adams Ceramics Staffordshire Potters and Pots, 1779-1998* (Pennsylvania, 1999)

John Gore,	'England's Eccentric Squires: Some reflections on the career of Jack Mytton', *The Sphere*, Saturday 25 May 1957
John Hinton,	*The History and Topography of the United States (1830-1832) – 2 vols*. (London, 1830)
Nimrod,	*The Life of John Mytton Esq. of Halston, Shropshire* (London, 1870)
John Ridgway,	Manuscript Journal dated September 1822 – January 1823, Potteries Museum and Art Gallery, Stoke-on-Trent
Samuel Scriven,	'Report to Her Majesties Commissioners on the Employment of Children and Young Persons in the District of the Staffordshire Potteries; and on the actual State, Condition, and Treatment of Such Children and Young Persons' (1841)
Nancy Siegel,	*Along the Junita: Thomas Cole and the Dissemination of American Landscape Imagery* (Pennsylvania, 2003)
R. G. Thorne,	'John Mytton (1796-1834), of Halston, Salop' in *The History of Parliament: The House of Commons 1790-1820* (www.historyofparliamentonline.org)
Henry Wedgwood,	*The Romance of Staffordshire* (1875)
Wikipedia,	'Black Ball Line (trans-Atlantic packet)' (www.wikipedia.org)
Wikipedia,	'Blow the Man Down' (www.wikipedia.org)
Wikipedia,	'Halston Hall' (www.wikipedia.org)
Wikipedia,	'John Mytton' (www.wikipedia.org)
Wikipedia,	'Patrick Henry (packet)' (www.wikipedia.org)

Chapter 9 – Dawn of the Twentieth Century (1833-1952)

Anon.,	'The Potter's Thumb – The Adams Historical Staffordshire Potteries', *The London and Provincial Magazine*, Vol. 5, No. 5 (October, 1910)
Diane Baker,	*Potworks: The Industrial Architecture of The Staffordshire Potteries* (London, 1991)
Dave Cooper,	*The Staffordshire Regiments: Knotted Together: The Imperial, Regular and Volunteer Regiments 1705-1919* (Leek, 2003)
Dave Cooper,	*The Staffordshire Regiments Vol. II: The Scrapbook* (Leek, 2004)
Mervyn Edwards,	*Potters in Parks* (Leek, 1999)
D. A. Furniss,	*Adams Notes*, Numbers 1-20 (August, 1988 – Winter, 1994), unpublished
D. A. Furniss,	'An Account of William Adams Potters 1779-1979', pamphlet for Greengates Factory Bicentenary published by Adams in 1979
D. A. Furniss, J. R. Wagner and J. Wagner,	*Adams Ceramics: Staffordshire Potters and Pots, 1779-1998* (Pennsylvania, 1999)
Andrew Derek Popp,	*Business Structure, Business Culture, and the Industrial District: The Potteries, c.1850-1914* (1997)
J. B. Priestley,	*English Journey* (London, 1934)
David Sekers,	*The Potteries* (1981)
Stafford (TA),	*The History of the 125th (Staffs) Corps Engr. Regt. TA* (June 1963)
John Thomas,	*The Rise of the Staffordshire Potteries* (Bath, 1971)
E. J. D. Warrillow,	*A Lantern Lecture on Stoke-on-Trent* (1979)

E. J. D. Warrillow,	*A Sociological History of Stoke-on-Trent (1960)*
Richard H. Weir,	*Six of the Best … A potteries Companion* (Leicester, 1988)
Wikipedia,	'Mary of Teck' (www.wikipedia.org)

Chapter 10 – The Last of the Adams Master Potters (1909-1966)

D. A. Furniss,	*Adams Notes*, Numbers 1-20 (August, 1988 – Winter, 1994), unpublished
D. A. Furniss, J. R. Wagner and J. Wagner,	*Adams Ceramics: Staffordshire Potters and Pots, 1779-1998* (Pennsylvania 1999)
Wikipedia,	'British Indian Army' (www.wikipedia.org)
Wikipedia,	'Indian Army during World War II' (www.wikipedia.org)
Wikipedia,	'North Midland Divisional Engineers' (www.wikipedia.org)
Wikipedia,	'78th Infantry Division (United Kingdom)' (www.wikipedia.org)

INDEX

Adams, Benjamin, 127, 129, 224
Adams, Cecily Janet, 25, 42, 44, 46, 172, 180, 219, 229, 233, 252, 278, 280-285
Adams, Christopher, 253
Adams, Clarice, 278
Adams, Dorothy (née Murhall), 62, 72, 74, 79
Adams, Edward, 24, 25, 131, 133-135, 139, 167, 180, 182, 214
Adams, Frank Pemberton 278
Adams, Helen, 122
Adams, Hugh Worthington, 277–78
Adams, Jane, 161, 167, 174, 203
Adams, John, 6, 11, 22, 25, 45, 53, 55-57, 62, 72–74, 104, 236
Adams, Joscelin Francis (Major), 250-53, 274, 275, 286, 287, 290-93, 295, 297, 299
Adams, Joseph, 107, 108
Adams, Laura Eliza, 243
Adams, Lewis, 169–73
Adams, Nicholas, 11, 12
Adams, Pamela, 275, 299
Adams, Percy Walter Lewis, 44, 110, 143, 149, 159, 167, 178, 183, 209, 224, 225-6, 233, 241, 243, 244-46, 248, 250-53, 257-68, 272–75, 277-8, 286
Adams, Ralph, 24, 57–59, 62, 272
Adams, Richard, 2, 3, 11, 19, 45, 72, 139-41, 143, 153, 236
Adams, Robert, 55-56, 74
Adams, Sarah, 124, 129, 135, 141, 143, 145, 147, 149, 153, 174, 183
Adams, Thomas, 12, 53, 105, 171, 183-84, 191, 208, 214, 219, 224
Adams, William (early), 1–3, 11, 16, 24-5, 29 53, 58, 72
– William Adams I (1779-1805), 97, 107, 108, 111, 113-25, 127–129, 131, 135, 153, 166-7, 193, 224, 235, 257-58, 268
– William Adams II (1750-1831), 74-75, 77, 79–81, 83, 86–96, 99, 101–5, 141
– William Adams III (1772-1829), 122, 131, 137-38, 140-143, 145, 147-49, 153, 155, 169, 174, 286
– William Adams IV (1798—1865), 141, 147, 153, 155-56, 159, 161, 167, 171, 174, 178-9, 182-4, 193, 202-3, 205, 207, 286
– William Adams V (1833-1905), 193, 205, 207-8, 214-16, 219, 224, 229-30, 232, 235-37, 241, 243, 250, 257, 277-78, 280, 285-6
– William Adams VI (1868-1952), 219-21, 233–235, 241, 243-44, 248, 250, 253-57, 273-75, 286
Adams, William Anthony, 247, 250, 252-53, 256, 274, 286-87, 290
Adams, William (junior of Greengates), 96–98
Adams & Co., 207, 224, 236, 265, 267
Adams & Sons, 159, 161, 246, 250, 254, 87, 298
Adams teapot, 62, 73
Alders and Harrison, 143
Alken, Samuel Henry, 37
Allan, Ramsay, 68
American market, 87, 129, 147, 155, 157, 159, 161, 167, 178, 183, 203, 246
Ashmolean Museum, Oxford, 3, 27
Astbury, John, 48

Bagnall, 16, 24, 45, 62, 69, 72-3, 79, 108, 131, 134-5, 137–41, 143, 147, 169, 259, 272-73, 286
Bagnall, Margery, 53
Bagnall, Sir Nicholas MP, 53
Bagnall, Sir Ralph, 53
Bartlett, William Henry, 91
Basford Hall, 180-83
Bellarmine, 28
Blanchet, Louis Gabriel, 62
bloodboats, 157-58
Booth, 139, 271

Bradwell (and hall), 37, 39-40, 45-6, 48, 50, 165, 200-1, 217
– Bradwell Wood, 48, 203
Breda, Carl Frederik von, 99
Breeze, Jesse, 161, 167
Breu, Jörg, 19
Brick House (and works), 12, 53–57, 59, 60-2, 72–77, 79-80, 87, 105, 108, 114
Brindley, James, 76, 108-9, 111, 113
Brindley, John, 108, 113
butterpot, 27–29, 33, 39

Charles Edward Stuart (Bonnie Prince Charlie) 62-3, 65, 67–69, 73, 193, 259
Charles I, 141
Charles II, 133–35
Cheddleton, 81, 86, 135
Chinese ware, 39–41, 49
Cistercian, 15–23, 88, 90
Clarendon Report, 207
Clews, Ralph and James, 99
Cliff Bank (house and works), 143, 145
Cliff Vale Iron Works, 198, 203
Cobridge (and hall), 25, 53–54, 74, 77, 79–81, 83, 86-7, 96, 99, 105, 139–41, 153
Combermere Abbey, 16, 19
Copeland, 271
Coombe House, 292
Culloden, 73, 74
Cumberland, Duke of, 65–69, 73

Daniel (family), 45, 53, 74, 87, 89, 105
Danzig, 92-3, 95
Darwin, Erasmus, 79, 109
Davenport Adams & Co., 278
de Adams, William, 2
de Audley, Henry, 15
Derby, 53, 65, 68-9, 72, 124
Dimsdale (and old hall), 39–42, 44-5, 48, 51, 217

Dissolution of the Abbeys, 22–25
Doulton, 271
Dunkirk, 251

East India Company, 39, 40
Edward I, 1
Edward II, 188
Elers, John Philip and David, 39–41, 45, 48–50, 265
Etruria Works (and see Wedgwood), 75, 79, 114, 116-17, 122, 175, 270-71
Evans, Charles M., 222–23

Fenton Hall (and Fenton Low), 124, 135, 137–8, 141, 143, 147–49, 151, 153, 286
Fulham, 40, 50
Greenfield (hall and factory), 129, 131, 155, 161-4 167, 174, 178, 183, 194, 203–5, 207-8, 214-15, 217-24, 229, 234, 236, 243-44, 246, 248-9, 253-254, 256-7, 268, 274-75, 278, 286–88, 290–97

Greengates, 12, 97, 107, 115-25, 127–29, 141, 166-67, 176, 224, 226, 233–36, 243-44, 246-47, 253-54, 57, 268, 287, 290–92, 296–99
Greenwood Hall, 72, 140-41

Hadderidge, The (estate and pottery), 53, 56, 59, 141, 143, 145, 147, 153, 155, 174-75, 183
Hales, John (of Cobridge), 74, 79, 81, 153
Halliday, Edward, 243
Halston (hall and estate), 184-93
Hamburg, 91, 94-95
Hamilton, William, 119, 129
Hayden, Arthur, 23, 86, 119, 121, 138
Heath Lewis, (and family), 55, 124, 141, 143, 145, 147, 153, 155, 175
Henry VIII, 11, 270
Henshall, Ann, 109

Hogarth, William, 70–71
Holden, 24-5, 29, 73, 131, 133, 139, 258
Holland, 39, 45, 139, 247
Hudson, Thomas, 69

Ivy House (works), 74-5

Jacobite Rebellion, 62-74, 109, 141
James III, 63

Keeling, Michael, 124, 143, 145, 147, 149

Langley, F. P., 230
Longbridge Hayes, 12, 45
Longcroft, 53-4
Lübeck, 91-2, 94
Lynam, Charles, 99

Machin, Arnold, 139, 272-3
Maddock & Seddons, 175
Mayfield, 72-3
Meakin, 271
Meir, 129, 203, 224
Meteyard, Eliza, 3, 32, 75, 77, 79, 114, 122, 124
Micratex, 290
Milton, 24, 25, 99
Minton, Thomas and Mintons, 141, 217, 221, 269–71
Monglott, Joseph, 121
Moreton House, 217, 229, 231, 235, 240-41, 281–83
Morier, David, 74
Mount, The, 169-70,
Murhall, 62, 69, 72-3, 79
Munday, J., 162
Mytton, John, 184-93

Nash-Peake, 211, 214, 237
Newfield (hall and works), 116, 193, 195, 217, 220-21, 236, 243-44, 290, 292
Nimrod, 188-89, 193
Norton Green Hall 133, 135, 137
Norton-in-the-Moors, 134-5, 140-1

Parson, Francis, 113
Pepys, Samuel, 29, 39
Plot, Robert, 3, 27
Podmore, Walker and Co., 203
Porthill, 219-20, 230-31, 260, 285
posset pot, 28-9, 50
Priestley, J. B., 247, 250, 273-4
Priestley, Joseph, 75,

Ravensdale Iron Works, 198, 202-3
Richardson, George, 28
Ridgeways, 141, 159
Roche Mount, 278
Rushton Grange, 19, 25, 55

Sandby, Paul, 33
Scarratt, William (artist), 2, 32, 48, 117, 124
Scriven Report, 175, 178, 182
Shaw, Simeon, 22, 24-5, 45, 164
Shaw, George Bernard, 272
Shrigley, John, 59, 75
Smith, Theophilus, 164–66
Smith Child, 107, 193, 195-6, 214
Smithfield (hall and estate), 161, 164–67
Sneyd Family 12–13, 40, 45, 216-17
Spode, Josiah, 98, 137, 149, 153, 169,-70, 269
Spode (manufacturer), 141, 271, 273
St Margaret's Church, Wolstanton, 12, 161, 195, 215-9, 285
St Paul's Church, Burslem, 101–3
St Peter ad Vincula Church, Stoke-on-Trent, 131, 140, 152-3, 268-9

Trentham, 76, 237
Turner, John, 115-6
Turner, William, 58, 107, 118, 124-5, 258,

Turnhurst Hall, 108–11
tyg, 28-9, 50

Upper Cliff Bank (House and Works), 82, 143,

Wainwright, Peter, 165-7
wares:
– Adams ware, 55, 159, 184, 220, 244, 258-9, 268
– 'American Landscape', 159
– basalt ware, 76, 79, 116, 161, 265
– Black Etruscan, 76
blue-printed, 99, 117, 141, 143, 161
– creamware, 76, 115-6, 131, 139, 265
– Calyx, 246, 250, 268
– 'Cries of London', 250, 268, 272
– 'Doctor Syntax', 268
– Egyptian Black (black porcelain), 76
  jasper, 40, 49, 108, 114–16, 118-25, 127, 129, 224–27, 243, 246, 257–59, 265, 267-8, 292, 298
– Queen's Ware, 53, 76, 117
– salt glaze, 25, 29, 45, 49, 56–58, 62, 131, 139, 258-9, 265
– slipware, 6, 29, 131, 258, 265
– stoneware, 27, 29, 50, 116, 129, 265
– Yi-xing, 40
Warren, H., 114
Watlands, The, 169-74, 184
Wedgwood, Josiah, 3, 32, 48-9, 53, 57, 74–77, 79, 107–9, 113-4, 117, 119, 122, 137–39, 143, 259, 268–71
Wesley, John, 35
Whieldon, Thomas, 50, 131, 135, 137–8, 140
Wiffen, Bethan, 20-1, 60–61
Wolfe's Big Works, 82, 143, 147, 153
Wood, Aaron, 137
Wood, Enoch, 35, 87
Woore Manor, 265–68, 272, 275
Wraxhall, Nathaniel William, 89

ADAMS POTTERY DYNASTIES 1460-1956

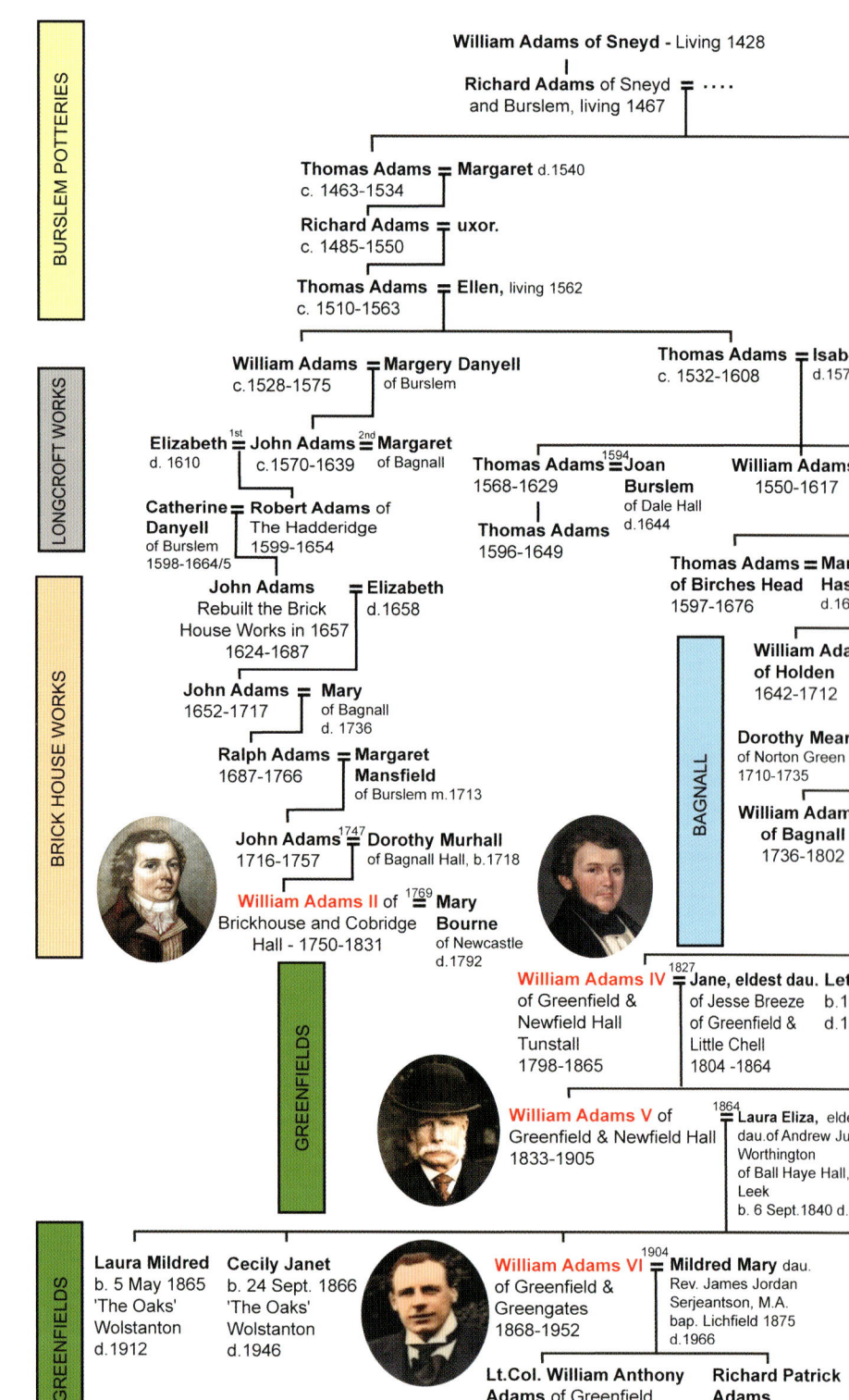

ADAMS POTTERY DYNASTIES 1460-1956

chard Adams of ═ A dau. of
eyd & Burslem   Nicholas Fynymore
530   of Burslem

Elizabeth ═ **Nicholas Adams** of Sneyd &
.1568   Burslem, 1490-1568

Richard Adams of Sneyd ═ **Alice**
& Burslem, 1533-1613   **Leacrofte** of Stone
                          d.1585

Joan ═(1st) **John Adams** of Sneyd Green ═(2nd) **Parnel**
d.1613   1569/70-1639   d.1648

Edward Adams of Sneyd Green ═ **Joan ....**
bap. 22 June 1608

John Adams of Sneyd Green ═(1664) **Alyce Ashley**
1636-1695/6   of Stoke-on-Trent

ohn Adams ═(1589) **Elizabeth Machyn**
f Birches   d.1632
ead 1569-1641

John Adams of Sneyd Green ═ **Alice**
bap. 2 Jan. 1669/70

William Adams ═(2nd) **Catherine**
f Bucknall Hall   **Hanson**
599-1676   d.1702

Joseph Adams ═ **Elizabeth**
St. Johns Square   d.1746
Burslem
1696-1772

John Adams ═ **Dorothy**   **Edward Adams** ═(1687) **Elizabeth Meare**
of Bucknall   **Pare**   Bagnall Bank House   of Handley Green
1645-1717   d.1711   1660-1727   d.1733

Edward Adams ═ **Martha** dau.
1709-1745   of Joseph Adams
                   bap. 15 Sept 1723

illiam Adams of Bagnall ═(2nd) **Sarah Braddock**
702-1775   née Wheildon
                                   d.1787

William Adams I ═(1771) **Mary** dau.
of Greengates   of John Cole of
Tunstall   Turnhurst Hall
1746-1805   1747-1805

Richard Adams ═ **Elizabeth Jackson**
of Cobridge   Greenwood Hall
1739-1811   d.1834

William Adams III ═(1793) **Sarah Heath**
of Fenton Hall   of The Hadderidge
1772-1829   1774-1846

William Adams   **Benjamin**
of Greengates   **Adams**
1777-1805   of Greengates
                    1788-1828

GREENGATES

dward Adams ═ **Mary** dau.   **Lewis Adams**   **Thomas Adams**
f Basford Hall   Jesse   of 'The Watlands'   of Stoke-on-Trent
r. Stoke-on-Trent Breeze   Wolstanton   & Liverpool
803-1872   1811-1863   1805-1850   1807-1863

Mary ═(1865) **Wm. Simms Bull**   **Thomas Adams**
b.1835   of Tyn-y-Coed,   1836-1905
d.1895   Arthog, co. Merioneth
                 d. 1919

ugh Worthington ═(1900) **Clarice Sophia**, 5th   **Frank Pemberton**   **Percy Walter Lewis** ═(1916) **Ada Gladys**, dau. of
dams   dau. of Chas. Bennett   **Adams** of Davenport   **Adams** of Greenfield,   Archibald Douglas of
370-1928   Roche, of Daventry, co.   Adams & Co.,   Greengates & Woore   Salwarpe,
oroner for N.W.   Northants   Silk Mills, Leek   J.P. & F.S.A.   co. Worcester
affordshire 1901   1874-1959   1872 -1919   1875-1952   d.1957

Major Joscelin Francis Whieldon
Adams of Greenfield
& Greengates & Woore Manor
1919-1991

GREENGATES

321